DIARY OF 66

THE NIGHT I BURNED ALIVE

Alexandra Furnea

DIARY OF 66

THE NIGHT I BURNED ALIVE

HISTRIA
PERSPECTIVES

Histria Perspectives

Las Vegas ♦ Chicago ♦ Palm Beach

Published in the United States of America by
Histria Books
7181 N. Hualapai Way, Ste. 130-86
Las Vegas, NV 89166 U.S.A.
HistriaBooks.com

Histria Perspectives is an imprint of Histria Books dedicated to outstanding non-fiction works. Titles published under the imprints of Histria Books are distributed worldwide.

English edition published in arrangement with Ilustrata Agency

Library of Congress Control Number: 2024931085

ISBN 978-1-59211-436-8 (softbound)
ISBN 978-1-59211-451-1 (eBook)

CONTENTS

To my mother, my father, and my sister.
To all those who suffered or died in the hospitals of neverhealing.
To those who manage to stay human in spite of the inhumanity that surrounds them.
To the angels dressed in scrubs who mended my soul by fixing my body.
To the music that kept me whole inside while my flesh was falling apart.

To a future Romania, where corruption has been destroyed, the medical system saves instead of killing, and the Colectiv Club fire is just a terrible memory of a tragedy that can never happen again.

PREFACE

In 2017, two years after I was injured in the Colectiv Club fire, I wrote on social media about the treatment I received at the Hospital for Burns in Bucharest. The reaction of the people who took time out of their lives to read about my experience was overwhelming. It is because of their love, support, and encouragement that I decided to keep translating into words the moments that make up the life of someone who is a survivor of a national tragedy. It's still hard for me to identify with this label. Using it seems unfair toward the 65 souls who never got the chance to share it with me.

Across the years, both friends and strangers asked me to write something longer about Colectiv. They didn't think that the posts I made managed to tell the whole story, and they were right. Even so, I hesitated because, to be honest, it still hurts. However, at some point I realized that much like the scars that now mark my body, the memories are an unerasable part of me. Within the shadows they cast around, lies a light that we can use to guide ourselves out of the darkness, toward a better world. I decided that going back in time, to the night of October 30th, 2015, and to what happened afterward, was worth it. It was time for the truth to come out. Maybe this way I'll be able to turn my hell into an instrument of redemption for others. I started writing the *Diary of 66* with this purpose in mind, and in heart.

It's called that, instead of, for instance, *Diary of a Survivor*, because something died inside each and every single one of us – those who walked out of the club, and then out of the hospitals alive. We all lost our lives that night and kept losing pieces of our being with every loved one who perished, with every pain that they didn't give us medicine for, with every humiliation, infection, and bathing procedure done without sedation, in inhumane conditions, in impoverished hospitals, which didn't cherish salvation, but corruption. We hate to admit it, but the fear we feel before each difficult reconstructive surgery, the resignation with which we sign the consent papers that list death as a possible side-effect of healing, the dark nights when grief haunts us, birthing longings, nightmares, regrets, and doubts, the moments when we ask ourselves whether it wouldn't be easier if we just gave up, are signs that either one of us could, at some point, become victim number 66.

After I was discharged from the Hospital for Burns, in the years that followed, I had well over forty reconstructive surgeries. Unfortunately, I'm not done, nor will I ever be. I must undergo surgical and rehabilitative procedures all my life, to fix both what the fire destroyed and what was ruined by the Romanian medical system. As I lie on the operating table, while the anesthesiologist places the oxygen mask on my face, I close my eyes and pray to God to help me wake up. I know there's a chance I won't. Then, before the nothingness engulfs my senses – before I'm swallowed by the darkness that annuls me, as the numbing drugs run through my veins and the knife cuts up my skin, I feel the horror of "66" seep inside me through the wounds, terrifying me.

Yes. We are in danger of adding our souls to the countdown of losses, as a late consequence of the same October 30th, 2015, that killed our friends. There's a price to pay if we wish to enhance our quality of life. We must acccpt that each surgery comes with risks, among which is death itself. This is the day-to-day struggle of the survivors of the Colectiv Club tragedy. But still, for us, perishing remains a metaphor, until proven otherwise. For the friends we buried, for their families, it's a heartbreaking and implacable reality. Their parents, who fall ill because of the grief, too love-sick to keep going, should be added to the list of victims too. Many have died early because they followed their children's footsteps toward the stars.

I chose to write a diary because I didn't want to create a beautiful text, but a deeply honest one, molded according to the thoughts that went through my mind in the most difficult moments of my life, when my hands were useless and couldn't put pen to paper. When my words, interrupted by sighs of pain and the dark revelation of the horrors I was being subjected to, were simple and raw. Some will see my confessions as screams for help. Others will view them as criticism against the systemic corruption in Romania. My diary will be different things to different people. For me, it's a way to give meaning to the suffering.

The names I used are not real, but everything else is. No matter how awful some of the scenes seem, please know that I neither embellished them nor made them up. Unfortunately, the things I describe really happened. I didn't reveal the true identity of those who helped me because I wanted to protect them. As for those who are shown in a less flattering light, I gave them pseudonyms because I don't want my endeavor to come off as vengeful. My goal is not to punish, but to recount what happened, as it was seen through my eyes. I leave judgment-making to the justice system and to God, and hope that it's going to be a fair process.

Initially, I published the *Diary of 66* on social media and on my website, www.genunderground.ro. My story has since been granted the amazing chance to become a book, through the generous efforts of two publishing houses: Histria Books, in the USA, and Humanitas, in Romania, who trusted me enough to release the English edition, therefore freeing my experience from the confines of a language with little international reach. I cherish this opportunity with all my heart and thank everyone who was kind enough to support me. Without the trust and encouragement I received, the *Diary* might have never shed its digital form to become the beautiful paperback volume you now hold in your hands. The physical version fills my soul with joy and brings me relief. Seeing my suffering embodied in a palpable form, with pages that have their own smell, texture, color, and weight, which give tangibility to my story, removing it from the immaterial recesses of my mind and of the internet, helps me separate myself from the horror I experienced, therefore allowing me to heal from it. For me, this is not just a book. It's a part of me. It's a fragment of my most intimate being. It is my heart, if it were made from paper and illustrated with ink. It's my soul, in the shape of a document.

I can't promise you that this is going to be an easy read, nor do I think that I wrote a masterpiece. Please show my diary the lenience and kindness fit for a testimony of someone's darkest trials. Don't expect it to be anything else but what it is: a collection of confessions from the hell we often unleash upon one another, but also a shy guide toward a better world, where corruption, and the cruelty it brings with it, have been eradicated and replaced with hope, respect, and love. A world where life matters more than the system, political power, and money. Only together can we transform the Colectiv Club tragedy into the moment when Romania decided it would stop accepting the unacceptable.

I can't end this preface without saying a few words about Goodbye to Gravity. As you read the *Diary of 66*, allow the band's music to resonate from its pages. Let it accompany you, like a soundtrack, sometimes loud, sometimes quiet, through the chapters. Grant it permission to give meaning to everything that happened.

We must not let the silence of oblivion mute it. The band's songs deserve to become contemporary hymns of change for the better, for Romania, and for other countries struggling with corruption.

I thank each and every single one of you who will read the current English edition. Translating it was an honor and a dream come true. Please never forget that you, the readers, are the only reason why my story – and anybody else's, for that matter – means something. By giving the *Diary of 66* a place in your libraries, in your homes, and in your hearts, you're actually sheltering a part of my soul and offering it healing. I am forever grateful to you, above anyone and anything else.

September 2023

I
THE NIGHT I BURNED ALIVE

It's six in the evening. After I finish writing the articles that I'm going to publish tomorrow, I rest my eyes on the framed posters on the walls. Most are autographed by the artists they portray, and the editorial office looks exactly like the one in my teenage fantasies: a big room filled with band photos, dominated by a sturdy wooden study right in the middle, at which I get to write about rock and roll. A feeling of intense joy overwhelms me. My teenage self is proud of the 27-year-old woman who managed to turn her dream into reality.

Five years ago, Nelu, the editor-in-chief, gave me the opportunity to write a few news bits for *Maximum Rock Magazine* to test my skills. I immediately accepted, and our collaboration grew to become a full-time job. I met him at a moment of doubt, when I was questioning whether I'd ever be able to work as a journalist for a rock webzine, and sure enough, here I am, doing what I love the most.

I press the save button one last time, turn off the computer, lock the door, and leave. The narrow street that hosts our headquarters is unusually dark, and, in the autumn dusk, it reminds me of a strange stony tongue, speckled chaotically with small houses, lost amidst colossal blocks of flats that swallow it whole, mercilessly. It's already cold outside and I can smell winter's breath in the frozen air. I rush ahead, moved by the soothing image of my home, grateful that I live close by. God, time passes so quickly over here. I sigh and sulk. There's no real reason to be upset, but I can't help wondering why the big-city nights are becoming lonelier and heavier lately. Their weight lays upon my young heart in the sleepless darkness of my shabby rented apartment.

I get out on the busy, bustling boulevard that sparkles indecently under makeshift advertisements and bright streetlights. My frown melts away under their warm glow and turns into a bitter smile, as I watch masses of agitated passers-by go about their business, unaware of each other. I put my headphones on, press play, turn up the volume, and lose myself in the crowd. I decide last minute to make a stop at the store, to buy some groceries for dinner. When I'm done, it's raining profusely, but I don't wait for it to dwindle. I start toward home, staggering this time, because of the heavy bags.

The sadness that took hold of me when I left the editorial office is back. Sometimes I ask myself too many questions. Is it a good idea to stay in Romania when so many friends are leaving the country in search of better opportunities? Should I find a job that pays more generously? If I go elsewhere, what's going to happen to my mom and my sister? Doubts like these keep rearing their ugly heads, and even though I'm mostly happy with my life here, I can't shake the feeling that things aren't working as they're supposed to, that a piece of my inner puzzle is missing. I stop carelessly in the middle of the sidewalk, holding the heavy grocery bags tight in my hands, and raise my head toward the leaden sky. Cold raindrops wash away the last traces of today's makeup, and the nascent tears in my eyes, relieving me of the unknown hurt that plagues me. Refreshing me. I don't know what's wrong with me. Sometimes it feels like I'm carrying the weight of the world on my shoulders. I make a run for it, trying to get home as unspoiled by the rain as possible.

I notice her late, while I'm already rummaging in my pockets searching for my keys. She's standing very still at the crosswalk, oblivious to the pattering rain that keeps getting worse. People pass by her in waves, but she doesn't falter, as if she's made of stone – a lonely cliff, in a tumultuous ocean of faces and hands. She's unnervingly calm under the attack of the sky. You'd think she's wearing some kind of invisible shield that protects her from the storm's wrath and from people's indifference. She's old, much older than my mother. She seems lost in this big, chaotic world. I wonder if she knows where she is. Her blue eyes are unusually bright. She's wearing bad clothes that have seen better days. I can tell that her coat is too thin for the weather, and her peeling, faux leather boots are worn out, with crummy soles. I look at her feet and I feel the dampness seeping in, as if they were my own. Now she's watching me, and she's whispering something as if she's talking to herself, but she doesn't take her tired eyes off of me. It doesn't take long, and she addresses me directly. She asks me, in a meek voice, if I can point her toward Emil Gârleanu Street, and nothing more. She glances at me with kindness and patience.

I'm taken aback by her firm, yet gentle gaze. I tell her how she can get to the address she indicated. She thanks me, then turns her head the other way, staring at the crosswalk as if she's waiting for some miracle that's running late again. I look at her for a few seconds, confused. I don't know what do to. Maybe I'd offend her if I offered her money. I decide I'm going to go upstairs, look for an umbrella, and bring it to her. I rush into the building, get in the elevator, reach my apartment, ransack it for an umbrella, then go back into the street, panting. The woman, however, is gone. It only took me a few minutes to return, but in that speck of time, fate decided to part our ways. How quickly she vanished, taking her sorrow-laden heart with her. I search for her. I cross the street and take a few steps in the direction of Emil Gârleanu Street, then go back. She's nowhere to be found. The rain suddenly stops and vanishes, leaving dirty puddles in her wake. Like sullied mirrors, they reflect the sharp headlights of cars driving by, dulling them, drowning them. I stare at the umbrella, hopeless, and blame myself for not having acted quicker. For not having asked her if I can help. What if I had told her something nice? Something that would have saved her a little, just for tonight.

At the red traffic lights, people stop, then cross in groups, anxious, mottled, their faces always different, in a permanent exchange of identities. Some are boisterous and young, others old and quiet, dressed in out-of-fashion clothes that bear the markings of time. Some are poor and lonely; others can't get enough of abundance. They play with their phones oblivious to everything else, to the things that don't chime happily, announcing some vapid message, or comment, to lights that come from within, and not from a screen. The old woman hasn't come back. She fell out of the world's variegated kaleidoscope, leaving behind a fading memory of her sad face and pale, mysterious eyes. She became invisible when what she needed the most was to be seen. But we're all blind down here.

Regret takes over me as, later that night, I prepare my humble dinner. It follows me the day after, and then all week. Day after day, I retrace my steps: I leave home, I go to work, I come back, never changing my route, in hopes I'll see her again at the crosswalk. But it never happens, and I wonder if this wasn't one of God's ploys, like in the fairytales. Maybe he throws angels in our path, disguised as souls in need, to test us and see if what we hold inside is worth something; to find out if we're good people. The thought is absurd, but as time passes and Autumn sinks deeper into darkness, I think about the old woman often, and my heart breaks every time I remember her standing all alone at the crosswalk, drenched in the heavy rain, lost in the big city. I close my eyes and ask her to forgive me. I pray she found what she was looking for, even if I was of no help to her. I ask God to forgive me as well, and to have mercy on this youth of mine that I'm rushing through in such a rampant hurry.

A few days later, it's October 30th — concert night. I leave the editorial office early so that I can go home and prepare. I've been waiting for the chance to see Goodbye to Gravity live for a long time. Even though I'm struggling to shake off the week's exhaustion, there's one thing I can't get rid of: the weight of the world on my shoulders, as anxiety takes over again. I sort through the wardrobe to find something nice to wear, and I decide last minute that I'm not going for the dress I initially eyed. It's much too cold for such an outfit, so I put my black jeans on, a matching t-shirt with shoulder pads, and my trusty blazer. I comb my long hair, freshly dyed black, and I lace my boots up. I'm proud of myself for picking the more prudent variant, and not giving in to temptation.

Before I leave the house, I get a text from my friend, Tamara. She's letting me know that she's on her way, so I write back that I can't wait to see her. I decide that I'm going to walk to the venue instead of calling a cab. It will only take me 15 minutes to get there. I stare at the crosswalk as I pass by it, but the street is strangely deserted. I realize I left my headphones upstairs, but it's too late to turn back, so instead of listening to music, I hum one of Goodbye to Gravity's songs to myself, in anticipation of the show, and to keep me company.

I gaze at the illuminated windows, etched in the tall, Communist-era buildings. There are hundreds of them, and in the dark October night, they look like openings into havens that shield people from the chaotic city below. I imagine the lives behind the bright lights, in the cozy and orderly apartments, or in the messy ones. What stories do the inhabitants recount to each other now? What good or bad news is discussed at the dinner table? Beyond the electric yellow of the windows, there's a family of four, just like mine used to be back in the day. The oldest daughter is getting dressed up for the party, and the youngest stares at her admiringly, wishing she'd grow up sooner, and be just as pretty. She's lying on her stomach in the bed, surrounded by colored pencils and markers, striving to draw her sister's portrait. She's the most beautiful girl in the world with her blonde hair and brown eyes. Their father is smoking in the kitchen, sketching caricatures of politicians on the same piece of paper where the day's numbers open their starving, gaping mouths, from amidst calculations of mortgages and debt. Mom is brewing coffee and sneaking loving peeks at her husband, who seems to have suddenly gotten older, hunched like that over their worries. No. That's not true. He's still young and handsome to her, and he'll always be that way.

"You'll live," I tell him. "You'll stay with them longer."

In spite of it all, the shadowy October night is gentle, and my figments make me smile. I'm convinced that, somewhere, these people I made up really exist, and they are happy.

The concert had already begun by the time I arrive. To make the club more fashionable, the owners installed a metal container at the entrance, as a nod to the industrial style that used to be trendy back in the day. I walk through it to get to the main hall, where the gigs take place. The band finishes up the first song and I catch some of the pyro show. The fireworks go off, illuminating people's smiling faces. I greet a few friends and head toward the other side of the venue, where I meet Nelu and my other workmates. The audience is busy applauding, and everyone is enthusiastic. Goodbye To Gravity's new album is masterful work, and I'm sure that it's going to become a landmark for the Romanian metal scene. The band members exude happiness, and I rejoice at seeing their animated faces. They worked very hard to make the songs sound this excellent. I exchange a few words with Ciprian, one of our editors, and with Mihai, his younger brother. Nelu signals me to take notes, so that I can later write a thorough review of the concert. I nod and turn toward the stage.

Mantras Of War, the record that is being released tonight, has a very strong social message. Metal has always dealt with this aspect, and the band members, through their work, managed to write a piece that succeeds at telling our generation's story. We're a haunted bunch, prey to inner conflicts, just as the first song of the evening, "The Day We Die", illustrates so well. It speaks about corruption, about the need to act collectively in order to stop this common enemy, through a plethora of harsh metaphors that evoke images of war fronts occupied by people who march together for change.

"Shadow Puppets" begins, and it too deals with these ills. The social evil has metastasized and the fight against it becomes even more personal. The war moves from the outside in, wreaking havoc on our inner being, subjecting it to all sorts of manipulations and games, the sole purpose of which is to lead us astray from our own soul.

The heavy, aggressive sound does justice to the themes. I listen to the lead singer's visceral voice, and I realize that there's no other way that he can express the crushing weight of the things he's calling out than the deep growls that give such an explosive edge to the band's specific brand of metal. He screams about the evils in our society that claim so many lives and wound our spirits so deeply. All of a sudden, I remember the first lines of the e-mail I sent to the Helsinki Sibelius Academy Admissions Office, to inquire about their Arts Management Master's program. "As a young professional in the field of event production, I am very interested in pursuing such an interesting and comprehensive degree that would allow me to enrich my experience significantly," I wrote, like a true geek, trying to impress the professors and find my way out of this dysfunctional country. What have I got to lose if I try to earn the scholarship, I ask myself, mid-concert, suddenly deaf to the music. If I don't do it, if I don't leave, maybe I'll waste the last chance I have to achieve a better life. But what if it's just a chimera? The feeling of longing for my family overwhelms me. I think of my nephews, of their fate here in Romania. How will this indifferent society protect them? What will happen to my widowed mother? Oh, enough of the dark stuff, I scold myself. I'm here to have fun, for Christ's sake! I'll have enough time to ponder these things after the gig.

I look around at the audience. I know most of the people here. Like me, they work in editorial offices, they write, they take photographs, and they strive to promote the alternative culture. Its curse in Romania is that it's deliberately kept in the shadows by prejudice and by the mass media's disinterest. The press doesn't see the point of promoting talented and wholesome artists if they're not sellable to the wider audience that is used to being fed facile, easily digestible junk. They call us "the underground" because we don't like the commercial sounding "mainstream," overly populated by shallow performers, barely good enough to be broadcast at the radio or TV stations that gobble them up and spit them out. We're "the underground" because we've been exiled in a place of bias, somewhere in the subterranean of culture, buried alive with our dreams. This place is not our home, but neither is what's "above" it.

Misunderstood, discriminated against, ridiculed, this movement's only flaw is that it doesn't feel represented by the fad of the moment in terms of music. Many artists get lost along the way because of the lack of a cultural infrastructure that is inclusive and friendly with diversity. They're defeated not because they're talentless, but because of the industry's unrelenting greed that dictates that something is worthless if it can't be sold. The consequences of this mentality translate into the way the bands are treated by those who should protect them. They're forced to perform in unsafe venues, by corrupt owners or event organizers, who humiliate them, deny them remuneration, and use them just to fill up a slot in a badly selling weeknight. They're punished because they have a passion that, for most of them, is a vehicle of salvation in a society that is still seeking its landmarks after thirty hard years or transition.

Journalists, photographers, musicians, we share the same fate. What we are is "the underground generation," taking refuge in niches where we uncover fragments of meaning. We're not comfortable with the main direction. Its only virtue is the semblance of normality. In reality, it's just that, an appearance that camouflages how rotten it is at its core. The mainstream reeks of fakeness and corruption. That's why we prefer the underground, even if it's harder for the truth to surface from down here. What would you call a world where values are reversed, where good passes for bad, and evil is so trivial, it's not even recognized as such? A dystopia. Romania has built its post-revolutionary structure against the grain of wholesomeness and true worth, something that is obvious even in the little things that make up the fabric of our world, like the music industry. Value is meaningless if it can't be put on an invoice. Long live the underground! Oh, we could escape it if we chose to leave, like I'm thinking of doing. But what will happen to those who can't run, to those forced to stay behind? In what heartbreaking ways will their souls be claimed by the monsters we let live?

The steady vibrations of my mobile phone against my back pocket throw my thoughts off course. Tamara arrived, and she's waiting for me to explain where I am, so that she can join me. I write back and, shortly after, her luminous, smiling face emerges from the crowd. Her petite figure floats lightly through the huddled bodies, contrasting with the ebb and flow of the mosh pit. By now, she's laughing. "Wow, these guys are really loud!" she shouts, barely audible. "They're doing a great job!"

Mishoo and Vlad's guitars merge in perfect harmony, while Bogdan's sturdy drumming leads the song steadily, like a heartbeat made up of musical notes, always faithful to the sonic beast called Goodbye to Gravity, conjured up by the five artists. The true puppeteer, however, is Pascu whose mathematically precise bass lines hold the structure of the compositions together. If Bogdan is the heart, then Alex is the brain, Mishoo and Vlad are the skilled hands, and Andrei is the soul. His voice, sometimes melodic, other times harsh, is an intercessor of sorts, forging a union between the world of instruments and that of man. Their talent and chemistry work together to create one of the country's best metal bands of all time.

The song ends, the audience applauds, and it's time for "Atonement." I feel like this song was written for me.

"I started running/ I wasn't gonna just stand there and wait/ For the changes that were sure to dissipate," Andrei sings, telling the story of my generation's fate, about the curse of being caught between worlds, suspended between one choice and the other, burdened by having to pick to either stay and fight, or leave. "I figured why should I risk it/I don't wanna venture and I don't wanna gain/Instead of making the choices/I'd rather be left with silence again." And it's as if no matter what we choose, it'll still be the wrong choice.

"For taking my time to find atonement/ Taking my time to feel the moment/ Taking the time to shun an omen/ For taking in all my time." We lie to ourselves that we've got so much time on our hands, but before we know it, we're old and lost within ourselves, and among others. Hesitance becomes chronic and turns into an inability to act. What should we do with ourselves in this blind and mute country, so overwhelmed by evil, yet filled with what is most intimately ours? Our home, hell.

Applause ripples through my thoughts as the audience dances front row, under the enthusiastic gaze of the band members. I awaken from my contemplation to witness the teenage fans forming playful circle-pits. They push and shove each other; they jump and fall, in a game that is a testament to their anxious youth. "Four Minutes of Rage" galvanizes them, and I witness their explosive unrest, amused. The musicians are smiling wide-eyed, thrilled to be able to offer them a safe space for their energy to come out. "Rise From the Fallen" follows and I notice that the band is playing the new record in the order of its track list. I wonder if I'll get the chance to listen to "I Won't Wait," my favorite song from Goodbye to Gravity, and the one I hummed on my way here. It's an older single, taken from the group's first release.

The band seems to read my thoughts, or at least partially, because the next song they choose to perform is "The Cage." It's one of their first ever releases and the fans react tellingly through loud applause and cheers. The next bit, "Unusual Suspects" is another favorite from the self-titled debut record, and it's received with the same level of joy. Front-row youngsters know the lyrics by heart, and accompany the lead-singer with their boisterous, collapsing voices. At one point, Andrei hands the microphone over to a boy who sings his heart out, proving that he's a worthy rock star himself.

The first chords of the Iron Maiden cover "The Evil That Men Do" rear their sonic heads, and I know that the performance is going to be one of the night's highlights. Iron Maiden is Pascu's all-time favorite band and the joy he experiences being able to deliver this song is overwhelming. It must be such an amazing thing for him to be able to honor his idols like this, in front of the people who love him, and his craft, the most. His smile encompasses the whole room, as he gives his heart out to the fans. Mishoo and Vlad join him, while masterfully strumming their guitars, to the progression of the song, electrified by the music, and by the audience's thrill. "It's your turn to sing the chorus," Andrei shouts, enlivening the people. He's completely happy in this moment in time, overcome with emotion and pure joy. I watch the artists weave our souls together in the common thread of music, and I tell myself that these people were born to be onstage.

"We've got Vlad Ţelea on guitars!"

The lead singer points to his shy bandmate, who, although intimidated by the attention and the roaring applause, delivers a perfect solo. He nods his head, as the musicians gaze at each other, thrilled to be here, in front of us, doing what they adore. Music brings them a sense of fulfillment that is captured and carried to the audience by the volatile sounds of their craft. It wraps itself around our hearts and binds us together in this ultimate moment of joy, a testimony to life's beauty.

These people give me so much hope. But then I think of their future outside of this concert, when they go off stage and have to face the careless music industry. Of my future, our future, when we leave this place, and go back into the outside world, so fraught with flaws and carelessness.

As the song draws to a close, I understand that we — each and every single person here tonight — are parts of the same whole, of this strange generation of people who experienced the privileges of freedom, oblivious to the captivity of dictatorship. We're young enough not to be overwhelmed by history, yet insufficiently removed from it to cease being prey to its mistakes. We're at the crossroads between what was, and what could be, in a purgatory called "Romania," where the past muzzles hope, silencing it and forcing it to stay quiet in the face of injustice.

We live our lives torn between the desire to get the hell out of here, and something akin to a mission that compels us to stay and wage the necessary war against the status quo. Goodbye to Gravity's music perfectly expresses this inner struggle; its music, but also its fate that so cruelly conditions the band to stay in an ignored niche, while its message remains unheard. We share its destiny, and the "sin" of wanting something else, something better, in a world of compromise and corruption. As I've said before: we are the Underground Generation, and whatever ill befalls its preachers, is sure to afflict us as well.

After a few repetitions of the chorus, the second round of fireworks goes off, followed by our applause. Tamara claps along, and smiles at me. There are so many beautiful people here tonight. Good energy flows from our young souls, reminding us that we are all in this together.

Something unexpected occurs on stage, putting a sudden end to the performance. The artists fumble and writhe. A sharp, unpleasant light washes over the lead singer's face. I can't tell where it's coming from. His frightened eyes stare fixedly ahead. He rushes to say that something caught fire, and that it's not part of the show. He demands a fire extinguisher, but there is none in sight. He looks at the pillar on his right, helpless. My eyes drift there automatically and that's when I see the flames. People are starting to fidget around me and Tamara. Some of them run toward the door that leads to the container. The only way out is through it. Why are they in such a hurry? Surely it isn't that bad. A few seconds later, the blaze reaches the ceiling and the whole thing ignites instantly. It takes me a while to get moving. It's as if I'm in a nightmare, and I'm desperately trying to escape the imminent danger, but my legs won't listen to me. I manage to tell Tamara that we must leave. The huge flames coming from the ceiling descend toward us voraciously, moving lower and lower every time. I glare at them confused, in disbelief. We've got no other choice. There's only one exit route, and it's already packed with frightened people, trying to escape faster. The fire charges at them from above, more intense in that part of the hall because of its proximity to the pillar.

She shouts at me with a shrill voice, so unlike her gentle timbre. "Through there? The ceiling's going to fall on us!" The thought of running to the restrooms and taking shelter there crosses my mind, but I can't remember if there are windows there that we can open and get out through. We hesitate, but we choose the container, since it's the only certain way out. Pieces of wood and flaming soundproofing foam are raining over it, crashing on top of people. The smoke becomes thicker and those coming from opposing sides of the venue meet in the middle, huddling together. Ciprian grabs me and asks if I've seen Nelu. I haven't, so I put my hand on his shoulder, hoping we'll stay together. Tamara holds on to me clumsily. She's small and frail amid swaying bodies that wrench at her. When we arrive at the door that leads inside the container, we feel the sweltering heat of the flames above us. Fear turns into panic. The fire's heat scorches us, and the pain drives the huddled people to push harder, in hope of a quicker advancement. I'm torn from Tamara and Ciprian by the desperate masses, and I remain alone underneath the hellish crumbling ceiling.

I try to protect my head with my right hand, but singeing pieces of wood and foam keep falling on me, burning me. A terror that I've never felt before overwhelms me and then turns into helplessness. The billowing smoke envelops and blinds us. I can feel the others shove against me, and when I finally manage to see something, I realize that I've been pushed to the back side of the container, where I come to a sudden halt. We can't advance any further because we're crammed together in the narrow space. Desperate screams from behind us prompt us to keep moving. Unaware that there's nowhere to go, those who are trapped in the main room keep thrusting. We're stuck in an inferno. I listen to their muddled shouts, and even though I can't — I won't — look, I know that some of the people left behind are burning alive. Beside me, squeezed into my right arm, a blonde man with a goatee whispers, with a shuddering voice, prayers to God, one after the other, begging Him to make this nightmare go away, hoping foolishly that it isn't real. He closes his eyes and folds his hands to speak to Him. His minute figure is crushed against someone else's back, and someone else is crushed against him, and someone else behind them is burning. Sharp elbows dig into his stomach, and his head, abandoned in between a stranger's shoulder blades, bobs aimlessly as he chants: "Please, God, it can't be happening. Please, God, this isn't happening." He recites "Our Father," crying.

The screams of those who didn't reach the container cover up his prayer, intensifying. And then it happens. Fire and smoke swoop from behind, swallowing us. I feel the flames on my naked skin, gnawing at my back with ferocious, seething teeth, excoriating me. As they envelop me completely, I cover my face with my hands. I'm trying to breathe, but this parching, sweltering thing isn't air anymore. It smells like melting chemicals, and it burns my throat, boiling in my chest, stinging, hurting. My fragile fingers bend against my will, and I hear how the flesh over them cracks open. The thick plastic frame of my glasses liquefies because of the unbearable heat and becomes molten. The liquid washes over my neck and chest, leaving behind streaks of skinned flesh. One by one, we fall on top of each other and continue to burn in the ashes made by our own decaying bodies. The fire eats us up whole and devours us, destroying our faces, our arms, our legs. Mutilating us. Stripping us of clothing. Stripping us of skin. Help. I'm burning. I'm on fire. I'm on fire. People are crying out in agony, and I can't tell if my voice has joined theirs or not, for we've all become one. I want it to end. Please, God, make it stop. It hurts! It hurts! The fire's unearthly groan deafens me and silences the screams. I see my sister and my mother, standing together in a recent memory. My last thought goes out to them. I know now that I'm going to die. I ask for their forgiveness, for the suffering I'll cause them by leaving like this, so early, just like my father. I'm crying, but the tears won't flow down my cheeks. The fire gobbles them up before they have a chance to form.

All of a sudden, a vast and heavy darkness cloaks me. I went blind. The flames killed my sight. I have died. Maybe this is how it begins, whatever lies beyond the threshold. Perhaps eternity is just an endless black ocean, shapeless, meaningless. Then there is light again. I finally understand that I am still alive. Beside me, a girl with long, burned hair is struggling to stay on her feet. Strips of skin hang from her arms like the ravaged wings of an angel who will never fly again. "Can you help me get up?" I ask her in a voice that doesn't sound like my own. She tries, but when her injured hands touch mine, she recoils. "It hurts too much. I'm so sorry. I can't," she replies, then starts bawling. Pity washes over me, and I thank her, resigned. "It's all right, don't cry, we'll be all right." I somehow manage to support my weight on my left hand, and, after several attempts, I get up. The floor itself is hot. There's not enough air inside the crammed metal container. It's become an oven. Fear starts to grow again in people's hearts, and they begin to push, and shove, desperate to get out, oblivious to the pain they're inflicting on each other. The exit is blocked by injured bodies lying on top of each other. Wailing has taken the place of screaming. A few young men push me out of their way to reach the door quicker. I fall down, and they stumble on me, collapsing on my back and legs. They're heavy, and they're crushing me. I can't breathe. "Please, I'm suffocating," I whisper, incapable of speaking out loud because of the pressure of their weight upon me. "Please," I beg, as it's getting darker and darker. My chest cracks and whistles under them, but they writhe, shouting, deaf to my cries.

An unfamiliar voice says my name, and then someone grabs my hands and drags me out forcefully. I scrape against the hard asphalt with my hips, and with my knees. Fresh air! Someone speaks to me, asking me if I can stand. I look at him, confused. Under the strangely dimmed streetlights, he looks like a tall blonde angel. I can't make out his features. Confused, I whisper the name of my first love. I tell him that I can't walk, so he sits me down on a curb, then goes back to the container door to try and save the others. I glare at my surroundings, searching for my friends. It's impossible to recognize anyone. Their faces are soiled with ash and disfigured by horror. Young people are lying motionless on the ground, moaning, begging for help with choked-out voices rising from their charred throats. Beside me, a man whose hair is completely burned off sits oddly, propped up by the wall behind us. His head has fallen into his chest, and his eyes are wide open. He doesn't blink. My mind refuses to accept what I see clearly. He doesn't have eyelids anymore.

I get dizzy and collapse next to him. When my skinned body touches the cement, the pain is so intense, it goes through me like a short-circuit. I scream like an animal and get up immediately. Shocked, I notice that my shoulder-bag is whole, untouched by the flames. I try to reach my phone, but pieces of flesh are hanging from my blackened, crooked fingers, and it hurts too much. Somehow, I grab the cell and dial the number. A voice within me shatters the chaos and tells me, in the clearest words possible, that if I don't get up to seek an ambulance, I will die there. When my mother answers, I'm already leaving the narrow alleyway where the club is situated. Something has taken over, like an autopilot of sorts, and it drives my actions.

"Mom, please come to Bucharest. The club caught fire, and I'm injured." My poor mother doesn't understand what I'm saying. She demands answers, confused, frightened. I start to cry and insist that I'm badly hurt, and I beg her to hurry. I end the call and reach the inner courtyard of the factory complex, of which the venue is just a small part. An ambulance appears ahead, and I dart toward it, but it passes by me, speeding, its tires squealing. I turn around and watch it hopelessly, unsure whether I still have the power to go back. It stops a few meters away, in front of a group of three people.

I recognize my friend, Flavia. Mihai is holding her up, as she shivers and shakes. Her face is black, and her hair is burned half-way. The cardigan she wore tonight is missing its left sleeve, revealing her swollen, darkened arm. There's no more skin on it, just a blistering mess of red flesh. A girl stands beside them, quiet, overcome with chills. I don't know her name, and I can't tell her features under the scorched tissue on her cheeks and forehead. Mihai is all right. He had gone out to another club and was on his way to Colectiv to meet Flavia. When he arrived, he found her in hell. Dragging my legs and gasping for air, I finally reach them. They recognize me too, and flinch, shocked.

"Your hair... it's... it's burned off," Mihai whispers.

I beg them to let me join them in the ambulance, and they hurry to say yes. The nurse takes the three of us in. Her hands are trembling, and her voice is subdued.

"Lord, have mercy, Holy Mother of God, pray for these children," she chants, appalled by what she's seeing.

She puts me on a stretcher, and the other girls on chairs. As I lay down, my body caves in, and releases the pain it kept at bay to allow me to run for my life. I stare at my hands in disbelief, watching them swell up. Weirdly translucent membranes fly off from my injured body, leaving behind pink, open wounds that hurt acutely, or black, gaping gashes that seem numb. My skin is detached from me, hanging like sick wings under the weight of death. The nurse keeps asking me my name, and how old I am, but I can't speak. Horror seizes hold of me. The pain is so terrible it silences me completely.

Flavia notices and diligently answers in my place, ogling me, worried.

"She's scared… We all are. Can't you give us something for the pain? We're hurting really badly."

"No, I… I'm sorry, I don't have anything suitable here. We didn't know this was so serious. We didn't come prepared."

She promises they'll take us to the hospital swiftly. "Where?" asks the driver. "The Hospital for Burns, urgently!" The ambulance drives off and hits a bump in the road that shakes the entire vehicle. I press my arm against the cabin and scream. My raw wounds stain the wall with blood and ash. The mark looks like the shadow of a sacrificed bird. God almighty, this pain… this impossible pain.

We arrive at the hospital and the stretcher-bearers take us inside. They leave us in the hallway among others, just like us. I gaze at the people who are sitting on the shoddy chairs. Their faces are sullied with coal, and their terrified eyes shine eerily under the neon lights in the waiting room. They've been brought here from the Hell that we barely escaped. Someone offers me a sip of water from a small plastic container, and another person tears off the stripes of flesh that hung from me like defeated angels. "Why are you taking away my skin?" I ask, desperate, unaware of the absurdity of my thoughts. There is no way that they're going to be able to make me whole again by using those pieces of dead tissue. "Dear, you've no use for them anymore!" the nurses answer. They transfer me to a bed in a neighboring ward. It's full of people like those in the hallway, staring their wits away with fixed, glowing eyes peering blindly from tarry faces. They can't see anything around them, because they're turned inward, to the flames that keep burning somewhere deep in their devastated minds. Some are sitting upright, completely stiff, others writhe in their sheets, sullying them with blood, shivering under grotesque wool blankets, with red and black designs. They can't get warm because they don't have skin to cover their bones anymore.

A teenage girl is crying for her mother. Some nurse tells me that I have to share my bed with her because there's too many of us, and too little space. Thirst scorches my throat and I beg for water. "You're not allowed! We'll take you to the operating room soon," she answers, but I ignore her. I wait for her to leave, then I clumsily grab an abandoned cup with the palms of my hands. The teenage girl's mother arrives, and I ask her to fill it up. At first, she says no, but then she gives in. Gulping, savage, I drink a few mouthfuls. "Thank you from the bottom of my heart," I sigh.

The cold liquid quenches my burning pharynx and soothes the stinging in my chest. With difficulty, I get up to go look in the mirror from above the sink. My heart is racing, anticipating a sight that nothing ever prepared me for. My eyes are the first thing I notice. They glance horrified back at me, haunted by the atrocities I've just witnessed. My forehead, nose, and cheeks are pinkish-red and swollen. I've got cinder on my lips. All that's left of my once long hair is a mass of grimy straws, huddled together on the top of my head. I sit back on the mattress, confused and appalled. Another nurse walks in and asks if she can remove my clothing. She takes out a pair of scissors and starts to cut it off. It's glued to my wounds. "You've got severe burns on your back," she interjects. Then she tears the fabric from me forcefully. It crackles and comes off with the skin it was stuck to. "It's melted in you!" she groans. I can't feel any pain. I'm not well. My breathing is getting worse.

An orderly walks in with my mobile phone, prompting me to talk to my mother, then shut it off because it's been ringing incessantly. I do as she instructs, and she leaves with it. A heavy claw made up of needles seems to be sitting on my chest, pressing into it, stabbing my heart. I can't tell if it's real, or just in my head, but the neon lights in the room are becoming dimmer and dimmer, as if we're in some strange cinema room, waiting for the movie to begin. The sound of sirens crying in the night can be heard from all around, like the city itself became one loud scream for help. A beautiful red-haired girl weeps and the tears leave pink streaks on her dirty cheeks. The child next to me got her own bed. She's not praying anymore, not sighing, she's just lying there, mute, shivering. Her mother – the woman who gave me water – keeps vigil over her, wringing her hands, swallowing her wails.

The world unravels, torn apart by the merciless claws of a beast too evil to be conquered. Someone is speaking to me, but the sound of their voice is muffled, distant. It climbs from somewhere in the underground, distorted. "We're taking you to the O.R., can you hear me? Hey! Quickly, she's fainting!" Then, all of a sudden, everything disappears, leaving behind darkness and silence. The life I knew is gone forever.

II
THE HOSPITAL OF NEVERHEALING

I open my eyes to the sight of my worried mother, whose silhouette I can barely discern through the edges of something that looks like a thick bandage over my face. She's standing in the middle of the room with my friend, Elena, staring at me, shivering and livid.

"You came...," I whisper to her, relieved, with a voice so faint, I have a hard time recognizing it as my own.

"Of course, my baby!"

The pain is overpowering.

"What happened to Tamara?" I ask.

"She's all right, she's not hospitalized. Her injuries are minor," Elena replies. "Keep calm, don't fuss. You just came out of surgery."

I have a weak perception of my own body. It feels like I've become a mass of butchered meat that greedy hands keep tearing at, until they reach the bone. My face is completely numb.

"Mom, do I still have a nose?" I babble, stunned by the anesthetic still flowing through my veins.

"How about lips?"

"Yes, dear, you even have lashes!"

All of a sudden, my mother puts her hand over her mouth and stumbles out of the ward. She left so that she can fall apart somewhere I can't see. I'm probably not doing very well. Maybe she thinks I'm going to die. Am I going to die? I don't know how badly I'm injured, but the pain in my right hand, back, and left shoulder is unbearable.

I drift between states, unable to stay awake. The girl in the bed next to mine is crying. She breaks my heart with her wails. Her whole body is bandaged, and tears dampen the gauze under her eyes.

"How could this have happened to us? I don't understand! God, it hurts so bad."

I'd love to console her, but before I manage to speak, I lose consciousness. I wake up after a while and notice that someone put the lights out in our ward but left them on in the hallway. Streaks of neon reach us through the slit in the door and make the obscurity less frightening. These wanton glowing strands and the colored flickers of the LEDs on the machines that monitor us are the only things standing between us and complete darkness.

I hear a long sigh that ends in a sob.

"I can't take it anymore. The pain is unbearable," cries the girl, defeated.

I want to help her, but I'm not even able to turn my head in her direction. Finally, I manage to ask.

"Didn't they give you something for the pain?"

"I keep calling them, but they never come."

"Let's call them together," I suggest, but her voice is too weak.

She tries to muster up some strength but fails. I fill my lungs up with air as best as I can, and scream:

"Nurse, nurse!"

Nothing happens for a while, then someone barges in. The woman is angry and unsettled.

"Why are you shouting like this? What happened?"

I don't like her aggressive tone, but I don't falter.

"The girl beside me is in very bad pain. She can't stop bawling. Help her, please!"

The nurse sweetens up.

"What else can I give you, girl? There's nothing left to give!"

"But please, it hurts so much, please. I beg of you!"

Her shy, imploring voice turns into tears.

"I'll see what I can find," says the nurse as she vanishes out the door.

The girl sobs and prays, saying words I've heard before. "Please, God, this can't be real. Please, God, I want to wake up." Her mantra brings back the aching memory of the man crammed beside me in the container. He too beseeched the Heavens to make it all go away, like some sort of fragile nightmare, waiting to be ended. How he hoped he'd open his eyes to his sweaty sheets, far away from any evil, his heart saved, his body whole. I wonder if he's still alive, if he's here with us, suffering in one of the hospital beds. Or maybe he never got out, and all that remains of his prayers are the ashes. I'm in deep pain. I'd cry too, but I hold it in for the girl's sake. She doesn't need more hurt around her. I don't want to think about death anymore, about the billowing, dark smoke, the devastating fire, our burned bodies falling apart like rags devoured by flames, the chemical smell that pervaded my entire being with its sharp, stinging stench. "It'll be all right, you'll see. Tomorrow will already be a better day," I whisper to her, trying to console her, but she keeps wailing, and wailing, as I lose consciousness again, surrendering to the agony.

Tomorrow never came for her. She died next to me while I was out cold. Nothing within me warned me, nothing shook, nor woke me. I couldn't shout for someone to save her. I couldn't call a soul. The feeble life that was left in her after she confronted hell caved in, overpowered by the pain her heart couldn't bear. I wake up the next day with her voice echoing in my mind, and I clumsily turn my head to check on her, but the bed is empty. My mother walks in the ward and starts recounting what the doctors told her about me. I can't focus.

"Where's the girl, Mom?"

She hesitates, then tells me that some victims were transferred to the intensive care unit overnight.

"Her too?" I insist.

"Yes, her too."

Deep silence follows her answer. I can tell that she's lying.

"She died, didn't she?"

I finally learn the truth. When her sister arrived at the hospital with a few of her things in a bag, the girl had already left this world. I try to understand what I'm hearing, but I can't. My brain goes over the news a thousand times, to no avail.

She cried all night. She begged for help. She died alone right here, beside me, while I was unconscious. Her disappearance shakes me to the core. A soul that I had shared this pain with climbed to heaven from right beside me, and I wasn't there for her. I couldn't do anything. We were twins in our suffering, but she's gone, and I'm still here. Why? If until now, I was shielded from the extent of the appalling truth of what happened to us by the veil of shock, by the struggle to escape and survive, now I see it in its full hideousness, and its evil nature paralyzes me. I stare at the darkness of this abyss that opened in front of me, mute and motionless. Mother keeps speaking, hoping she'll chase away the haunting with her words. She tells me that I'm not one of the easy cases. Doctor Petrescu, the Chief of the Intensive Care Unit, confessed that I'm in very bad shape. I have deep, full-thickness burns on my back, hands, and head. The burns on my face, while relatively shallow, aggravate my prognosis because they will lead to severe swelling. The only reason why they didn't transfer me to the ICU is that I don't seem to have any airway burns.

She speaks, and speaks, but it's like I'm deaf. Pain flows through me, molten, incandescent, scorching me from within, as if the fire had found shelter somewhere inside, still burning, inextinguishable. I'm nauseous and dizzy, but above anything else, I'm scared. I ask to see my reflection in a tiny pocket mirror. I can't recognize myself. My head and body are wrapped in a mass of thick gauze, with slits for my eyes, nose, and mouth.

"You look like a tiny mummy," Mom says, trying to cheer me up.

I have a hard time discerning what's going on. The rest of the day vanishes by in a haze. I swing between an odd, dream-like state, and moments of lucidity, made even more real by the excruciating pain. The only thing I remember clearly is being transferred to a bigger ward, where there are three more girls and a boy. I recognize Flavia. She's sitting upright in her bed, sighing. Her entire upper body is wrapped in bloodied gauze.

"Alex!" she shouts. "God, I didn't realize it was you! I'm so happy you're here!"

The red-haired girl who was crying in the triage ward is also with us. Her tears left streaks of injured pink skin behind, as they were falling across her ashen cheeks. I don't recall us being introduced, but I know her name is Iris. She's vomiting black tar in a hospital tray, wailing, groaning. It's as if she wants to eliminate all of the darkness from her being, to free herself from the evil that permeated her body while she was burning alive. Iris vomits the horrors of last night, bit by bit. Sandra, another victim, sits beside me and, even though I don't know her, I tell her that she's pretty. We've never met but I'm glad she's alive. The three of us have our heads, backs, shoulders, and arms covered in thick bandages. Neither one of us knows what wounds they hide underneath. The boy in the ward turns out to be Ciprian. He gives me news about Nelu, who is hospitalized someplace else. Every once in a while, a nurse walks in with bedpans we have to urinate in. This room doesn't have a bathroom of its own. The only toilet available is far across the hallway. We can't get there alone, because we can't walk more than a few steps, and even if by some miracle we managed to, we couldn't use our burned hands, wrapped tightly in dressings. Our parents and our siblings help us with bodily hygiene, and feed us, as if we were little children. Around evening time, the effect of the painkillers diminishes, and I become fully aware of my surroundings. The price I pay for my lucidity is this vanquishing, indescribable pain. It wears me out, and it steals every ounce of hope from me. My body is swollen, and I'm cold. There's not enough skin left to keep me warm. As chills torment us, the only sounds heard in the ward are our cries, and the chattering of teeth.

The pain is immense. Overwhelmed by its spasms, we ask ourselves if, perhaps, it had been better if we too had died. We struggle to go on, but every once in a while, someone weeps, devastated, and we follow suit. Our agony is profound, and our loneliness, absolute. All our tears, combined, cannot wash the cinder off from what is left of us. And how could they if we're secretly still burning? I lose consciousness and wake up late at night. I look around desperate, making sure neither one of us was taken. Sandra notices my fright and speaks to me. We talk for hours about everything that's happened, about the people who survived, and those who have died, about how badly it hurts, about how it just doesn't seem real. It's become our dark leitmotif, this feeling. We try to soothe one another with what little force is left in us, even though our world has fallen apart. We'd hug each other, if we could, but we don't have arms for that anymore. Our embraces are folded tight in the bandages that hide the tragedy of our bodies from our sight.

At 6:00 A.M. sharp, a nurse walks in the ward. The woman is dressed in a green robe, and she's wearing a bonnet. Her eyes are meek, and her voice is gentle.

"Good morning! Bath-time starts today."

One by one, they'll take us to the hygiene ward, and they'll wash our wounds. They're starting with me. I'm exhausted because of the suffering, and I can barely move. She helps me sit in a worn-out wheelchair. It's cold in the hallway and it smells like chlorine. The sun has not risen yet and the darkness beyond the windows contrasts heavily with the sharp hospital lights. Shorter and shorter are the days, as the merciless night grows, famished, gulping us up. "It's November 1st," I whisper to myself, trying to keep track of time.

The hygiene ward is large and chilly. To the left, I see a green rubber tub with foldable edges. Next to it, there's a faucet connected to a plain shower head. By now, I'm freezing. I shiver and feel nauseated by the pain and the movement. It hurts. It always hurts.

"Your name is Alexandra, am I right?"

"Yes, and yours, madam?"

"Please call me Alina, no madam, no nothing, otherwise I'll feel extremely old!"

I smile as the woman puts on a pair of surgical gloves. I ask her what's going to happen next.

"Alex, I'll help you climb in the tub, then I'll remove your bandages and I'll wash your wounds with soap and water. After that, your doctors will come to see you."

"May I have a painkiller? It's very early, and I haven't received anything since yesterday."

"The nurse will come by and give you some Ketoprofen."

Alina helps me sit on the edge of the tub, then puts my legs in, one by one. A tall, dark-haired woman enters the ward, holding a syringe. She removes the lid from the cannula they placed on my left foot – one of the few body parts that has not suffered any injuries – and injects some drug into my veins. The liquid is cold, and it stings as it enters my bloodstream. I sigh but I let myself be consoled by the idea that the medicine will lessen the pain of the procedure. I don't know what to expect, but I think it can't be worse than what I feel right now, this desperate throbbing, as if something alive, a beast, is constantly burning underneath the gauze, writhing to escape. Maybe I'm so numbed by it, I won't even notice what they're doing to me. If it was that bad, they'd have given me something stronger.

Ketoprofen... The name is familiar. My sister used to take this drug when she had tooth aches.

"Alex, first I'll check the dressing, and if it's clung to the wound bed, I'll drench it in water to release it, so that I don't have to pull it off, all right?"

"All right, Alina."

With careful movements, the nurse unfolds the gauze, layer by layer. When she gets to the last one, I feel the cold air on my skinned shoulder. I suddenly remember the stripes of flesh that were hanging all around me two days ago, and I shudder, nauseated. I gulp hard, so as not to heave. I still can't see my injuries, but the bandages are very bloody. Alina picks at them, trying to remove them gently, but it's as if they're glued to me. I scream when she pulls on the dressing on my right hand. It makes a grotesque tearing noise, but it won't budge. The woman blushes and gives up.

"Let's try soaking them, OK?"

"Yes..."

I'm scared. She grabs the shower head and starts the water, checking its temperature on her arm. Minutes go by and I feel colder and colder. I shiver as the pain gets worse. My raw body can't take the low temperature, so I start to shake uncontrollably. Before the fire, whenever I had the chills, I took a warm bath, and all was well again. I used to love soaking in the hot water, letting it soothe me. Absurdly, I think the same thing is going to happen now, so I wait for it, with my flesh wide open in the Hospital for Burns' green tub, as if it's a blessing.

"Alina, I'm freezing. Is it going to take long?"

"I know, dear, but the water is still cold. It won't heat up. I don't know what's wrong. We keep telling them that the faucet is broken, but no one listens to us around here. I'll have to wash you, regardless. It'll warm up in the meantime. I'm so sorry..."

I nod, resigned. The nurse moves the shower head over my right hand. As the icy spray of water penetrates whatever wounds lie underneath the adherent gauze, my heartbeat becomes erratic. I start to cry, suddenly confronted with the unexpected revelation of the horrible, inhumane pain. It can't be real.

"Ali... Alina, I can't... please, stop. I can't. It hurts too much, please."

"I know, I know it hurts, but there's nothing I can do about it. Bath-time is painful, especially the first few washes."

"Please, can't you anesthetize me? Can't you at least sedate me somehow? It's unbearable."

"Dearest, all they wrote down for you is Ketoprofen. We never anesthetize patients during bath-time."

"But Alina, I can't..."

Her hands start to shake, and consumed with doubt, she calls the nurse again. The same dark-haired woman walks into the ward, and they whisper to each other. The other woman looks at me, unmoved. Her expression is dry, unimpressed. She shrugs and rolls her eyes.

"There's nothing else I can administer. If her doctors only wrote down Ketoprofen in her record, that's what I'll give her. She should talk to them, not to me. This is none of my business."

She exits without glancing behind her. Alina wrings her hands, turns to me, and gently caresses my uninjured foot.

"Alex, come on, be a strong girl. I'll get it over with quickly!"

I'm appalled. How can I disapprove of this in the awful condition I'm in? I'd leave, run away, but I'm so weak I can't even get out of the tub alone. Alina douses me. I want to cry, but nothing comes out. My mouth drops open in a silent scream. I hear it inside, shattering my sanity. As the water dampens the dressings, blood pours profusely from my wounds, and some of the gauze falls off, revealing the true extent of my body's ruin. Now, the spray hits the open gashes directly, and I roar and wail, choking, shaken by chills. After she removes all the bandages, the nurse grabs a small package from a box and opens it. It's an ugly-looking sponge with a side made up of hard silicone bristles. From a huge container that has the name "Dexin" spelled on the front, she pumps a dollop of foul-smelling soap. She disengages the dead tissue from my wounds with the device's plastic teeth. It makes a tearing sound that horrifies me. Scrub, scratch, scrub. I implore her to stop. She doesn't.

No. No. The human body is not made to endure something so horrendous. Alina turns the sponge over and washes me with the soft side, squeezing the stinging foam inside me. I cry now, and bleed, completely naked, skinned, robbed of my humanity. "Please, God. This can't be real. Please, God. Make it go away. I want to wake up." I pray and as I do so, I remember the boy in the container again. With folded hands, he begged God to wrench him to safety from his nightmare to no avail. He still burned alive. Then I see the girl who died beside me, and I hear her thin, vanquished voice, whispering the same inane mantras in the silence of the dark ward, before disappearing from the world. "God, it's not real, God, it can't be true." But it is. And she... she is no more.

My right hand is so swollen, they had to cut it in the middle, to avoid it snapping open on its own. It's cleaved by a deep incision that uncovers my fragile white tendons. There's no more skin on my forearms and arms. My raw flesh lies there, exposed, vulnerable, aching. I turn my head in horror, only to witness more decay. The left shoulder looks like a mad sculptor's ill creation. It's sunken, deformed, as if the fire had bitten it hollow, to appease its hunger. Thick crimson blood squirts from the gaping entrails of the injury, filling up the tub, making a puddle around my helpless legs. Abhorrence. It's not real. Nightmare. Wake up, wake up! Uselessness. It's all true. I can't see the wounds on my back, but when the nurse tears at them with the sponge, the pain is so immense that I soil myself.

"Forgive me, Alina, forgive me..."

"It's all right, child. Hang in there, we're almost done. Be brave!"

A tall male orderly walks in and looks at me. He exchanges a few words with Alina. I can't hear what they're saying.

"Little girl, please stop crying. Look, I'm George. I came to lend a helping hand."

He puts on a pair of gloves and runs his hands through my hair, gathering burned strands in between his fingers.

"You used to have beautiful hair, but see what's left of it? Gunk. You've got some awful burns on your scalp. This filth shouldn't sit so close to the wounds. Would you be upset if I cut it all off?"

I think my answer is "no," but I can't be sure. It's like something inside me broke, leaving me prey to a deafening silence. George shaves my head with an old, bulky machine. It makes an uneven sound as it works through the mess. Clumps of hair fall in the tub, looking like rotten clew of scorched wool, glued together by blackness. They smell foul, like chemicals, like the night before yesterday, like the scathing container. Alina washes my face, cleanses my nose, and pours water on my scalp. Thick droplets of blood trickle down my forehead, staining my cheeks, with tears of mourning after beauty lost. The water stirs my wounds as if someone was rummaging through them with coal-steel. The light in the ward starts to fade, as if someone's dimming it on purpose. Is it getting dark in here? Or maybe I'm dying. Dying because of the pain.

"I think she's ready. Hey! Little girl! You're ready!"

Alina stops the faucet. Her eyes are teary behind her mask. She avoids looking at me.

"Now we wait for your doctors, Alex, and then, after they see you, we'll take you to get new bandages."

I cry and shake in the green tub, naked to the core of my being, splayed apart, body and soul, in this ward that's become my slaughterhouse. I can't understand what just happened to me, how something like this was possible. There's no escaping the thought that what I experienced was appalling, inexcusable. The coldness of the room stings the exposed nerves in my wide, bleeding wounds, and it's as if I've caught fire again. I swallow continuously to alleviate the nausea, praying that I don't vomit. God, if you can hear me, I'm freezing. God, please warm me up somehow. Wrap your arms around my body and make it go away. Why are they keeping me like this, bare and on display like some sort of horror? Why don't they cover me with something? I shiver, my teeth chattering, dressed in nothing but this inhuman hurt and the abominable injuries, and they sit there, in the corner of this hell, looking down at their feet, their eyes averted from the spectacle of my unraveling. Help me. Please. But the words can't leave my lips because my jaw is shaking relentlessly. I'm muted by the pain.

Minutes go by until two doctors arrive in the ward: a woman and a man. She's dressed in a medical uniform with teddy-bear prints, and she's very young, probably in her early thirties. Her hair is tousled to perfection and her make-up is flawless on her serious, frowning face. She smells strongly of perfume, and I notice her beautiful hands. The manicure is done scrupulously, and it looks fresh. My hands... they used to be that way too, before all of this. Now, they're just masses of swollen, destroyed flesh. He, however, is middle-aged, somber, and dressed in a monotonous uniform. They introduce themselves: Doctor Preda, and Doctor Moldovan. They examine my wounds intently, exchanging unreadable glances.

"Call me Silvia," the young woman says and asks permission to photograph me.

I agree reluctantly, under the condition that she attaches the resulting pictures to my medical record, so that I can have access to them later, if I survive...

"Please stop crying. You're making yourself sick."

"I'm sorry... it's just that the pain was indescribable. It's not like anything I've ever experienced. I don't think this procedure is normal, at least not the way it was done, without any analgesics."

"Oh, come on! It wasn't that bad. It's over now. This is how they clean burn wounds everywhere in the world. It's part of the international hygiene protocol."

"Will there be more procedures like this?!"

"Of course!" she bursts out, annoyed. "You won't heal without bath-time!"

"Then could I at least receive a stronger painkiller next time?"

"No."

"But... why?"

Her tone becomes hostile. She hesitates.

"Because your respiratory function is... affected by the fire. A potent drug wouldn't suit you."

"But these procedures... they're too much to endure completely awake, completely aware."

"You've got to be strong, period!" she exclaims, glaring at the older doctor as if asking for support.

"Your sister is a very ambitious woman, isn't she? She made a lot of calls and reached out to all sorts of people, demanding information about you. I can't say I was thrilled," he intervenes, visibly offended.

I don't know what to answer. I have no idea what he's talking about. I've been naked under their petrified gaze all this time, shivering from the cold, the nausea, and the overwhelming hurt. I don't understand the purpose of his scolding. I haven't spoken to my sister since before the fire. Alina's eyes shift to the floor, ashamed.

"Anyway, you'll have surgery soon enough. Your burns are very deep in certain areas, so we'll have to transplant skin from your buttocks to cover the injuries."

"Please stop crying already, all right?"

"She's a very brave girl," Alina interjects shyly from her corner. Silvia throws her a dismissive glance and exits the ward, accompanied by Doctor Moldovan, without greeting me or the staff.

The nurse picks up a green sheet from a shelf and wraps me in it. She takes me out of the tub and helps me sit in the same chair she brought me in with.

"There, there, Alex dearest. I'll take you to Iulia now. She's going to bandage you."

"Thank you, Alina."

The woman doesn't answer. The habitual "my pleasure" doesn't fit the situation at all.

In the dressing ward, Iulia is caring for an elderly patient. She is young and pretty. Her red hair shines, bathed in the timid dawn light that washes over the room through the large windows. There are three beds here and lots of tall cupboards filled with surgical utensils.

"Who are you bringing in, Alina?" she asks.

"A very strong girl. Alex."

"Oh, she's one of the girls from the club. Poor little thing! Come on, help her get on the bed. Don't lie her down, just have her sit up."

Alina does what she's told. When she's done, she pets my leg gently, says goodbye, and leaves. There's a mirror in the corner of the ward. I manage to catch a glimpse of my reflection. A strange, bald figure, with gasping wounds on its head, stares at me from a mass of crinkly, blooded green sheets. Its red, swollen face looks back, searchingly, from a completely foreign world to the one I once knew. I have flashbacks of me putting my lipstick on a few minutes before walking out of my apartment on October 30th, flashbacks of my long, black hair flowing in the autumn wind, flashbacks of my neatly done make-up. I don't know who I really am.

That girl or this emaciated specter, peering at me with teary eyes, begging for something unattainable, for an escape, for an end to this madness.

I avert my gaze and turn my head to the man in the ward. He's an elderly gentleman with burns on his feet. He hasn't even noticed me because he's been staring at his wounds in rapture. Every once in a while, he sighs and chants: "I'm not healing," "I'm not healing." I feel sorry for him... When Iulia is done with him, she changes her gloves and comes to me.

"Tell me, dear. What happened over there?"

I realize that people don't know anything about the fire yet. I recount how beautiful the night was before the flame on the pillar ignited the entire surface of the ceiling with a surreal speed. I confess that, if it weren't for the fear in the lead singer's eyes, for his words of warning, we wouldn't have moved as quickly as we did, Tamara and me. I describe the infernal heat, and the stifling smoke that smelled like sweltering death. I tell her about the boy who prayed next to me. The fire that enveloped us. The darkness that swallowed us. The light. My blurry-faced savior, and the unrecognizable faces of those who managed to get out. The man without eyelids. I stop. The words refuse to be spoken further. Deafening silence falls between us, as I choke back tears and she becomes aware of the horror of it all.

"It's... it's going to be all right, Alex. Come, let me see what's under this sheet. I want to know what I'm dealing with."

She removes the shroud from my wounds. It's soaked in blood, and it's clinging to me. It hurts. It hurts so bad. Her gestures are gentle, merciful, but to no avail. When it's over, and I'm naked, her eyes widen as she takes in the grim sight of my injuries. She sighs.

"Is it... bad?"

"Well, it's not very good, but you're young and your body is strong. You'll heal."

She brings over the tray with medical utensils and chooses a pair of large tweezers. Gradually, she picks at the strips of dead skin that were torn off my wounds by the silicone bristles. It's like she's skinning me alive. I let her work without saying a word, drained of tears, powerless. Bath-time ruined me. She washes my burns with antibiotic. It stings and burns like I never left the hot container. She squeezes out cream from a tube labeled Flamazine and applies it to some of my wounds. She cuts out pieces of something called Atrauman and places them on the others. God, the pain. Make it stop. She wraps me up in thick gauze that she fixes with dressing rolls. It's done. She hands me over to another orderly, a petite woman called Stephanie.

"We're going to take a few steps together, all right?"

She grabs my waist to support me because she can't hold my hand. My aching fingers and seared palms lie mutilated under the bandages. We walk, halting regularly, to my ward, where Flavia and Iris are waiting for me. Alina has already taken Sandra, and Ciprian has been moved to another room.

"How... was it?" Flavia asks.

I can't find words to describe the agony. The orderly lays me in my bed and walks out. I burst into tears. I don't understand what's happening to us. The pain throbs in my body, insatiable, impossible to tame. Sandra hasn't returned yet, but they come after Iris, then Flavia, until every single one of us has had her taste of bath-time, the torture they disguise as healing.

Later that day, my sister and my mother come to visit. Cristina traveled all the way from Târgu-Mureș, my hometown, as soon as she heard about the fire. Her tired eyes are red and swollen from all the crying. They make small talk, hoping to get me to smile, at least a little bit. They want to keep me here with them, anchored in this life that is slipping away from me through the bleeding gashes on my body.

"I want to buy you something nice, a present. What would you like?" Cristina asks.

"Something nice from Sephora..."

It's our favorite store. I'm moved by how worried they look. I thought about them while I was burning alive. About the pain I'd cause them by dying so young, just like my father. After he passed, I begged God to make it so that I'd be the next to go, because I didn't want to experience the pain of loss again. I was just a naïve teenager. I had no idea what I was praying for. Maybe this ordeal is the answer to that prayer. Maybe these truly are my last days here, on Earth. One morning, they'll arrive at the hospital, and someone will hand them a bag with my belongings. "She died," they'll say. "She's gone."

How do I tell them about bath-time? How could I possibly explain? What name should I give to the atrocious pain, to make them understand? And if I manage to convey the terror, is there anything that they can do about it? I fumble for words as my thoughts become more and more confused. I'm powerless to offer them shape and meaning, so I give up. I abandon myself to what remains of this cruel day. I let my tears fall, hoping that they'll wash away the unspeakable darkness that pulls me under, to a place of anguish and silence.

I'm numb with pain and my fever keeps rising. I'm burning inside-out, as the freshly washed wounds become incandescent under the gauze that covers their horror. The hours pass, and the dressings become wet, soaked in my blood and in the stinging medicinal creams that melt inside me. I feel filthy and destroyed. The burns on my face swell, engulfing my eyes, blinding me. I can't breathe properly. Felicia, one of the nurses, keeps coming in to wash our eyelids and put eyedrops in. She changes the IV bags and helps us urinate in the bedpan. She sighs, and sighs, endlessly. The old, worn-out beds are broken, which means they can't be adjusted automatically.

"Even if you had a remote, you still wouldn't be able to use it," another nurse says, pointing at our contorted, bandaged hands. "Plus, they've all short-circuited at some point in time. I assume you don't want to electrocute yourselves as well," she explains coldly, as if what she's saying makes complete sense.

She leaves, but Felicia stays with us. All day, she carries unopened boxes filled with IV flasks and places them under our mattresses to raise them so that we can sit up, instead of constantly laying on our wounds. Maria, another orderly, feeds us and tells us funny stories about her baby granddaughter, trying to cheer us up. Her vivid blue eyes speak volumes about how much love she holds in her heart for the child. She talks and talks. She hopes her stories will keep us here, with the living, but we're drifting farther and farther away. As she stuffs a spoonful of soup in my mouth, I realize that I've become completely helpless. I swallow. And weep.

Iris's sisters arrive. All our loved ones look alike. Their eyes are red from all the crying and their hands shake when they try to touch us. Their forced smiles turn into heartsick grimaces. Even though they're falling apart, they want to shield us from the suffering. They can't. They don't know if we'll make it either. The girls fold Iris's remaining hair in a topknot and caress her leg, while she keeps asking what happened to him, to Theo. They stay quiet. Anca shakes her head and averts her eyes. Diana covers her face with her hands. Theo died, but neither one of them can utter the words.

Iris understands the meaning of their silence and faints. She falls back lifeless on her pillow, hurting her freshly dressed wounds, washed without anesthesia during bath-time. She doesn't speak for a long time after she wakes. In the stillness that Anca and Diana couldn't fill with the news of Theo's salvation, her heart has shattered. The pain of losing him is greater than the one inflicted by her dying body. As she cries, something unravels in all of us. We comprehend that Hell never truly ended when we walked out of the container. It continues here, in the hospital, and who knows for how long, and how many of us it will swallow. Iris, the girl who vomited darkness, could not free herself of it fully. We see it now, seeping through the windows, falling out of our loved one's lips, nestling inside us death by death, tragedy by tragedy, deeper and deeper with every ounce of skin we lose.

I learn that in order to convince my mother and sister to go eat and rest, I have to pretend I'm sleeping. They would never leave my side if I didn't lie to them like this, for their own good. After they walk out, Sandra and I talk in whispers. Even though we didn't know each other before the fire, we became sisters in suffering through it.

"I saw my left hand today, at bath-time... They told me that they don't know if they can save it. I'm an architect. I'm never going to be able to work again if they amputate it."

She's crying now, and all I can do is lie to her too, telling her that it'll all be all right, that we'll heal soon. Sandra's delicate face is hidden under patches of gauze, stuck sloppily over the wounds on her cheeks and nose. The tears well up in her eyes and fall on her bare chest. We're all naked, but we're in too much pain to feel any shame. We're not allowed to wear clothes, and even if we were, we wouldn't be able to. We can barely tolerate the bandages.

"Mihai was my professor, but above anything else, he was my friend. He never left that hellhole. Neither did Cătălina. They died together. I don't know... I don't understand how something like this was possible."

We mourn them as best as we can, talking about them until late in the night. We can't sleep anyway because of the pain. Every once in a while, Felicia walks in to add or remove a box of IV flasks from under our mattresses, to change our position. No matter what she does, they still torture us. They're hard and rigid at a time when our wounds beg for gentle touches that are nowhere to be found here. We're feverish, so she gives us Tylenol. We fall asleep but wake up soon enough, screaming for the bedpan. There's no other way to reach the nurses except for shouting. The emergency buttons don't work.

We pass around a worn sponge of sorts, pinched and deformed by all the bodies it's seen before ours. We use it to support our hands because we must keep them elevated to prevent blood clots from forming and to lessen the pain. It's the only one we have. Its case is missing, so we have no idea what it was used for before it became a medical device in the Hospital for Burns. First, I lay my hands on it, then it's Sandra's turn, then Iris, then Flavia.

The night fades slowly, through the tears and the hurt, which the first rays of daylight cannot alleviate. If we doze off, we're swiftly woken by the nightmares that force us back into the container, where we burn alive. The sensation of flames on naked skin never leaves us. It's nestled there in our wounds. They seem to have swallowed the fire whole, so they keep seething from the inside. We open our eyes terrified, confused, and exhausted, searching for an escape, for a familiar sight, for the bed we were supposed to lay in to rest after a fun Friday night; anything that would prove to us that it was all just a bad dream. All we see is the monotonous whiteness of the ward. All we hear is the meaningless chit-chat of the medical personnel, the hums and chirps of the machines that monitor us, the ordinary sounds of yet another day in the hospital. It's as if we're staring at the world from a shattered planet, like shipwrecked souls on a sterile ashen rock, adrift in a monstrous universe, always ready to devour us. We're afraid, but above anything else, we're cold and we're shivering. Our teeth chatter from the fever. We're tormented by the constant pain and by the lack of skin. We lie in our beds, unraveled; our flesh torn from our bodies, alone on these filthy mattresses held up by God knows what, mourning the dead, and our life - the life that, for others, has already begun to go on. I can hear footsteps in the hallway, accompanied by the screeching of small wheels. They're getting closer. It's Alina, and it's bath-time again.

Doctor Moldovan and Silvia tell me that the burns on my left shoulder and right hand have deepened, so I must have surgery. As they said before, they'll collect skin from my buttocks and graft it over the gaping wounds. They urge me not to eat or drink anything after 8 P.M. because they'll take me to the O.R. first thing in the morning. It won't be hard to fast. I can barely touch food because of the pain, which is so intense, it makes me throw up. They've stopped giving me pain-killers a while ago, since the second day, so I'm completely aware of it and of eve-rything else too. The suffering is indescribable. Every time I ask why they won't prescribe something for it, the answer is the same: my respiratory function is im-paired, and more drugs would hurt my lungs. They allude to the fact that I might even die if they administer strong medicine. Won't I die anyway, though, just like the girl who lay beside me, on the night of October 30th? Her name was Delia. I didn't recognize her in the ward, but we had met before. Flavia told me we shared the ambulance on our way here. And now... she's gone. We should have stayed together. We should have all lived.

My sister bought me perfume, eye shadow, and lipstick. She's keeping them safe for me, for when they discharge me. Today, her big brown eyes drift around the room, red and cried out. She can't look at me. Poor Cristina. As if she didn't have enough problems already. I pry, trying to find out if something happened, but she comforts me. Everything is all right. She has a hard time opening the gift box because her hands won't stop shaking.

"See how nifty everything is? Here, smell it. Amazing, right? I knew you loved this one. And check out the lipstick. The color is hardcore. And the eye-shadow kit is awesome too. I can't wait for you to come home. We'll put make-up on and go out, and you'll wear everything I got you. Don't worry, don't stress. You're having surgery tomorrow. I spoke to Doctor Moldovan. Your burns are deep, but you're all right. You'll be all right."

Mom walks out of the ward suddenly. I watch her fumbling with the door handle, struggling to exit. I realize something is wrong, but I don't want to address it.

"I... I know. I'll fight this. I'll be fine, just like you said."

I can't bring myself to share my fears with Cristina. I can't tell her what I think will actually happen to me. She doesn't have to know about the nightmares or the pain, so I lie. I lie for their sake, so that they believe I'm strong and I'll overcome this. The truth is too ugly to be expressed. The truth is that I don't know if I'll survive this surgery, and they don't either. At night, I open my scorched eyes. My body is burning with fever and my mouth is parched. The thirst is visceral, unbearable. I suck water out of the cup voraciously, bending the straw.

"Alex!" shouts Sandra. "You're not allowed to drink!"

"Damn it. You're right! I completely forgot. But I'm so thirsty..."

Sandra shares my fear that one of these days, the bed beside her will remain empty with another life lost. She scolds me and promises that she'll tell the doctors about my mishap when they come to take me to the O.R. A few hours later, as they walk into the ward, she snitches on me.

"Alexandra drank water last night!"

Silvia laughs and calms her down.

"She's being bathed before the surgery either way, so enough time will have passed between the water accident and the operation."

My legs go numb with fear the instant I hear about "bath-time." It fills me with horror to know that I can't fight this procedure in any way. I'll have to lie there, completely naked, defenseless, watching as they tear me apart wound by wound, taking it all in perfectly awake and aware. The nurse walks in with her useless Ketoprofen syringe and injects the drug into my cannula, as I shiver and shake, exposed. If she didn't come, if she didn't give me anything, it wouldn't make a difference at all. The medicine is too weak to work. It's just a formality. I'm their prisoner in this dysfunctional, upside-down world and I lie there helpless, incapable of stopping the atrocity. I ask myself if these people understand how much pain they're inflicting upon me. I don't think they can or want to. I don't think they care.

Water washes over me for a time that's impossible to measure in earthly numbers. I don't know if the ordeal lasts an eternity or just a few minutes. All I can perceive is the hurt. I hear myself crying endlessly with wails that, after a while, begin to sound distant, as if they're coming from someone else. I only know it's me doing the bawling because I see blood in the water, getting redder and thicker with every stroke of the bristled sponge. The nurse combs through my decaying injuries with the brush, ripping me apart. Scrub, scratch, scrub go its teeth, ripping and chewing off pieces of me while my body struggles to survive the anguish. I beg for painkillers through the chatter of my teeth. Their "no" shatters my heart every time it's uttered. After the last of the remaining pieces of gauze is torn from my gaping sores, as the soiled dressing falls off, it takes with it not only my skin but also fragments of who I used to be, leaving behind less and less of myself. The burns are deeper and more painful. Bath-time doesn't seem to be helping.

I used to have a favorite birthmark on my right forearm. I inherited it from my father, and it was very dear to me because of that. It was a sign that something of his lived on through me and gave him a sort of continuity beyond his early death. During my first bath, I could still distinguish its outlines. They were purple and swollen, but they were still there. As the days passed and the bathing continued, an amorphous gash took its place, erasing it forever.

When Alina walks in with the wheelchair, I close my eyes and recite "The Lord's Prayer." I keep whispering its verses in the hallway, and in the green tub where they're interrupted by my faltering breath, yet somehow still come through.

"Our Father... Who art in heaven, hallowed be... Thy name; Thy kingdom come... Thy... will be done on... Earth as it is in heaven."

But when the harsh spray of water tears my wounds open with its pressure, even my thoughts become silent. Any trace of reason is muted. There, in the tub, the chaos of absolute pain reigns supreme, and I latch onto my tears to stay human in this man-made hell. When Alina removes the gauze from my left shoulder, fresh, fat blood pours out of the burns. I don't understand what I'm looking at. I don't understand why there's so much missing of me. My right hand is still split apart. The fingers are black, contorted, and I see the fragile white tendons underneath the mass of damaged flesh. My body has become the stuff of nightmares. "Our Father, who art in Heaven, Our Father who art in Heaven, Our Father who art in Heaven..."

At last, they wrap me in the same green shroud as always. I force myself not to heave, not to soil myself. A nurse from the operating room enters the ward and asks me if I can walk there. She doesn't wait for an answer, she just shouts over her shoulder.

"Come on, let's get going. They're waiting for you."

She doesn't care that I'm too weak. She knows that I have no choice. Before, someone always accompanied me to my ward after bath-time. They've stopped doing that for a while now. It's no use asking them. They'll just shrug their shoulders and point me to the door. I struggle to move, drowsy, exhausted. I take each step carefully, with effort. "Don't fall," "Don't faint." I encourage myself as best as I can. With the green shroud stuck to my wounds, I drag my tired, swollen legs, leaving behind a stream of bloody water. It's a sign for God, so he can follow it and find me, so he can save me. I'm cold and my wounds throb under their cover, staining the fabric, dousing it. My lips burn because of the thirst, and my heart races. I'm so afraid...

Once in the O.R., I can barely climb into the tall bed. The nurses lay me on my back, pulling clumsily on my burned, immobile limbs. Someone grabs the shroud and tears it off. I shout. There goes my skin again. They throw the dirty laundry in a corner of the O.R. carelessly. I'm completely naked under the expressionless eyes of these strangers. I shiver. I shiver all the time. My teeth chatter and no matter what I do, I can't stop the chills.

"Where should we give her the injection? Her hands are useless."

"She's got a cannula there, near her ankle. We'll use that one and we'll see what we can do later."

"Alexandra, first we'll put this oxygen mask on your face, all right? Count to ten and think about something nice."

I close my eyes, shaking, but all I can see behind my scorched lids are the flames engulfing the club's ceiling, and then washing over us. One, two, three, four, five, six, seven... darkness, like in the container. It eats me up and I disappear.

They put the lights out in the ward. I wake up in complete obscurity. My chest hurts and I can't stop coughing. I'm lying on my stomach in the bed that's been adjusted with new boxes. Someone put a towel roll under my torso. I rattle my throat and shout for help. I'm suffocating. Felicia arrives and changes my position. She removes the roll and gives me water. She turns my head on the other side, and I sigh. Please, not on the burned ear. My tummy hurts.

"I can't move you too much. They've put grafts on your back as well. You'll have to sleep like this tonight, so that they take."

"But why does everything hurt like this, Felicia..."

"They removed skin from your buttocks; they've shorn you pretty good. Your belly hurts because of the urinary catheter. Calm down, all right? Try to sleep."

She leaves and I notice Sandra looking at me.

"Are you in pain?"

"Yes... My shoulder and back are killing me. And my right hand too. It's like the tips of my fingers are on fire."

My voice is ragged, and my throat is raw because of the intubation procedure. I cough hard a few times, but there's no relief. I keep swinging between a state of cloudy, tiresome sleep, and restless wakefulness. The night passes with new torments that my body cannot understand.

The next morning, they separate us. Flavia and I get a two-bed ward because we have the same doctors. If we share a room, they'll be able to perform the medical visit simultaneously and save time. Sandra and Iris receive a similar one. Both have private bathrooms, a rare occurrence at the Hospital for Burns. The orderlies crack bitter jokes about how they gave us the "premium" wards, which were only used for "special" patients in the past. What they meant by this was that the doctors had people come in under the excuse that they had to undergo reconstructive procedures, but they performed plastic surgery instead: breast augmentations, rhinoplasties, and so on. They wrote down a fake diagnosis in the paperwork, and *voila*. Problem solved. This way, state insurance would cover the expenses, and the surgeons would keep the fee, in cash, for themselves. "State-owned boob jobs," as one of the orderlies put it.

The good thing is that, from now on, my family, and Mihai, Flavia's boyfriend, can spend more time with us to help us. The personnel can't handle the large number of patients, so they turn to our folks for aid. They become our full-time keepers, feeding us, cleaning us, taking us to the bathroom. The joy of moving is eclipsed by a sad revelation. The mattresses aren't any different from the ones in our previous ward. They're not made for patients with severe burns either and they don't protect us from the emerging eschars that plague us because of the inadequate conditions. Their hardness worsens our pain and because the beds are unusually tall, we can't get out of them, or in them, without help. At least they don't need boxes filled with flasks to stay up, but neither are they any more practical for people like us, who can't use their hands. The only way to move them is by using a rigid crank, which only Mihai can budge.

"Are these music boxes? Who gives crank beds to burn patients?"

After the surgery, I keep getting worse. All I can do is lie in bed, prey to the most excruciating pain. I can't even sit up because of the wounds on my buttocks, where my donor sites are. Every step I take is tortuous and going to the bathroom is agonizing. The orderlies put me in diapers, and I feel deeply ashamed every time I urinate in them. They forget to change me for hours and I sit there, in my own dirt, completely helpless. I cry because of the mortification and the hurt. I'm useless. The number of IV bags grows every hour, every day. They're new antibiotics that I've never heard of before. I steal their names, written by hand, from the bags and repeat them until they're etched on my memory: Colistin, Moxifloxacin, Levofloxacin, Linezolid, Meropenem. The nurses keep probing me for new veins where they can set cannulas because the old ones keep failing. Adina finds an untainted blood vessel somewhere on my neck and fixes the drip there, asking me to be mindful of how I sleep, so as not to accidentally remove it. She's so beautiful with her long, black hair. She always has something nice to say, and her light touch allows her to do her job with prowess. At night, she steals glances at us through the cracked door of the ward, making sure we're asleep. But we're just pretending. We always pretend. The fever gets worse, and I spend my days ridden with chills, unable to move, unaware of myself. My entire body swells and swells. The internal medicine doctor treads heavily through the ward, worried. She keeps palpating me, measuring me, asking questions. I receive blood transfusions, iron, and albumins in hopes that I'll get better. Judging by my sister's cried-out eyes, I'm not so sure that'll ever happen.

Mom warms up yet another bag of AII, RH Negative blood. The nurses asked her to hold it on her tummy or under her coat and "massage" it so that it doesn't clot up. She rocks it back and forth, tucks it in, then rocks it some more, as if it were a baby in need of love. I watch her standing there, with her head fallen in her chest, fumbling with the bag absurdly. Humble and beaten, she bears the weight of my salvation, alone.

"Atta' girl, Mrs. Furnea! Keep it nice and hot. We don't want to hurt the kid, now do we? We're not giving her spoiled blood!"

Mom startles and latches onto the bag with desperation, kneading it fiercely. She stares at me with big, unsettled eyes, terrified. God forbid she'd hurt me! She doesn't want to harm me. It's so unfair that these people put such a burden on her frail shoulders. Aren't they supposed to have a special device that keeps the transfusion bags in order? Why should a mother be responsible for them? This is ridiculous. I swallow my tears and with them my mother's fear. I store them both in a new place in my heart, where I add, daily, new things of fright. I call it the Bestiary of Horrors.

I found my father lying on the floor in the hallway of our large apartment. He had taken his shoes off in front of the storage closet and had probably gotten sick immediately after. His face was unraveled and his lips, already turned blue, seemed to have wanted to gulp for air, famished for the breath he never managed to take. I tried to resuscitate him, but I had no idea what I was doing. My teeth hit against his as I blew air into his mouth, to no avail. I pressed and pressed on his chest, but all it did was make a dry, empty sound, while his still, unblinking eyes stared fixedly somewhere above me, toward something unknown. I ran for help from the neighbors. When my mother and my sister arrived home, the paramedics were already packing up their things. They sighed and told us that Daddy was dead. One of the men leaned over him and, with his big hands, shut his lids forever. Cristina fell to her knees and stayed like that for a while, unable to move, unable to hear, horrified. They helped us take his body to his workroom, where he had his computer and his guitar. We stayed there with him, caressing his cold forehead, saying goodbyes we didn't want to utter. His face, now devoid of his warm smile, became, as the dark hours poured over it, less and less his own, harder, and harder to recognize. We couldn't bring ourselves to leave his side until late at night, when exhaustion overcame us. The lights stayed on in his room for hours to come. We didn't want him to be alone in the dark. We walked away from him and sat on the couch in the living room, sobbing quietly, torn apart, unaware of what we were supposed to do with ourselves. Father was right there, next to us, yet he was gone forever.

My mother locked herself up in a tower of silence afterward. She never spoke of her pain. Her life went on, propelled by her immense inner strength. Only she knows what terrible monsters she tamed and with what heartbreaking longings she fought to stay whole for us. All the love she would have showered him with, she gave to me and my sister, and this gift soothed what was left of her shattered soul. And now this... How could I have done something like this to her? In the hard hospital nights, vanquished by the absolute loneliness of suffering, I pray to God to spare me for her. I don't want them to remember me the same way we remember Dad: mangled, robbed of who he used to be, terrified. I don't want this to be their last image of me: a maimed, scorched body, covered with unhealed wounds, an unrecognizable face; a closed casket with an anonymous body in it.

A few days later, at 6:30 A.M. sharp, still dizzy after a few minutes of sleep stolen from the dark hours of pain, I notice Alina standing at the ward's door. She's leaning on the old wheelchair. My heart races and my cheeks flush.

"Alex, baby... it's bath-time again. Flavia is next."

My legs are shaking. I can't control the fear. Flavia's eyes well up with tears. We cry together, one for the other. On my way to the hygiene ward, the pain flares up in my injuries, tormenting me. Moving makes me nauseous. I can't sit right. The wounds on my buttocks sting because of the pressure. I feel them smearing the chair with their fluids.

"What's your favorite thing in the world, Alex? Tell me."

Alina tries to distract me from what's about to happen.

"Music," I answer. My voice is faint because of exhaustion.

She stays quiet for a while, but then she finds the courage to speak up.

"Would you like me to sing to you?"

"Oh, please Alina, please do!"

She comes up with a song on the spot. The sad lyrics tell the story of a girl and the lover she lost. I close my eyes and focus on the melancholy tune while Alina puts me in the tub. When the water soaks the heavy dressings that are tangled in the stitches, the melody becomes a gentle soundtrack to my agony, keeping me sane. I don't know how long it's been since I've heard any music. They don't play any in the hospital and, until now, I didn't realize how much I missed it. It always saved me whenever I felt like life was too hard. Through Alina's voice, it's come back to me, to be by my side once again.

"Your voice is beautiful, Alina." I can barely speak because of the chills.

She removes my diaper and throws it in the trashcan. When the water washes over the donor sites, the room starts to spin. Next, she unravels my bandages carefully, so as not to tear off the fresh skin grafts that should be lying underneath. On my right hand, just parts of the new skin adhere to the wounds. I can still see the tendons rearing their delicate arches from the incision's belly, where the decompression cut is. The crimson flesh is torn and surrounded by stitches that no longer hold anything in place. They float eerily near the corners of the gash, like blue ghosts at the edge of a precipice. The left shoulder looks bad. More stitches that should have sewn the healthy skin on the burn lie scattered, clinging to nothing, amid pieces of detached grafts that look like continents set adrift by a violent ocean of fire. They're not part of me anymore. They're just sick patches of lace thrown clumsily over a chasm, neither covering it nor fully revealing its depth. They sink into it, blackened in the middle, consumed by the hollowness. They're too fragile to withstand the hunger of the wound below that devours them, starving for healing.

"Am I supposed to look like this, Alina?"

"Here comes the water, Alex!"

Her answer never arrives, but even if it did, I don't think I'd have heard it. The nurse squeezes the foamy sponge over the botched surgical sites and cleans me with a lower pressure flush that she improvises by holding her hand over the shower head. I'm certain now that I never left the club, that the fire was never extinguished. I don't know if I closed my eyes or if it simply became dark inside me, because no matter how hard I try, I can't see anything else but blackness. I feel everything: the weight of the water in my wounds, the tearing, the stinging. I hear the dizzying scrub, scratch, scrub sound made by the silicone bristles. My entire body is an open sore that isn't healing. "I'm not healing, I'm not healing." I remember the old man's voice chanting the same desperate mantra the first morning after the fire, in the dressing ward.

Alina takes me to Iulia after bath-time. She looks at me, displeased.

"The grafts didn't take. Let's see what the doctors have to say."

They arrive smiling, exchanging intimate glances, distracted by the conversation they're having.

"Are you crying again?!" Silvia asks, exasperated. "You've got to be more optimistic! Morale is an important part of the healing process."

"I don't know how much longer I'll be able to undergo bath-time without sedation. Today was terrible."

"I thought I made myself clear when I said that we can't give you a strong drug for the pain! What? Do you want something bad to happen to you? Ketoprofen is perfectly fine!"

I'd ask her how she knows this since she's standing right there, in front of me, perfectly whole, without a scar on her body, without ever having been touched by fire, and then drenched in water and detergent, awake and utterly lucid. But I keep my mouth shut. I feel too powerless to speak up.

"She's a very strong girl, Doctor," Iulia intervenes. "She's a fighter, she never gives up."

Silvia ignores her and approaches me with her phone. She takes pictures again, then examines the freshly grafted sites. Doctor Moldovan joins her.

"How am I?"

"Some grafts are all right, others aren't," he says, with a dry voice.

"But why, Doctor?"

"Your sister says that you're not eating enough, and you lie on your back all day," Silvia interrupts, annoyed.

"I sometimes don't have an appetite because of the pain and nausea, but I try my best to eat as much as I can, I swear! And I don't want to lie on my back, please believe me. I only do it because it's impossible to sit otherwise. The mattresses are not adjustable and..."

"It's bad to lie on your back, period! It affects the skin grafts. You must force yourself to eat even if you can't do it, even if you're not hungry. And work on your morale, for Heaven's sake! All the other girls are laughing and having fun. You're always depressed. Cheer up!"

I stare at her, confounded. I think about the girls. Iris is still mourning Theo, sobbing day and night. Sandra is desperate because she doesn't know if the doctors will be able to save her left hand. Flavia cries at night with her face buried in the pillows, hoping no one can hear her. I think of my ruined body, the endless antibiotic IVs, the blood transfusions, the ever-rising fever, the wounds, the diapers, my skinless hands with exposed tendons, my dead friends, bath-time, my helplessness. Our shame. The hard, inadequate beds, their squeaking cranks, and the boxes of serum flasks from under our heads. Then I look at her long, freshly manicured nails. I stare at her methodically curled hair, and at her neatly contoured eyes. Doesn't she understand that our bodies are rotting, while our souls unravel? Doesn't she see that we're dying? Of course she does, but she couldn't care less.

"Debride her and slather Flamazine all over. That should do it."

Iulia listens to her, nodding. Shy and meek, she holds her hands behind her back, as a sign of respect. After Silvia leaves, she puts her gloves on, picks up the tools she'll use, and comes to me.

"Don't mind her. She's always been like that. She's allowed to behave badly because she knows she's got protection."

The tweezers tear off the dead strips of flesh that used to be held together by stitches. I can't feel anything except for the pain. There are no more boundaries between me and the hurt. We've become one. The physical suffering takes hold of me and cancels the world around me. It gets dark again, just like it did in the container. All I want is for all of this to stop. Please, make it go away. These are the only words that manage to escape the blackness inside my mind, and they describe a simple, yet completely inaccessible wish. Please, let it end already. It doesn't. The torture continues, and it's just the beginning. I cry in spite of the doctor's advice. I cry to stay sane.

Today I find out from Cristina that the man who pulled me out of the club on October 30th is Mihai, Ciprian's brother.

"Their mother told me. He's really traumatized by what he saw. He got people out of there for a long time after he saved you. You're not the only one. That boy is a hero, but he doesn't want anyone to know about it. He's not looking for fame or gratitude."

"Can you please ask him to come see me for a bit?"

After a while, he shows up in the doorway. His head hangs low. Just like our parents, he's exhausted. He saved my life, but he can't look me in the eye. He's too humble.

"Mihai... is it true?"

"Yes," he whispers.

"Thank you. I'm alive because of you."

We burst out in tears, overpowered by the revelation of life's fragility, appalled by the unerasable horrors we've witnessed.

We count deaths to record the progression of our days. Our friends, those who escaped the club, can't seem to get out of the hospitals alive. It's as if we pass through time reaping loss, drawing bloody cross after bloody cross in the calendar of our souls, to mark the dates for mourning. The fire keeps engulfing us even after it was extinguished. What was not claimed by the night of October 30th is devoured by these cursed weeks in which not all those who struggle to survive manage to conquer death. Early in the morning, I found out that Alex Pascu died. He was the bassist of Goodbye to Gravity. During bath-time, I also cried for him, not just because of the pain, struggling to remember him as I had last seen him: immeasurably happy on stage, overwhelmed by our joy. He wasn't just a talented young man, but also a symbol of the fight for integrity in a society that has lost its way. He believed in art until his last breath, together with his bandmates. They were murdered by the very things they were trying to change as they knew best, through the music they made. Their songs spoke about everything that's wrong with our country, with us as individuals. And it also tried to save us. However, when the time came, no one and nothing saved him, or the others. They died, and they'll keep dying, killed by our powerlessness, by the powerlessness of Romania.

Suddenly, under the harsh spray of the water, as I lay in a puddle of blood and rotted pieces of myself, I understand what happened the night of the fire. I shiver, cry, and vomit in the green tub, realizing that what ultimately took Alex's life is the very wrong he tried to fix, the same thing that once drove me to write to the University of Helsinki, seeking a way to leave the country. That's why we burned alive: because of corruption. It got Alex, it got Delia, and maybe it'll get me, Flavia, Iris, and Sandra too.

I wake up burning after a nightmare about fire and death. I need to use the bathroom, so I shout desperately for an orderly or a nurse. No one comes. They stopped putting me in diapers because the donor sites have become infected. They say it's because of the warmth and the moisture, but I'm starting to doubt their explanations. More and more, they sound like excuses. I manage to sit up after writhing and fumbling but fall back down because of the pain. I can't use the toilet alone. I can't even get out of bed to go to it. I stare at the burned tips of my fingers, peeping through the bottom of my shoddy dressing, and understand that I'm completely helpless. The revelation of the humiliation I'm about to experience guts me. God, I'm going to soil myself. I try to jump off of the tall bed in a last effort to spare myself the shame, but I miscalculate my movements and almost crash to the floor. I scream because of the deep, stinging hurt caused by the bandages rubbing against my wounds. I sweat and squirm, dragging myself back on the mattress, away from the dangerous edge. I force myself to stifle my physical needs until the sensation makes me nauseous and my belly starts to hurt. "Please, someone, help me! I need to use to bathroom!" Nothing. My body, swollen from all the perfusions, caves in and I feel the hot urine spreading underneath me. The mordant smell of warm ammonia seeps out of the sheets. I'm mortified. Such shame, such horrible shame. I weep, utterly humiliated, stealing glances at Flavia who's sleeping. She hasn't closed an eye for days and now she's finally resting. What use would it have had to wake her? She can't help me. She's just as injured as I am, and she can't use her hands either.

The wet patch gets colder and colder, as my shame becomes deeper. Much later, an orderly appears and enters the ward, annoyed. When she sees what happened, she pulls me out of the bed and pushes me into the middle of the room. My body can't withstand her. I'm too weak to fight back. She tears the dirtied sheets off and reveals a grotesque, soiled mattress, filled with stains made by all the bodies before mine, by all those who suffered here ahead of me, by all those who died in this hell. I lose my balance, but I manage not to fall. I rock back and forth, with trembling legs, chattering my teeth because of the cold and the fever, holding back the vomit. I'm so weak, I'm so terribly weak. The orderly throws the linen on the floor, screeching and piercing me with her fiery eyes.

"You peed on yourself like a sow!"

"Please forgive me... I didn't want to..."

My voice cracks and I start to sob. I'm done. Instead of telling her that I kept calling her, that I'm full of the IV fluids that they keep pumping me with, that my hands are destroyed, that I'm feverish, that I'm sick because of the pain, the thirst, the unearthly thirst that tortures me every second of every day, I just give up. I stand there, in the middle of the ward, overcome with shame, incapable of defending myself.

"She called for you all night! It's not our fault that you make us lie in these horrible beds that we can't get out of alone. Can't you see that we're helpless? It's not with joy that we soil ourselves!"

Flavia fights with the orderly, protecting me. The woman's shrill screaming woke her up and now she's angry. After the orderly changes the sheets, peering at me with disgust every once in a while, she helps me climb up in bed and starts for the door.

"Thank you," I tell her, but she doesn't bother to turn around.

I cry until late in the night, while Flavia tries to cheer me up by conjuring up memories of the concerts we went to together. She tells me how happy she is that we get to share the same ward. She talks and talks, laughing in between. She feigns happiness and suppresses the horror in her, the pain and the suffering, to be there for me, to show me that I'm not alone. Her once clear green eyes are dry and expressionless. Networks of red veins cloud them, forming odd patterns that turn into maps that draw the agony of her devastated body, slave to the terror of bathtime and to the eternal, unremitting fever. Even so, she looks inside her broken heart for a leftover fragment of joy that she can give to me. Maybe its light will erase the dark stain of the humiliation I just experienced.

"I love you, Flavia..."

"Love you too, Alex."

We only fall asleep close to dawn and wake up when Alina's knock raps gently at our door. She's wearing her worn rubber apron, in the same shade of green as the tub that waits for us, gaping and famished, just a few feet away.

I'm not healing, and I keep getting worse. The skin grafts died, and the dirty dressings cover wounds that keep getting deeper. My body has doubled its size because of the severe inflammation, and I have trouble recognizing my legs. The nurses insist that I take walks down the hallway, but it's getting harder every day to just get out of bed. My breathing is shallow, I'm constantly shaken by chills, and the pain... I don't have words to describe it. It's as if someone whose sole purpose is my unraveling tears me apart slowly, consistently, piece by piece.

My mother and my sister help me walk by holding me up by the waist. Apart from the scarf they tied around my hips, I'm completely naked, but no one seems to care or notice. We're all dying here. Nudity stopped being a taboo a long time ago. My fever rises all through the day. It's high in the morning, then dwindles after the first IVs. Around lunch, it's grown again. It comes in waves, ebbing and flowing until late in the night when we receive our last drugs. They decide to run some tests on me: an abdominal ultrasound and a chest x-ray. An orderly takes me downstairs in a wheelchair and stops in front of the internal medicine ward. She has me get up and leaves, taking the wheelchair with her. She needs it for another patient. My legs shake from the effort of standing. I get the chills again because it's so cold here. All I've got on are the dressings and the scarf around my waist. A nurse finally arrives. She points me to the x-ray room, and I wobble there, already exhausted. Afterwards, she ushers me into the doctor's cabinet for the ultrasound. It takes a while for the results to arrive. When they do, he looks at them, shakes his head and stares at me. His eyes are unreadable.

"Is it bad, Doctor?"

"Well, there's a large collection of fluid in your tummy. Same goes for your lungs. I'll speak to your surgeons to let them know."

"But... can anything bad happen to me?"

"Let's hope it won't be the case."

Later that day, Cristina brings news from the surgeons. She spoke to them about my situation.

"They said you brought pneumonia 'from home'," my sister explains mockingly, rubbing her forehead. "Apparently, you didn't catch it from the hospital. You already had it the night of the fire! We have to get you out of here somehow. We'll pay for everything, we'll take a loan, it doesn't matter, but you've got to leave. I'll talk to all my acquaintances to find out what we can do. No one here wants to discuss the possibility of transferring you abroad. It's like someone glued their lips shut."

It's probably the second or third week of November. My body keeps swelling. The pain is incessant. Bath-time is more terrifying than ever. It feels like I'm stuck in a loop of suffering, every new day a repetition of the other, a mirror of horrors within a mirror of horrors, reflecting torments that never end. What if, in reality, I actually died the night of the fire and went to Hell? I chase the thought away by humming a song to myself. It's "Dark Light," by the band HIM. It's my go-to lullaby that I listen to every time I think that I won't make it to morning. It was inspired by *Mørke Lyset*, a novel by Norwegian author Mette Newth. The book tells the story of Tora, a 13-year-old girl with leprosy, sent to die in a quarantine hospital in Norway, sometime in the 19th century. Day by day, the girl learns about life, by dying. I first heard the tune when I was 18. I had undergone surgery and was hospitalized. At night, to keep the sadness at bay, I'd listen to the band's albums on my shoddy CD player, until exhaustion made me fall asleep. I didn't know anything about physical suffering before the operation. There, in the darkness of ward number seven, I learned about pain through the wailing and weeping of the other patients, some of whom were terminal.

At first, the doctors didn't know if they could save me. I waited too long to seek treatment and my autoimmune condition had gotten worse. I asked my mother to bring me a rosary so I could keep track of the prayers I made for myself, and for the woman I shared the room with. I still have it. It sits next to the kind minister's Bible. He came by the hospital one day to give his blessings to the ill. He was very young and humble. It touched me that he didn't want to enter the ward without wearing sterile equipment to protect us. From the threshold, he spoke to us about healing and gave us comfort as best as he could. He left the tiny book on the chair that my mother used to sleep on. Back then, I had to stare deep into the eyes of Death and either make peace with and let go or decide to fight. I chose to keep going with "Dark Light" playing in my headphones and in my heart, with Tora's delicate, emaciated face smiling in my mind. How I understood her... Like only a sick child can understand another. I forgave my body for its weaknesses and eventually, unexpectedly, I healed and was sent home.

Now, I don't know if I'm going to be that lucky. I often close my eyes as my thoughts wander to Tora, the quarantine hospital she died in, the young minister, and the humble rosary, with worn wooden beads. I sing "Dark Light" quietly in the night, like I'm crooning myself a lullaby, like I'm humming a gentle dirge, creating a soundtrack that mutes the loudness of death, howling all around me with its shrill screams. It's getting closer, but the music still manages to chase it away.

Dear Tora, my body is unraveling just like yours once did. I'm also learning to live by dying. I hope you found your peace.

Shivers run through the spine/ Of hope as she cries/ The poisoned tears of
a life denied/ In the raven-black night/ Holding hands with/ Dark light/ Come
shine in her lost heart tonight/ And blind/ All fears that haunt her with your
smile/ Dark light/ In oblivion's garden/ Her body's on fire/ Writhing towards
the angel, defiled/ To learn how to die/ In peace with her God.[1]

Music is light and in the darkness that surrounds me, it's my secret beacon that guides me towards salvation.

"I managed to speak to V. through S. He said he'll try to help get you out of here. He's not sure it's possible, but he's looking into it. There's no one I can talk to in the hospital. They don't care. Every time I tried to speak to them, they told me to sod off. They don't even want to hear about transfers abroad. It's taboo."

S. is a relative, and he's been living abroad since college. He and V. became good friends because they were both humble students looking for a better life far from home. V. felt guilty about leaving Romania, so he became a volunteer for charity organizations. He started off by buying drugs, out of his own pocket, for patients who couldn't afford them. Then he helped them go abroad to receive better treatment. It's what he's trying to do for me now. He wants to offer me support so that I can get transferred to another country.

I can't think straight because of the state I'm in. More often than not, I'm confused as to what the best course of action is. Between the spasms of pain, the torture of the fever, and the terror of bath-time, I must make a choice. I don't feel capable of doing it. I can't act. With my skin torn from me, sick to my core, and forever in anguish, I'm at a crossroads. I stare paralyzed at the new path ahead of me and I don't know if what awaits me on the other side is the light I've been searching for, or darkness. Doctor Moldovan and Doctor Preda reassure me that there's no difference between the care I'd receive abroad and the one here, that bath-time occurs identically. "The protocol is the same everywhere in the world," they claim. There's no way to know if it's true. I never set foot in a hospital outside of Romania. I think they're lying, and Cristina does too. Who should we trust? I stopped believing in their honesty a long time ago, but they're our only landmark

---

[1] "Dark Light" is a song that belongs to the Finnish band HIM. The lyrics were written by singer and songwriter Ville Valo.

in these times of horror, our only source of accurate information. What if they're hiding something, though? What if they're playing God with us precisely because we're lost and vulnerable? Maybe I'm giving away my chance at survival out of ignorance and fear. Maybe I'm a lot worse than they say and I'll die if I stay here.

Not long ago, they brought Călin to the dressing ward, in a wheelchair. Iulia was already working on my bandages when George rolled him into the room. She got upset and scolded her colleague.

"Can't you see I've got a naked girl here? Couldn't you just wait?"

"Do you think he's got eyes for something like that? Look at him!"

The boy threw me an empty glance and sighed. The skin on his cheeks and scalp was gone. George ignored Iulia's pleas for patience, sat Călin on one of the beds, and left. Our teeth were chattering so hard because of the cold and the fever, it was all we could hear in the room. We didn't look at each other, not because of shame, but because of the horror of what we'd see. A few days later, while Iulia was painstakingly removing the green crusts from my wounds, I heard George talking to someone in the hallway.

"They found Pseudomonas in Călin's burns. So, what? How could they not?"

I shuddered. It was the first time I heard that word and even though I didn't know what it meant, I realized that they were talking about some sort of superbug. Pity for the boy's fate washed over me and turned into worry. What if I was also exposed to it?

"Cristina, please ask them about me. They keep taking samples from my wounds, but they never tell us what the lab results are. Ask them if I've also got Pseudomonas or other infections. Insist on the transfer. Demand an opinion. If I'm infected, I want to leave, I don't want to stay here and be eaten alive by germs."

Not long after, my sister comes back with the answers.

"So, I spoke to Dr. Moldovan... He said your labs always come out sterile. He said you don't have any germs, you're just too sensitive, that's all. He said that if his own child was in your situation, he wouldn't transfer him. He *accused* you of being depressed, of not eating enough, of sleeping on your back. According to him, it's your fault that you're not healing properly. I explained that there's no other way for you to sleep on these awful beds. I don't know what to believe anymore. I can't get rid of the feeling that he's lying to me. This is an extermination camp, not a hospital."

Since they keep claiming that the pneumonia I "brought from home" has affected my respiratory function, flying isn't forbidden, but it's "somewhat of a risk." My sister sits on the chair beside me staring across the room, blankly. She feels helpless in this fight she leads against something much bigger than her, than her will to save me. We don't know what it is. It keeps vigil over me from the shadows like a voracious, featureless monster, a faceless evil that cannot be cast away. It's sick with power and it cares only about itself. I'm not safe here. I don't think that the things they're telling me are true, but I've lost the strength to challenge them. And so have my loved ones. How can you fight back when the people who hold your life in their hands argue repeatedly, that it's your fault that you're so sick?

But if I'm not infected, then why don't the grafts take? If I'm not allowed to lie on my back, then why don't they have special adjustable mattresses designed for burn victims? Is it really normal to be bathed like that, in a rubber tub, without receiving any pain medication or sedatives, one after the other? Is it enough that Alina sprays it in between patients with some anonymous disinfectant and then rinses it with cold water? Is this how it's supposed to be: they make you walk alone to the O.R. naked, dripping blood on the floor?

"There's no point in leaving if I'm not infected. I'm scared of flying if my lungs are in bad shape, Cris..."

My teeth start chattering because of the chills and I can't talk anymore. My sister looks at me, saddened. She's disappointed. She doesn't know what's best for me either. She doesn't think my labs come out sterile, but she has no proof that they don't either. No one shows you the results here. She doesn't want to pressure me to leave because she's afraid, just like I am. So, eventually, we give up.

"She's clean, that's what they told me, at least. She also has a bad case of pneumonia, and she doesn't have the courage to fly. She feels too sick to travel."

She's talking to V. I hear his sad, worried voice through the phone. He's not convinced we're picking the right path. My sister sighs, ends the conversation, and walks to the window. She stares out of it, crestfallen, wracking her brain for solutions. I'm restless. My cowardice appalls me. I made the wrong choice. Yes, I tell myself. Yet another fault I take upon myself and add to the bestiary of horrors. Perhaps this was my chance at salvation, and I missed it.

Day after day, the sterile coats that our folks have to put on when they visit us deteriorate. Our parents and loved ones wear them at all times while cleaning us, feeding us, and taking us to the bathroom. The gowns should be single use only but, in the evening, before they go home, our parents hang them on the rack in the hallway, stained and torn. The personnel asked them to reuse them because the hospital wants to save money. The hypocrisy is shocking. While the management demands that everyone wear "protection gear," that no one enter the wards without it, they forget to mention that the coats and slippers are only useful if they're truly sterile. This is not the case at the Hospital for Burns and Plastic Surgery. Everything gets recycled here one way or the other. In the end, my mom and sister buy their own coats and shoe guards from the pharmacy. They refuse to use the ones hanging on the rack, with their blood stains and ripped seams. They're getting sadder and angrier by the day. Cristina argued with Silvia because she wouldn't let an employee from a private medical gear company see me, to assess whether or not he could build me some sort of customized support system for my back, so that I don't have to always lie on the grafts.

"I commissioned those people, I said I'd pay for everything. They told me they'd bring you something special, like a backrest. The technician came yesterday to measure your bed while you were at bath-time, and she kicked him out. She told him you don't need anything, that they have everything they need. The man called me and told me she insulted him. I asked her why she did such a thing and she shouted at me. She yelled that they're doing everything humanly possible, but your body is just too weak. It's clear to me that they don't want other people to see the poor conditions they offer. I'm disgusted..."

I wish I had the power to feel outraged, but I can't find it anywhere. Later, I find out that I need to have more surgery. This time, they'll take skin from my legs. The wounds on my buttocks aren't even healed yet, and they'll make new ones. The surgeons tell me that this time the grafts will take, and I believe them, not because it's true, but because hope is all I've got left. I'm not capable of doing much these days. The fever keeps rising, my body swells and swells, the pain is worse than ever, and the IV bags multiply. I'm lethargic and completely devastated by the physical suffering. The only thing that consoles me is the presence of my family, of Flavia, and of her boyfriend. Our folks laugh, joke around, tell us funny stories, and caress us. They love us as they know best. But when we close our eyes to pretend that we're sleeping, to offer them a few moments of relief, they take a break from the show they put on for us. And they unravel.

They take turns collapsing on the chairs beside our beds. They look out the window or around the room with a blank, expressionless stare. Sometimes their eyes shift to the floor. They sigh and writhe, all the while watching us with crestfallen eyes, wrought with the fear that any moment now we might vanish from the world forever. They exchange whispers or glances, understanding each other without words. They go outside to smoke or eat and come back cried-out, shivering from exhaustion and from horror. They never tell us, and we can't find out alone, but we know that we lose people every day. Something inside us feels it. Even without hearing the news, we know that our friends perish one by one.

In the quiet autumn afternoons, feverish nightmares wake us up from the brief moments of sleep stolen from the pain. We open our eyes to tears after we caught fire again, or we said goodbye to someone we hadn't heard about in days. Our own closeness to death makes us more sensitive to such heartbreaking departures. We can't watch the news or read about it on the internet, but our souls know when someone left this world, and they never stop counting the dead. Maybe one of these days, someone will add us to the growing number of victims.

My right leg is about to burst with pain. I want to stretch it, but moving it is even more agonizing. I scream and my sister startles. She squeezes some water on my parched lips.

"Calm down, Alex. They just brought you back."

Before I lose consciousness, I remember I had surgery today. Bath-time, the pain, the tears, Alina's songs, walking alone to the O.R., the cold, the chills, the oxygen mask, and the darkness. My head spins as the memories mix together forming an incoherent whole. I fall into an abysmal sleep, as deep as death itself. I come to my senses in the evening. My head, back, and shoulders are killing me. This I expected. But I don't understand what's wrong with my legs. They throb and ache under what seems to be gauze. God, did they skin them?

"What did they do, Cris?"

"They took skin from both your thighs, and they grafted it on your back, shoulders, and hands. Again... They tried sewing together the edges of the burns on your scalp. You had extensive surgery. You have to be careful not to move too much."

I wake up in the middle of the night, sobbing. I feel the moisture of the tears on my cheeks and hear myself wail, but my mind is numb. Something broke inside me. Between the part of me that observes my condition rationally and the one weeping because of the physical suffering, there's a precipice. It's as if I'm torn in two. I free myself from the frightening feeling of dissociation and come back to myself, where it hurts. Oh, how it hurts. Flavia shouts after the nurse and Tela arrives quickly. She injects something into my IV bag.

"I gave you some Tylenol, all right?"

"Can't you give me something stronger?"

"Unfortunately, I can't, darling..."

I'm too sick to protest. I give up. Tela jokes around while she adjusts the IV drip. She doesn't walk out immediately, but stays with us for a while, talking softly about life, the weather, the lonely hospital nights. She's kind and gentle. She helps me sit up and strokes my foot. She tells me that my mom and my sister are amazing ladies. She wants to help me keep my mind off the pain, but I'm vanquished by it. My heart races and I sweat profusely. Suffering washes over me in waves. My body is a torture weapon. It's as if my flesh wants to tear itself from me and run away, escape the ordeal. I'm very nauseous. I can't stop vomiting in the tray that Tela brought. I stop feeling sick a couple of hours later, after Tela pours me a glass of watermelon juice. It's Flavia's. Mihai brought it for her that afternoon because it's her favorite. It's still a little cold, and it's delicious.

"Thank you, girls..."

The nurse leaves and, soon after, even the little effect that the drug had on the pain wears off. I'm in agony again. The first rays of dawn find me lying awake, with bloodshot eyes, exhausted. Another night went by without sleeping.

Mom and Cristina bought me ten brand-new pillows of all shapes and sizes. With their help, they build a soft structure that I can lean on so that I don't lie directly on the hard mattress. They adjust it a few times a day. That way, the weight of my body doesn't crush the freshly grafted areas. Initially, they weren't allowed to bring anything "foreign" in the hospital, but after a few weeks, they don't care about the so-called "rules" anymore. Not when I'm in this amount of pain, and they won't give me anything to alleviate it.

"It's not the pillows that they should be afraid of. The real dirtiness is in these walls and on their hands."

The suffering is atrocious and any reprieve from it, no matter how it's achieved, is lifesaving. The pillows soothe my wounds and make the pain more bearable. Cristina, Mom, and Mihai also bought two pairs of plastic ladders to help us get down from the tall beds. One day, Flavia wanted to go to the bathroom alone because there was no one there to take her and she didn't want to spoil the sheets. Our folks hadn't arrived yet, and the orderlies weren't responding to our calls either. She put titanic efforts into getting up, but when she tried to step down from the bed, she lost her balance. The distance between the mattress and the floor was unusually large. Flavia fell to her side, putting pressure on her wounds with the weight of her body. She let out a sharp scream. When Mihai walked in, we were both crying. I wept because I couldn't do anything to help Flavia, and she sobbed because of the pain. Her swollen ankles were hovering above the floor helplessly, without touching it. To prevent something like this from happening again, our loved ones decided to equip the ward as best as they could, out of their own pockets. For weeks, they asked the doctors and the medical personnel to take measures to improve the conditions. To no avail. No one listened to them. No one acted. Why would they? They had everything they needed...

My mother takes me to the bathroom, puts me on the toilet seat, washes me, and holds me up while we wait for my sister to finish building my improvised pillow fort. I climb on the plastic ladder and sit on the mattress, while Mom and Cristina grab my swollen legs and lift them up in the bed. I can't do it on my own. They've become victims of the fire too. Victims of this place that, instead of being a haven of healing, is home to anguish and torment. The Hospital of Neverhealing.

I open my eyes in the cold entrails of a dreary November morning. I slept for an hour because the pain wouldn't allow for more. The light in the ward is blind and milky. It's very early. I look to my right side and notice that Flavia's bed is empty. My heartbeat becomes erratic because of the panic. Like in a nightmare, I want to call out to someone, but I can't make a sound. My voice writhes inside of me, muted, incapable of becoming material. "She died," I hear a whisper within. It becomes louder and louder, growing with the desperation, until it becomes a deafening and monstrous groan. "She died like Delia next to you, while you slept. You should have stayed awake. You should have been there for her! You should have helped her!" In the wee hours, the silence in the hospital is vast. Only the chirping of some machine or the light steps of a wandering nurse interrupts it. Once the uproar in my mind quiets down, I hear the shower spray ripple against rubber, and then a visceral, almost inhuman howl that becomes a wail as the flush tears through the flesh. It's Flavia. She's alive. It's Monday. It's bath-time again. Today, they came for her first.

Later, with a few milligrams of Ketoprofen in my veins, it's my turn to lie in the tub. The water washes off the lacerated remains of the dead skin grafts. The same blue stitches that no longer hold anything in place hang from the ever-deep-ening wounds on my left shoulder. Alina loosens the thick, green secretions that cling to the burns. I cry, and she sings. My once beautiful and smooth legs have been skinned to the hips. They took almost all the healthy skin off my thighs, and I bleed profusely, filling the shallow tub with parts of me that I lose forever. The wounds they make to "heal" me are useless. The fresh flesh they cut off to cover the burns dies, sickened by the germs they claim don't exist. "What a shame," I think. What a shame that everything they sacrificed perished. Another surgery has failed.

I ask myself how much more I can take. Pain pours over me, molten, burning me alive. One of these days, I'll go mad. One of these days, I'll either die, or I'll get out of this tub, fleshless as I am, and run away from this place on skinless legs. I know I won't make it far... I'll crash in front of the hospital. But at least I'll be outside. I'll collapse on the dirty asphalt with my even filthier wounds, stripped naked of everything I used to be, of all my humanity. A puddle will grow from under my ravaged body, pestilent and dark, thick enough for them to see their monstrous faces reflected in its murky mirror. But no. That's not going to happen, is it? I'll never escape this place. It's getting harder and harder to believe that I'll survive. And even if I make it, someone else will walk out of those gates, not me, not the girl I was before. With every second that passes, something rots inside me. On me. The flesh that keeps dying covers a soul that's just as tormented, as it lays under the surface, strangled in the vise of suffering and indifference, destroyed by every "no" they shout back when I beg for painkillers, sobbing. Nothing will be the same again, no matter what will happen.

After they bring Flavia back in, she looks at me with her bloodshot eyes and whispers, exhausted, that it was worse than last time. That it hurt more.

"I screamed like an animal, Alex. I cried because of the pain, mortified that something like that came out of me."

That's what we always say. Every bath-time seems worse than the other. Our body is still shocked by the torture. Something inside us refuses to accept that the things we feel are real. We bury the memory of the harsh shower spray tearing through the open flesh, dousing the exposed tendons, but only until the next procedure, when we're reminded that it's not a nightmare. It's our day-to-day gruesome reality. Swollen from the pus and the creams that melt in them, the dressings stick to the live nerves in the unraveled muscle tissue. Once they're wet, their weight leans on the devastated wound, crushing it. When they fall off, they take the dead grafts with them, revealing the true extent of our decay. Then, the water, sometimes cold, other times scorching, washes over the naked flesh, devoid of skin, digging its way to the very core of our being. This pain might not have a name, but it does have a face.

When I was a small child, I dreamed of darkness after watching a horror movie. I was staring into the shadows, frightened, knowing full well that the true terror is about to begin. The night that had swallowed me was but a curtain hiding the horror waiting for me behind it. Then, from within the wall of tar, the face of a monster came out. I didn't look it in the eyes. I forced myself to wake up. The memory of the apparition stayed with me for years on end, as an embodiment of the great evil in the world, until life archived it. I had grown up and had, therefore, stopped believing in the boogeyman. But long after that, the mutilated beast, with its hate-filled features, reappeared in my life during bath-time. I saw it painted on the pitch-black canvas of my closed eyes while I was lying in the tub, collapsed in the darkness within, praying to God. It sprung out of the black hole that I had buried it in, a symbol of my shattered mind trying to make sense of what was happening to my body. An old nightmare had come true.

This pain might not have a name, but its features are those of the monster in my nightmare, the face of the evil we do to one another. Maybe the boogeyman is not a lie after all, but a truth too devastating to be uttered out loud.

Our Father, who art in heaven, hallowed be Thy name...

I'm still praying in the tub to the tune of Alina's singing, when Silvia walks in. She sees that I'm weeping, and she rolls her eyes.

"I can't believe that you're crying again! Alina, give her the sponge. She should just wash herself if she's such a wimp. Maybe we're more efficient that way."

"But Doctor, how is she supposed to hold it? She can't use her fingers."

"Come now, at least try, all right?"

She gives it to me, and I grab at it with my left hand, unable to grasp it. I finally manage to retrieve it, but it doesn't sit right in my weakened palm. Somehow, I put the silicone bristles on my wounds, but I can't do anything. My fingers refuse to move even though I'm forcing them to. I try to rub the green gunk off one of the burns, but it's impossible to keep going. The pain is excruciating.

"Oh, please, it shouldn't hurt at all! It's just dead skin. The others washed themselves just fine!"

"I can't... It's not that I don't want to. I just can't..."

"Not good at all," she interjects and takes pictures of my injuries while inspecting them.

"How am I?" I ask.

"Well, truth is we don't know what to do with you... You're simply not healing. Some grafts took, others didn't, just like last time. We sewed the edges of your scalp wound together, and, well, look at it now... It's wide open again! We'll have to graft that site at some point."

She says these things in a monotonous, clinical, and emotionless tone of voice. She doesn't encourage me. She doesn't tell me that it's going to be all right. It's my fault. Obviously. My body is a piece of flesh, bad and rotten flesh, that won't let itself be molded by her skillful hands. "At some point." What does that mean? Will I live to see that moment, or will I die before I get the chance to see my body covered in skin again? I don't answer anything. I just wait for her to leave. In the dressing ward, Iulia cleans the grafted areas, removing the dead tissue. Blue stitches fall on the floor as the wounds open their gaping, hungry mouths, begging for relief. My poor legs are bleeding on the sheets, staining the fabric crimson red. They were shorn for nothing. The surgery was a failure.

Mom waits for me on the threshold of the ward I share with Flavia. She has dark circles under her eyes because she hasn't slept again. She wrings her hands, further damaging her dry, scaly skin, that's started to peel off because of the harsh disinfectant soaps she washes herself with, to avoid contaminating me. She grows older by the hour. She's getting smaller and more hunched every day. The effort of caring for me takes a toll on her. I'm so sorry I did this to her. She's finished building me a new fort with the fresh pillows she cleaned and sterilized at home. Every night, she takes the dirty ones with her and washes them at 90 degrees Celsius. She brings them back and starts over. She doesn't care that she's infesting her home with dangerous superbugs. All she wants is to alleviate my pain. She's exhausted, but she never complains. She feeds me, she takes me to the bathroom, she tells me happy stories to chase away the fear and the desolation, to help me hold on to life and to reality.

Cristina is here too. She left her kids at home with her husband to be able to be by my side, to nurse me like a second mother. Two times a week, she makes the long journey from our hometown to Bucharest to take care of me. She's lost a lot of weight. She hides her trembling hands in her sleeves and gives me a smile. She sits on the chair next to my bed and unpacks the boxes of food she's cooked for me. She didn't sleep either because she worked all night to bring me fresh dishes filled with nutrients. The hospital food is neither good nor plentiful. They can't afford to feed us properly. Some nights, they boil wieners, put them in plastic bags, and serve them for dinner. Our folks are not only our full-time nurses but also our chefs.

"I made you the spread you love so much," Cristina says, her beautiful brown eyes examining me with compassion.

I nod my head and swallow my tears. My poor, poor girls.

A little later, the nurse arrives to set up the IVs I'll receive today.

"Why do you give her so many antibiotics?"

"Well... prophylactically. So that she doesn't develop any infections, you know?"

"You give her five bags of drugs as a preventive measure?"

"Yes, that's how we do it here."

After the woman leaves, Cristina sighs.

"You can't really talk to these people. No one's telling the truth around here."

My sister is convinced that the reason why I'm not healing is because I'm infected. She recounts that one of the nurses told her that a medical company offered to donate special beds for burn victims to the hospital, but the director refused to accept them, claiming that they have everything they need and there's no use for new beds.

"If they hadn't said no out of pride, you'd have better conditions now. At least you'd suffer a little less. They keep saying they don't need anything, but if it wasn't for these pillows of ours, you and Flavia would have gone mad because of the pain."

Mihai wants to change the diaper blanket from under Flavia's body. We sweat profusely because of the fever and when we're alone here, we lie in our own moisture, shivering. These blankets absorb the sweat and help us stay dry for longer. He sits her up, then encourages her to climb out of bed, using the plastic ladder. She's in the middle of the ward now, naked, shaking like a broken marionette. Blood drips from under the gauze that barely covers the gaping wounds on her back.

"Honey, there's no diaper here... It's just the sheet."

"I heard them talking this morning that they're fresh out of blankets."

"That's impossible. We brought a few new boxes ourselves. Alex, how about you? Do you have one?"

"I honestly don't know. I can't feel anything through the bandages on my buttocks and legs."

Cristina checks.

"She doesn't have one either. Poor girls! How would they know with all those bandages?"

Mihai goes to ask the nurses to give him two blankets. A few minutes later, we hear shouting in the hallway.

"If we gave them to everybody, there wouldn't be any left!"

"But we're the ones who brought them to you! We bought them out of our own pockets, boxes, and boxes of those damn diapers. Friends of ours brought some too, and donations were made. What do you mean you won't give them to me? How dare you! Please, bring me two pieces now!"

"I'm not bringing you anything! Talk to the chief nurse. She's locked them in her office!"

"What do you mean, she *locked* them?! Our sick girls suffer on wet beds and you're replenishing the hospital's stock with blankets bought with our own money? They need them now, not after they've healed."

But he can't get through to her. When he comes back, he's seething with rage. Together with my sister, they leave for the pharmacy to buy us new blankets. From now on, they'll bring them from home. They're not leaving them here anymore, because they know they'll vanish. It's not the first time that something like this happens. A few days ago, the silicon scar gels that some other company donated to us were locked in the chief nurse's office too. We didn't receive any. Iulia took a few tubes and gave them to us without telling anyone.

"Contraband donations," Cristina interjects.

As soon as the sun sets, the show begins. Flavia and I pretend to sleep so that our loved ones can go home and get some rest. Every time, before leaving our side, they watch us from the half-lit hallway with immeasurable sadness in their eyes. We know that, because we spy on them, through our squinting eyes. They don't want to go. They know that we might not be alive tomorrow, so they do everything in their power to stay with us as much as the nurses allow them to. We want them here because we're afraid we'll die without getting the chance to say goodbye. We are used to feigning tiredness by now. It's the only thing that convinces them to leave, but sometimes, in spite of our best efforts, they sleep on the hard chairs next to our beds until morning, when they wake up and start taking care of us again. When they really go home, however, we listen carefully to the sounds of their departure, to the exhaustion in their voice as they greet the nurses, to the light tread of their footsteps getting fainter and fainter, to the rusted squealing of the door opening and closing. We count each step they take on the stairs, until the distant pit-pats sink into silence. After the quietness conquers the night, extinguishing their presence, we open our eyes to behold the heartbreaking loneliness we're left with. There's no one here to lie to, so we resume our dying.

We talk to distract ourselves from the pain. We honor those who have died, and we mourn them. We recall our lives before the fire. Only the past is real. The present is uncertain. It only seems to be true because of the physical torture, which is too intense to be made-up. Without it, we wouldn't know if we're still alive, and that this isn't hell. We don't dare to think about the future. We're not sure it'll even exist for us.

The night brings back the fever and the thirst that plague us. Mihai brought Flavia watermelon juice again, and it's still cold as ice. When the nurse arrives to remove our IV bags, she pours us a glass and helps us drink. It's the best thing in the world and it alleviates the nausea that torments us every waking moment. I fall asleep late, when dawn already lights up the ward, coloring the darkness in pink. In two hours, we'll hear Alina's steps in the hallway, and the creak and wobble of the wheelchair.

Another one of my cannulas broke today and the nurses keep poking my legs in search of a viable blood vessel. After trying and failing a few times, they give up. There's nothing they can do. I need a central venous catheter. A young doctor walks into the ward and does a shallow check-up. He tells me they'll take me to the O.R. to insert the device.

Later that evening, while Cristina is busy building a new pillow fort, they come to get me. Mother ties the wide scarf around my hips, and I leave with Nurse Miruna. She tells me she'll wait for me in the hallway to take me back as soon as they're done. A team of two other nurses greets me in the O.R.. They help me lie down on the surgical bed. It's freezing cold in here and I'm in pain because these mattresses are even harder. The young doctor who saw me earlier walks in and stares at me. His glassy eyes look bizarre under the strong neon lights. He's wearing a pair of odd, doll-like contact lenses. While he talks to the nurses, a cold shiver runs down my spine in anticipation of the procedure.

"Doctor, will you sedate me?"

The man mocks me and laughs.

"Come now, Miss Furnea, I've inserted catheters in pregnant women without anesthetizing them. It's a trifle!"

I gulp and shut up. Everything's a trifle here. One that tortures us beyond human endurance. A trifle, of course, since it's not their flesh doing the unraveling.

One of the nurses turns my head to the other side and places a sterile blanket over my face. I don't ask why. I'm too scared. "Lidocaine," I hear the doctor's harsh voice thunder. His heavy hands are pressing down on my clavicles, searching for something. I feel a sharp stab in the delicate skin above the bone. I scream and tears flow down my cheeks unexpectedly. The needle, or something like it, writhes inside me back and forth, left and right, in vain. It wiggles around aimlessly. It can't find anything.

"It hurts, please..."

The doctor grunts and pulls the thing out of me. The room goes completely quiet. All I can hear are his annoyed sighs. The nurses don't utter a word. Not long after, I feel his heavy hands upon me again, pressing my chest down once more. Then comes the same violent stab, this time a little higher. The pain is like a sudden short-circuit that numbs the right side of my body. I groan. The needle begins to writhe through me again. It tears me apart. I endure the torture as long as I can, but, in the end, I give up.

"Please, I beg you, sedate me. Please, please..."

"It's not my fault that your blood vessels are so thin! I just can't find what I'm looking for. I didn't catch it this time, but we'll try again."

"But I can't take it any longer, not like this. Please give me something. At least something light."

It's like they're all deaf. I feel like I'm in a nightmare again. Three people who are stronger than I am are sitting on top of me and kneading my body with their merciless hands while I implore them to help me lose consciousness. My weak voice struggles to make itself heard, but it doesn't get through to them. They keep working on me as if I were a piece of lifeless clay. It's my fault once again that I'm a ruin. Ever since I got here, they blame me for everything bad that happens to me. Or that they do to me themselves.

The thick needle wiggles through me over and over again. Each time it goes in deeper, I hear the doctor shout out the word "Lidocaine!" The pain becomes worse.

I sweat and suffocate under the sterile blanket, begging them to give me a sedative, a painkiller, or anything else. To no avail. They ignore me, deaf to my cries. As they graze against the hard bed, my burn wounds ache and ooze. The fresh grafts on my back tear open and I bleed through the gauze. At this point, I'm bawling like a child, while a needle digs inside my chest, looking for something it can't find. All of a sudden, my left arm goes completely numb, and I feel a stabbing pain where my heart should be. I don't know how many more attempts the doctor made to find the blood vessel. I stopped counting when I reached nine. In the end, one of the nurses removes the sterile blanket from my face and looks me in the eye with pity.

"I'm done. I'm calling Doctor Petrescu."

The young doctor is drenched in sweat and upset. He's angry, but he doesn't dare refuse. Not long after, the chief anesthesiologist makes his appearance, thundering through the O.R. doors. He's visibly bothered by the fact that they disturbed him with a call, and he scolds his subordinates, screaming. He tears off the sterile blanket from my face, throws it on the floor, grabs my head, and twists it to the other side, digging his fat finger into my neck.

"Put it here!"

"She's burned there, Doctor. We can't," says one of the nurses.

"Please, Doctor, I just had surgery and I'm in pain."

"In pain? Shut up! You're not in pain!"

He turns my head from side to side like I'm a broken toy. After he lets go of me, I hear him exchanging whispers with the others. They'll call someone else to do the procedure. The young doctor sits in the corner quietly, staring at the floor. No one talks to him, no one even looks at him. The chills are back, and they take hold of me, making my teeth chatter. One of the nurses covers my face, blinding me once more.

After a while, I hear a new voice in the room. A woman approaches the table and I feel her light fingers touching my neck. Then she scoffs.

"Is this the needle you used for *all* the attempts? You didn't change it? Can't you see that it's blunt? You could have torn something inside this child! Please, give me a new kit!"

I freeze and close my eyes, getting ready for a new round of torture. I feel something pricking the skin. My tears have wet the pillow, and the moisture stings the burns on my cheeks. I'm exhausted. My body is a naked, throbbing nerve, scintillating with pain. The female doctor works confidently, with skillful gestures. She doesn't complain that my blood vessels are too thin, she doesn't hurt me by digging inside me with broken needles. She stops. Tired, but full of hope, I ask if it's finished.

The anesthesiologist removes the blanket from my face, stares at her colleagues, and asks, bewildered, if I was awake all this time. She doesn't get an answer. Silence engulfs the room filled with eyes gawking at the floor. "I've inserted catheters in pregnant women without anesthetizing them."

"Yes, young lady, we're done here..."

The doctors walk out of the ward without saying goodbye. A nurse calls Miruna to come get me and another one sits me up and dries the tears on my cheeks with a piece of gauze. She can't look me in the eye. Miruna appears and has a brief chat with them. She shakes her head and steals glances my way. She approaches me, grabs my waist, and helps me get down from the bed. I crawl out of the ward, leaning on her. I can't walk straight. The new catheter hangs down from my neck. The insertion site aches and throbs. It's swollen and sore.

"Why the hell did it take so long? It's been over an hour since you left. Your folks are worried sick! What did they do to you?"

"They hurt me, Miruna. The young doctor couldn't insert the catheter and he refused to sedate me too."

As soon as I walk into the ward, Mom and Cristina grab me and help me lie down. Crazy with worry, they talk over each other, trying to understand what happened to me. For some reason, I can't hear what they're saying. I feel sick. I can't focus or keep my eyes open. My breathing is shallow, and I'm fighting to stay awake. I don't want them to notice that I'm unwell because I don't want to scare them. I'm frightened. I feel like I did in the container when those boys fell on top of me. There's a heavy weight on my chest, pressing down on it, making me wheeze. I'm suffocating.

"I feel sick, please, help me," I whisper, struggling to breathe.

Cristina runs out to get the nurse and comes back with Adina. She injects something into my catheter and examines me.

"Her blood pressure is too weak, and her oxygen saturation isn't great. They've given her too much Lidocaine. She's also probably having a panic attack. I'll give her something to calm her down."

"What did those bastards do to you?"

"Cristina, walk with me a bit, all right? We need to talk."

When my sister returns, she's livid. The nurse told her what happened in the O.R.

"Is it true?"

"Yes..."

"I'll be right back. I'm going to look for that 'doctor'. He owes us an explanation."

Not long after she leaves, I hear voices in the hallway. My sister found the doctor and is demanding explanations. The chief anesthesiologist shows up too after a while, probably alerted by his staff. The civilized conversation becomes a shouting match. He screams at Cristina from the top of his lungs, silencing her.

"What? Is it his fault that your sister has weak veins?"

"Is everything in this hospital the patient's fault? Then how come the other doctor managed to insert it quickly? What's your explanation?"

"I don't owe you an explanation, miss!"

A pair of heavy steps trod away, becoming fainter and fainter, leaving behind silence. Cristina is alone now in front of the closed door of the ward. I can hear her breathing shallowly, fighting back tears. When she finally walks in, she collapses on the chair next to my bed and hides her face in the palms of her hands so that I can't see that she's been crying. The pain in my neck, around the catheter site, has gotten worse. So has the swelling. I feel an overwhelming pity for my mom and my sister. For this useless torment they're going through because of me. It makes me angry that I can't be feistier, that I'm not strong enough, that I let these people do whatever they want to me. There's a war going on between the trust I was taught to have in them and the awful reality of their sheer incompetence. Its theater is my dying body. I escaped one hell to end up in another. Cristina stifles her wails in the wide sleeves of her oversized shirt, pretending to massage her temples, while I pretend that I'm sleeping. We're putting on this show for each other, to hide from the horrifying truth. I'm not safe here. I'm not receiving proper care. I'm probably infected. I might die. All their lives, my sister and my mother will blame themselves for letting me rot here, in the Hospital for Burns. They'll strive to remember me like I was before the fire: their sweet girl, with her long hair, and her unscathed body. They'll bury somewhere deep inside their maimed souls the image of me lying here, burnt, swollen, anguished, begging for mercy. They'll struggle to forget the smell of decaying flesh emanating from my filthy dressings, as the germs ate me alive. But they won't succeed. No matter what they'll do, it will come back to haunt them. They'll always have nightmares about me like this: disfigured, destroyed, robbed of my humanity.

Defeated, Cristina weeps in the chair next to my bed, while Mother strokes her shoulder. She looks at me with the desperation I know so well, as if, from one moment to the other, I might disappear forever, and she wants to make sure it doesn't happen. She wants to anchor me to life with her loving eyes. Mihai stares at the floor and Flavia gawks out the window, wiping her tears with the bandages on her wrist. We've lost the battle tonight.

I open my eyes and smile, lying to them that I'm feeling better. The nap I took helped me calm down. Oh, look how late it is already! I'd like to sleep, and it's time for them to go home and rest. Mom is clutching a pillow that she wants to place under my head. Cristina smiles mischievously, promising me that she'll make sure everyone gets what they deserve. I ask her to leave things be, to stop worrying so much. It's fine. It passed! I do it for her because I love her too much to allow her to endure more humiliation. I know she can't change anything, no matter how hard she tries. No one is ever going to answer for what they're doing to us. The hearts of these people died a long time ago. Their empty eyes and unforgiving hands are signs that they're not whole. Someone or something shut the lights inside them and it's so dark in their souls that nothing can spark a reaction, not even a sister's tears. Afterwards, they'll terrorize me. They'll tell me she's nosy and distrustful. They'll insult her during bath-time or after it, while I'm being bandaged, or when I'm alone in the ward. They'll take advantage of my vulnerability and laugh at her to my face. As the pain takes away, even the little voice I've got left, that's when they choose to humiliate us and our loved ones. I won't be able to defend her then. I won't be able to stand up for her. Or for myself.

"Don't bother, Cristina. Let it go. We'll get through this, won't we?"

But I don't believe a word I'm saying. Tonight, I don't think tomorrow will come for me. Mother sets up my pillow fort and leans forward to stroke my cheek but withdraws her hand frightened. She remembers that she's not allowed to touch my wounds. We talk for a while until Adina walks in with the last IV bags I'll receive today. She hooks them up to my new catheter, pulling gently on the tube. I feel a sharp ache, followed by throbbing. Flavia seems to have dozed off, and I imitate her, closing my eyes. Our loved ones get up to leave. They try to make as little noise as possible, fumbling, shushing each other, and taking small, inter-rupted steps. They're heading toward the door slowly, and they never stop staring at us. I squint and see Cristina on the threshold. She's standing there, looking at me with the saddest eyes. Her lips quiver, and before she starts to cry again, she vanishes in the hallway. Once outside, they talk in whispers because they're con-vinced that we're sleeping. They're not ready to say goodbye yet. My sister is crying quietly and my mother hushes her because she doesn't want to burst out in tears herself. Mihai tries to comfort them with kind and hopeful words that he doesn't believe. They leave late, without greeting anyone.

When they're gone, I open my eyes wide. It's dark in the ward and the sounds of the night have taken command of the hospital, replacing the concerned voices of our loved ones and the chatter of the nurses with the muffled whispers of strangers and their distant wails. Somewhere on the other side of the hallway, a device beeps discretely, calling someone to the bedside of the dying. An unknown hand lowers the volume on the old-fashioned TV in the nurse's office. Everything quiets down, except for the throbbing of my heart. The fear makes me nauseous. I count to ten slowly – one, two, three, four, five, six, seven, eight, nine, ten – to calm myself down. After a while, terror turns into sadness. I look at Flavia, who is still sleeping. I don't think she's pretending this time. Often, I hear her sighing alone in the darkness. She doesn't want to disturb me. She doesn't know I'm awake. During the day, she feigns optimism to give us hope, but when night falls and our folks go home, pain silences her and replaces her laughter with sorrow. It tears off her mask and leaves her naked and defenseless in front of the horror. Then, Flavia falls apart.

"All the other girls are laughing and having fun. You're always crying!" Silvia's words pierce through the silence, deafening me. I stare at Flavia's unraveled face. We never look rested, not even when we're sleeping. Pain disfigures us at all times. How could someone mistake the grimaces we make for smiles? They don't, not really. They're just pretending. Today they told her that she's not healing because her skin is... "too white and thin." That's why the grafts don't take. Flavia believed them, just like I once did when they told me that I'm too skinny, too sad, too lazy to live. "All the other girls are laughing," but I still hear Flavia's visceral screams from that morning when I thought she had died, and they took her from me.

I close my eyes and keep counting. The contents of the IV bags flow inside me through my new catheter. My jaw hurts and I can taste the saltiness of the saline drip. My neck becomes numb around the fresh wound they dug in me tonight, but I'm too weak to call the nurse. I give up. I don't care what'll happen if the device isn't inserted correctly. The numbness extends to my chest and continues to spread. The ceiling is spinning and something is burning in the corner, but not with red, like flames, but with black and gray shadows, writhing to extinguish themselves. Outside, the late-night uproar of the big city manufactures loud ghosts, churning them out on the dusty streets. A few youngsters shout and laugh in the distance. Hasty cars rush down the highway, heading toward unknown destinations. I wonder... If these people knew what goes on behind the gray walls of the hospital they pass by daily, would they come to save us? Would they care? The seething shadows continue to agonize on the ceiling, mixing their murky blood with the sound of engines roaring. 61, 62, 63, 64, 65, 66. The numbers follow each other until they lose their contours and join the specters on the walls and the urban soundtrack made up of wheels and scattered voices. Am I falling asleep or losing consciousness? Maybe I'm actually dying...

Three days later, I'm naked in the green tub again and I'm shivering. Alina pushes the catheter back into the incision site and fixes it in place with a band-aid. Some of the stitches that were holding it in place fell off. It hurts, but compared to what I'm going to experience next, it's nothing.

"Your neck is quite swollen, Alex. I'll tell them to give it a look."

How can water be so cold and, at the same time, burn like this? Hurt like this?

After bath-time, the band-aid comes off because of the moisture. The catheter hangs along my chest, pulling on the blue stitches that keep snapping. Alina hands me over to Iulia and points to my neck. She shakes her head. I don't notice when the doctors walk in. Today I don't want to ask them anything. They'd answer vaguely and arrogantly as always, and I'm not in the mood to deal with their attitudes. They examine the catheter site and talk to each other like I'm not there.

"Have someone come over, remove it, and take it to the laboratory to test it. Have them take samples."

"I'll talk to one of the nurses."

Before they leave, they take pictures. They walk out of the room without saying goodbye, just as usual.

"Alex, I'll wash you with a new disinfectant we got from Germany, all right? I'm very pleased with the product. It'll sting a little, but it'll help you a lot!"

I close my eyes and count. Numbers replace prayers when my soul, muted by the pain, can't speak with God properly. Iulia drenches me in antiseptics, dries me, then drenches me again. Sometimes she uses the dreaded tweezers. She prepares the Colistin solution, pours it on gauze, then squeezes the medication on my burns. The cream comes next. Afterwards she wraps me in layers over layers of bandages. When I finally get back to the ward, I'm shivering and nauseous. The fever rises mercilessly. Mom arranges the clean pillows and helps me find a position to lie in; one that isn't as painful. She caresses my foot as I shake, chattering my teeth uncontrollably. I smile to comfort her. Felicia brings more IV bags.

"Hey, beautiful girl! I'll remove the catheter and we'll insert a cannula someplace else, okay?"

"But Felicia, they tortured her to put that catheter in. Is it really necessary to remove it after only three days?"

"I know, I know, but she's very swollen, Mrs. Furnea. Her neck looks awful. It's not a good sign."

The nurse cuts off the remaining stitches, takes the catheter out carefully, and places it in a bag that she then seals shut.

"This goes directly to the lab,' she says.

"But why?"

"So that they can check if there's a problem with it."

My mother and I exchange glances and realize that we're thinking the same thing. Infections. They're worried that the catheter might be contaminated. Felicia cleanses the wound, walks out with the samples, and returns with a kit of brand-new butterfly needles. She palpates my neck, my ankles, my feet, looking for a viable blood vessel, and ultimately finds one at the back of my knee. It's going to be hard to walk with the cannula sticking out of that area, but there's no other way. She pricks the skin and, luckily, finds the vein immediately. She fixes the device in place and hooks me up to the IV.

"It won't last more than two days, but at least I got rid of that piece of garbage in your neck..."

She leaves before Mom gets to ask any more questions. We feel like we're part of an odd conspiracy of silence, sporadically interrupted by explosions of honesty that never turn into real confessions. We know and don't know that we're infected.

My sister hasn't given up on the idea of sending me abroad. She tells me she spoke to V. again on behalf of me and Flavia. He's going to visit us today, together with two doctors from Germany. This time, Flavia and I decided to agree to be transferred. We've learned our lesson in the weeks of torture that we've experienced since the fire. We realized nothing can be worse than what they're doing to us here. This is the real hell we should be afraid of. We hear voices in the hallway. Our doctors are speaking in English with three other men.

All five of them enter the ward, wearing protective gear. Seeing Silvia and Doctor Moldovan with masks and sterile gowns makes me think that they've put on a show for the foreigners. Whenever they come to see us, when no one is looking, they're never dressed in anything but scrubs. V. waves at us from behind them. He's young and kind. He's staring around wide-eyed.

"Girls, I'm V. Maybe we can find a way to help you!"

His voice is warm, and I can tell that he's touched by our suffering. He's also surprised by how humble and precarious the ward and the gear are. We thank him for offering us support as best as he can. It's what matters the most to us in these troubling times.

The German doctors introduce themselves and gawk at us, surprised, inspecting the shoddy environment while frowning. Something is making them anxious.

They ask us how we're doing. We answer that we're not well. They ask if we're pleased with the care we're receiving. We answer that we're not. They tell us that there are two free beds in the hospital they work in, situated somewhere in the western part of their country. They spend some time talking to us, then walk out. Once outside, they continue their conversation with Silvia and Dr. Moldovan, asking for details regarding the treatment protocols used at the Hospital for Burns and Plastic Surgery in Bucharest. We eavesdrop, hoping to catch their answers, but we can't make them out.

"I bet they'll lie that everything's wonderful around here. The German doctors should have come to see us during bath-time, not now, when we're lying in bed, all wrapped up."

When they return, the German doctors are not anxious anymore. Their agitation is gone. They ask a few more questions about our general health. The younger of the three shrugs, resigned. V. is quiet, and he seems doubtful. He's fidgeting from one leg to the other.

"We spoke to your doctors. The protocols are similar in our hospital as well. You seem to be well taken care of, from what they've told us. It doesn't make much sense to transfer you in this situation."

Flavia and I remain quiet. We don't know how to react. We exchange confused glances. Flavia wants to say something, but she changes her mind. We agree to keep in touch, and they say goodbye. In the hallway, their voices mix with those of Dr. Moldovan and Silvia, who is chirping away in English, trying to be charming. V. however, keeps his mouth shut. He's not convinced that they told them the truth. Their steps become fainter and fainter as they approach the large wooden gates of the medium care department until they disappear into the silence.

"What do you make of this?"

"I have no idea..."

"I don't know what to believe anymore. If it's as they say, then what's the point of leaving? So that they can wash us like in the slaughterhouse, but in a different country? Wouldn't it have been more telling if they saw us without bandages? How can they know that we're well taken care of if they don't see what's underneath the gauze?"

"I don't know. I'm at a complete loss. I don't think that they question what they've been told. They trust our doctors because, at the end of the day, they're colleagues, they believe in the Hippocratic Oath. They're not used to lying. They can't imagine why someone would deceive them like that. Flavia, I don't understand..."

"Me neither. I simply can't tell the truth apart from lies anymore. If they can't offer more than what we have here, why travel so far? Where will our folks get the money to join us? It's hard to get by as it is. Food, diaper blankets, a little bribe here, a small gift there, and so on."

"Exactly..."

Later that night, after debating for hours, in the absence of appropriate medical advice from our doctors, in the absence of an informed assessment based on the reality of our wounds and not on sweet words, in the absence of certainties regarding the infections, we decide to stay, just like before. Why leave if we can't escape bath-time no matter where we go?

"At least here, we can beg for mercy in our own language..."

"To what use, Flavia, if no one's willing to show us any?"

Cristina, Mom, and Mihai are each sitting in a different corner of the ward. They're lost in thought and riddled with doubt. They won't say it, but they're really upset with us. At the Hospital for Burns and Plastic Surgery, every attempt at salvation is met with a lie strong enough to chase hope away. Or maybe we're crazy. Maybe we've lost our minds. Maybe they're telling the truth, and this really is all they can do for us. We spend the rest of the evening pretending to sleep, convinced somewhere deep inside our hearts that we've made the biggest mistake of our lives. We trusted them again.

Today they tell us that we have to move. They want to turn our wards into isolation rooms for the new patients that have arrived recently. They have infectious diseases, and they have to be locked in. At least we're going to be closer to Sandra and Iris. However, it won't just be the two of us anymore. We have to share the small ward with a woman who was injured in a house fire. This room has a common bathroom with the next one. Seven severely ill people, often suffering from diarrhea because of the harsh antibiotics they pump us with, will have to use the same toilet. The woman has no one to take care of her, so my sister and mother become her part-time nurses. She's all alone here, and they feel bad for her, so they help her with everything she needs.

After bath-time, they told me that I have to have another surgery. It'll be my fourth. They're going to take skin from my thighs again. The inner parts are still viable, and they think they can harvest enough healthy tissue from there to cover the wounds on my back, shoulders, right forearm, neck, and scalp. The grafts on my hands took pretty well last time, so they'll leave them alone. Whatever is left open will close "by itself," they say. As the day of the surgery draws nearer, the horror inside my heart grows. I wonder how much more this mangled body can take, overpowered as it is by the fever, the pain, and the never healing wounds. The night before the procedure, Mom takes me out into the hallway for our routine evening walk. It's a habit encouraged by the hospital personnel who keep telling us that we'll get blood clots if we don't move more. The donation sites on my legs are still open, so I can't stand up straight. My anguished body resists the movement, and I have to fight against the urge to lie down. I sweat, take a step, wait, then start over, hunched under the oozing dressings, bending my knees because of the stinging. Thick yellow cream drips from under my bandages, soiling the floor. The fever melted it. I leave behind filth. Mom cleans it up with wet napkins.

"Be careful not to pass by the ward at the end of the hallway. We isolated a patient with Clostridium there," says one of the nurses as we approach her.

However, the door to his room is half-open.

"It's too warm for him in there so we allow him to keep it like that," she adds, after Mom asks her what "isolated" actually means in the Hospital for Burns.

She shrugs and vanishes in the hallway leading to the other wing of the hospital, where the ICU is. A few minutes later, a disheveled head peeps out of the infamous isolation ward. After checking the hallway, the patient with Clostridium tiptoes out of the room and sits on Iris's favorite armchair, the one she always rests on after her evening walk. The man's hands and feet are bandaged too tight. We stop, frightened. We don't want to get any closer, so we decide to end the walk. He throws us a hopeless glance and shakes his head.

"You're one of the girls from the club fire, right? Such a pity you ended up like this. You used to be beautiful."

Instead of making me sad, his words amuse me. In a second, the entire absurdity of this whole thing becomes clear to me, and I laugh out loud. The "isolated" patient sitting carelessly in the armchair in the hallway, prey to an infection that slowly devours his burned body, decries my wounds while I stand there paralyzed, afraid of his disease, when my flesh harbors God knows what horrible germs. "The antibiotics are administered prophylactically," "You probably brought pneumonia from home," "You caught a cold from someone in the club." I wonder what lies they tell him. What did he do to catch the Clostridium? At least his illness has a name.

Early in the morning, the nurses who pass by our half-open doors exchange whispers. Sometimes they talk about their husbands, their children, their families, the little joys, and sorrows of everyday existence. These snippets of their reality – of "normal" life – have become so alien to me. It's like they barely mean anything, coming to me from a different life, one that I've lost forever. It must be really good waking up whole, in your bed, ready to face another day. It must be soothing to go to sleep without the fear that you're not going to make it through the night. How does not being in pain feel? I eavesdrop on their stories, famished for them, disregarding the fact that once they'd have seemed foolish or uninteresting to me. Now I cling to them desperately just to keep believing that something else exists beyond this hell, something I could still reach one day, something that doesn't hurt or burn. I rejoice when they're happy and suffer when they're sad. I experience the things that are denied to me vicariously, fighting to stay human by learning about other people's humanity, while mine slips through my fingers with the stitches that fall from my unhealed wounds, taking the dead grafts with them.

Rarely do they talk about the patients. About us. Their voices change then. They're no longer light and lively, hovering near the threshold of silence, morphing into awkward murmurs that recite strange words like "Pseudomonas," "Staphylococcus," "Klebsiella," "Clostridium."

"Did you hear that they found multidrug-resistant Pseudomonas in Călin's wounds?"

Nothing. Quietness fills the gap between their chatter. The other person doesn't answer. She lets the echo of the revelation die. Then, hidden lips whisper unknown sentences that I can't make out. The bodies stop moving for a while, only to rustle onward on their path, in tandem, heading to the hygiene ward or to the operating room. They take their secrets with them.

Pseudomonas.

Maybe it's just Călin. He's the only one who has it, and I'm all right. I'm healthy. My labs are sterile. But then why am I not healing? Why do I keep getting a fever? Why do my teeth chatter from the shivers? Is it just the fear, or is it something worse? I wonder if their words would make more sense if instead of "Călin," they'd have said "Alexandra." In the early hours, when dawn grows sharp teeth that will tear us apart in the green tub, when we should be sleeping, unaware of their mindless chatter, the truth haunts the hospital hallways, disguised in whispers and questions without answer.

On the day of the surgery, Alina takes me to bath-time earlier than usual. It's colder in the hygiene ward than I expected.

"They left the window open overnight. They sprayed the place with formaldehyde and then forgot to close it once they were done. I'm sorry, Alex."

She's talking about the hospital staff's habit of sterilizing the hallways with a device they call "the froggy." It sprays vapors of formaldehyde which are supposed to disinfect the place. Sometimes, around 9 P.M., the nurses close the doors of the wards, stuff our blankets under the threshold, and demand that we stay inside. The strong scent seeps in through the cracks and intoxicates us and our loved ones who've stayed behind to care for us during the night. Mom got sick once from the vapors. One of the nurses gave her an IV to stop her coughing, but it only made it worse. She was so ill that she vomited in the taxi on her way back home. Ever since, I forbade her to stay with me when they bring out the formaldehyde froggy.

Freezing cold water washes over me, burning the wounds under my dressings. When the gauze falls off and the spray hits the gaping gashes, I cry, and I don't stop until I'm in the O.R. and someone forces an oxygen mask onto my face. I beg God to help me survive the surgery. Then I fall into a deep sleep before my tears get a chance to dry.

A few hours later, the pain wakes me up from my sickly slumber. The white light of the early winter afternoon flushes through the windows and casts a ghostly pallor on my mother's face. Every once in a while, just like last time, my sister wipes my lips with a sponge soaked in water.

"She's burning. Good job, Al. You made it!"

The pain is like a monster ravaging my flesh with its hungry claws, picking at me, pulling me apart. I feel nauseous and dizzy. I'm lying on my back on the dead-hard mattress. I beg my mom to slip a pillow underneath my back. She and my sister sigh. They're not allowed to move me. I have to stay in this position until tomorrow. God, it hurts so bad. I have to urinate, and the orderly walks in with a worn-out bedpan. She hoists me up and pushes it under me. My heavy body, not yet fully woken from the anesthesia, slips over it without my control and I rub my freshly grafted back against the harsh bed. I weep because of the shame, the helplessness, and the anxiety. I hope the new skin didn't break. I hope the new skin didn't break.

I vomit all night long. Every time I try not to force myself. Effort worsens the agony. Cristina pats my broken lips with the sponge and strokes my leg with trembling hands. They've taken skin from my thighs again and I can't bend my knees because of the hurt. Will this torture ever end, and if so, how? I don't want to die. God, I don't want to die.

The chills are getting worse, and the nurses walk in and out of the ward, bringing new IV bags, taking out old ones. I'm freezing, and someone throws a red wool blanket over me. It smells funny, and it looks exactly like the ones they put under the threshold of our doors when the formaldehyde froggy sprays disinfectant vapors in the air. Or like the ones they covered the burn victims in the triage ward with, on the night of October 30th. Before I lose consciousness, I wonder if they're the same ones. They trundle them on the filthy floors, then they put them over our bodies as if we're just as besmirched as the surfaces their merciless feet step on, like they step on our dead skin, like they step on our dying souls.

"Why are there new scrapes and bruises on her cheek and hand?"

I hear this from a distance as if someone were speaking to me in a dream.

"See this? She has a large scrape on her left forearm. And look, here, on the cheek, where the burn had healed, the skin is cracked. The pillow is drenched in blood under her face."

I open my eyes and try to lift my arm to look at it, but I can't. A stabbing pain shoots through me and I sigh.

"What happened?"

"We don't know. You have new wounds..."

Cristina walks out of the ward, and Mother grabs the pillow. She holds my head up while she turns it on the other side, so that I don't have to lie in my own blood. She helps me drink some juice. God, how I miss my pillow fort. When my sister returns, she's angry.

"I asked about these new injuries of yours. One of the nurses shrugged and said that they either dropped you while they were turning you on the operating table, or the orderlies that brought you in hit you while they were putting you in bed. And they have the guts to call this place a hospital! Good thing they didn't crack your skull or break your bones. I'm going to speak to the doctor about this. I'm curious about what she has to say about it."

My body caves in and I faint. I wake up at night in pain. My sister is by my side. She fell asleep on the chair and her head rests on my bed. She's exhausted because of all the traveling back and forth, the cooking, and the endless conflict with the doctors, who never give us information freely. It has to be pried from them. From the illuminated hallway, I can hear the faint chatter of the news program reporters. They're counting the dead again. Our friends who didn't make it. Flavia opens her eyes and looks at me, grief-stricken. We cry quietly so as not to wake Cristina. She deserves some peace and quiet after keeping vigil over me for hours. For a while, I don't disturb her, even though I need help. When I can't take it anymore, I beg her to soothe me somehow. I need my pillows. I can't lie on the hard mattress anymore. The freshly operated wounds throb and ache because of its firmness. The pain is excruciating. Cristina hesitates. In the end, she understands and gets to work. She pulls out clean pillows from the plastic bag left by Mom. She improvises a structure capable of supporting my body, without putting pressure on the surgery sites. Her hands shake because of exhaustion. When she's done with me, she helps Flavia. Ever since they moved us into this ward, someone always sleeps on the chair next to us, either Mom, Mihai, Cristina, or Olivia, our friend. They wake up to take us to the bathroom, to give us a sip of water, or to rearrange our pillows forts. They wash us, they feed us, they sit with us in our darkest hour, tending to the needs of our bodies, but also to those of our souls.

When we open our eyes in the dead of the hospital night and we see them there, resting by our sides, their familiar presence comforts us. Somewhere deep inside our hearts, beyond the threshold of sleep, the famished flames that burned our bodies take shape again, becoming nightmares. When we climb up from the maelstrom within, we cling to our loved ones to take us back to the shore of sanity, away from the raging ocean of death that froths inside us, troubled and filled with terrors. Their tired hands, with chafed skin from all the washing, wipe our tears away when fear threatens to engulf us and when we think that we never made it out of the club in the first place. We never got out of the container. Out of Hell. They're here to tell us that we're no longer burning, even though a different kind of fire, just as devouring, consumes our flesh, preventing us from healing.

"They operated on you supervised by a Romanian doctor who works in France," says Cristina. "I eavesdropped on their conversation while I waited outside Dr. Moldovan's door. They grafted artificial skin on your back, shoulders, and scalp. The surgeon brought the product with him from abroad. Apparently, it's called Matriderm, or something like that."

"Did you ask about the wounds on my cheek and arm?"

"Yes. I took Silvia by surprise, but she regrouped quickly. She denied anything had happened in the O.R. She said you probably hurt yourself. I asked her how she thought that was possible since you can't move your hands at all. She literally turned around and trotted off without answering, leaving me in the middle of the hallway. Her level of disrespect is astounding. She thinks she's the master of everyone's fate."

My sister shrugs, resigned. Nothing surprises me anymore. How could I have done this to myself when, for a few weeks now, I've become completely immobile? My joints are stiff because they force me to lie in these inadequate beds that cannot be adjusted. My mother replaced the worn-out sponge that was being passed around from one sick person to the other with the clean pillows she bought. I use them for the same purpose: to hold my arms up, because I'm not allowed to lay them beside me. One day, tired of seeing me struggle with the dirty sponge, which was so pinched and frayed it no longer offered any support, Mom took it back to the nurses and told them we wouldn't be needing it anymore. She asked them if it had ever been washed. She didn't receive any answer. If I simply put my arms down, the pain is excruciating, and, after a while, my hands start to swell and throb. The inflammation can lead to blood clots, so there's nothing I can do. I must obey the recommendation of propping something under my limbs. I must improvise to live. For a burn victim, staying in the same position all the time means losing mobility, because the joints become rigid. I can neither straighten nor bend my elbows anymore, which makes Silvia's hypothesis that I scraped myself sound not only absurd but also impossible.

It's five o'clock in the morning and I open my tired eyes to the pale dawn of a new day. I only managed to sleep a total of two hours. The damp dressings, drenched in the blood I lost overnight, cling to my wounds, worsening the pain. Every movement I make feels like torture. The pillow fort my mother built yesterday fell down and something is rubbing against my left shoulder through the gauze. The sensation is nauseating, and I'm convinced that the new skin didn't take, because only an open sore can hurt like this. Right now, the mattress seems even harder than before. It's skinning me alive with its rigidity, tearing off the stitches from my grafts. I try to adjust my position to stop the feeling that my flesh is igniting under the bandages. The fire from the container never stopped burning. The growing pain makes me sicker and sicker, and I start to count to take my mind off the agony. I can't pray today. My heart beats so loudly that I can hear it in my ears, deafening me with its desperation. One, two, three, four, five, six, seven, eight, nine, ten. The numbers roll off my lips, but they're of no use.

There's noise in the hallway. The day-shift nurses arrive one at a time and, just like every morning, I eavesdrop on their simple chatter, the type that only healthy people can have. I listen to their jokes as the chills take hold of my body. It's so cold in the ward. The windows are not well insulated and, even though Alina took pity on us and loaned us the small electric heater from the hygiene ward, it's no match for the mid-December frost. I wish I could sleep a little longer, but I can't. I remember that it's the third day after my surgery, and a new week of agony begins. My heart skips a beat when I realize it's bath-time. Now is when it hurts the most. Like a nightmare that comes true, I see Alina's frail silhouette in the doorway.

"Alex, join me..."

She looks at me with merciful eyes. Her hands are resting on the wheelchair and, before she walks into the room, just for a second, she hesitates. When she takes that first step, I start to sob. My tears fall on the new wound on my cheek. I don't have any control over my body. I'm a scared animal that knows it can't do anything to save itself from the suffering that awaits it. I choke back my cries as desperation takes hold of me. I'm shaking because of the cold and the fear. Today, I am more afraid than ever that I'll die in the green tub, while the nurse tries to remove the dead skin from my injuries, without anesthetizing me. Alina wants to comfort me. She sings me her lullabies all the way to the hygiene ward.

When we enter, it's so cold that I begin to shiver uncontrollably. Someone left the windows open overnight again and I can smell the crude scent of winter in the air. It tries to overpower the stench of hospital disinfectants and decaying flesh, but it can't. Nothing can.

"I know it's cold again, Alex... I'm so sorry. The water doesn't seem to be warming up either."

Just like the wounds don't seem to be healing. Just like I don't seem to be getting better. Maybe I will indeed die in the end.

In my mind, Alina's words are distorted, as if she's talking to me in a nightmare. She grabs the plain shower head and starts the water. Here, in the abode of misery, ordinary objects have become torture devices. Alina rinses the tub and helps me climb inside. The worn-out rubber is frozen, and its touch makes me heave. Pain shoots through my limbs, sickening me. My tormented wounds throb under the stuck gauze, anticipating the hurt that is to come. I beg them, like countless times before, to give me something to make this more bearable. A nurse arrives and injects Ketoprofen into the cannula on my ankle.

"Please, give me something stronger, at least today, please..."

"You already know that's impossible. Why do you even bother asking?"

She shakes her head like I'm a naughty child, too spoiled to understand the meaning of the word "no." Will the cruelty ever end? Will they ever see what they're doing to us?

Water sprays out of the shower head forcefully, tearing through the gauze. It's completely cold, but it feels molten against my wounds. Pain burns through me, while I weep, devastated. The Ketoprofen does nothing. I feel everything, utterly aware, lucid to the core of my being. The boundary between the desperation I feel and madness is a thin thread, just like the one separating life from death.

I sob and sob. Alina removes the bandages from my wounds with shaking hands. The gauze comes off, pulling the necrotized tissue apart and tearing away the dead skin grafts. It leaves behind gaping gashes that weep blood and paint the water red. Some dressings won't come off just with water. When they're that stuck, the nurse just rips them. They make a slashing sound that I hear through the wails. Someone is ravaging my body, going through the entrails of my soul with hot coal steel. The harsh shower spray penetrates the skinned muscle and douses the exposed tendons. The pain is immeasurable, infinite. It's going to stop my heart. The tub spills over because of the dirty gauze splashing on the floor, sullying it with human tissue. Pieces of me lie on the linoleum; pieces of me clog the drain. The doctors say that I'm not infected. That's not why I'm wasting away like this, they shout. But I know now. They can't lie to me anymore. "They found Pseudomonas in Călin's wounds." It can't be just him. They wash us one after the other in this thing, with cold water. They barely disinfect it afterward. If he has it, we have it too. I have it too.

Once upon a time, these patches of dead skin that fall off me like from a cadaver were my beautiful skin. Now they've become garbage, eaten by the monstrous germs they hide in this place.

Alina picks up the gruesome, bristled sponge. She drenches it in Dexin soap. Every time they wash me, I stare at the disinfectant labels and read them over and over again, until I know them by heart. On each and every single bottle, the same brand name, "Hexipharma," is written in big letters that stand out. I gawk at the bottles, at the cheap, worn-out furniture, I fix my eyes on the door. My soul knows what my mind — hollowed by the pain — cannot fathom. I want to get out of here. I want to run away. But I can't. My body is their prisoner. The cruel hands of strangers knead it like it's some sort of bad dough. Nothing will come out of it. Except for pus. I bawl without realizing it. Every once in a while, the nurse shushes me gently, like she would a scared infant. Tears mixed with blood stream down my cheeks and onto my chest.

Now it's time to clean the back. The bristles tear through the dead skin and get stuck in the stitches, ripping them off. Scrub, scratch, scrub. Scrub, scratch, scrub. My wailing becomes howling. I beg her to stop. I wish I could vomit the dark agony out of me, like Iris once did. I want to free myself from the torture, but nothing happens. It goes on and on.

Alina takes a break, but then the silicone teeth bite me again, and I bleed, and bleed. "I want to faint," I tell myself, trying to force myself into senselessness, but my brain refuses to yield. It knows that if I let my guard down, I'll die. My body keeps me awake to save me. The price I pay is this gutting hurt.

"Please, sing to me," I whisper, and with a fragile voice, Alina hums a ballad.

I shiver and heave. I cry and pray. I listen to her singing. It's the only beautiful thing in this hell, and I need it. Her song is a painkiller for the soul in a world where the body must endure the agony awake.

The nurse tries to reduce pressure so that the spray doesn't tear through the wounds like that. She thinks it'll hurt less. Perhaps she's right, but she can't prove it. The spray stays the same no matter what she does. Sometimes frozen, sometimes hot, it rips into me, while I shake and howl. My teeth are chattering. I can't take it anymore. I can't. Alina puts the sponge away and continues to wash me with her hands. Her otherwise delicate fingers rub and pinch me, tearing at things. They leave behind holes and lacerations that will never heal. I look at myself, but I don't understand what I see. I don't have skin on my legs anymore. My hands and shoulders are raw masses of ravaged flesh. The index finger of my right hand is bent over. A big, green scab covers the joint. It didn't look like that before. On my left hand, there's a big hematoma, pooling with dark violet blood. It's new too. It's clear to me that something happened in the O.R. or after the surgery, when I was unconscious. The fresh scrapes and bruises sting when they come into contact with the surgical soap. Frayed remnants of what was probably a graft hang down from my right wrist, together with a few blue stitches. "They either dropped her in the operating room or when they brought her to the ward. Something happened," said the nurse to my sister. "Nothing happened!" shouted the doctor, denying. But there's no other explanation for these new injuries. I close my eyes because I can't watch anymore. I realize that the fire that engulfed us on October 30th has not been extinguished. Its flames rise from the water, scorching me.

"You're done," sighs Alina, relieved.

She covers me in the green shrouds and takes me to Iulia, who is working on another patient. After she finishes, she moves on to me, sits me on the bed, and starts prying the sheets from the wounds. As always, they're stuck to me. I already soiled them with pieces of my body. Once again, when they come off, they also remove the skin that adhered to them. Day by day, bath-time repeats itself, identical, like a recurring nightmare. Or like a curse. I shiver when Iulia uses the tweezers to clean the grafts that have survived, ridding them of the scabs and the pus.

"You look better than last time. It seems to me that you're slowly starting to heal."

I remember what my sister told me about the foreign doctor who operated on me in secret, using products he brought from France. We never found out his name. Iulia is working on my left shoulder. I can't take it anymore. My heartbeat becomes erratic and the ringing in my ears deafens me. The pain is inhuman.

"Come now, it's over. I've finished. Now we wait for your doctors, Alex, all right?"

My skinned body sits there, in the middle of the room, ruined and shivering. I've never felt so vulnerable in my life. It's not about the nudity, but rather about the nakedness of my broken heart. My flesh, my muscles, my fragile tendons, they're all wide open and in agony, exposed to the cold air that smells like chlorine and pus. The doctors are late, as always, and I try to stifle the chills because I'm afraid I'll bite my tongue if I keep shaking like this. I just want to lie down. Please, hurry up... They finally walk into the room, casual and unbothered. She's holding her phone, and she uses it to take pictures. Again. For the first time in weeks, I decide that I'm going to stand up for myself. I'm going to be strong. I'm going to demand answers.

"What were the results of the catheter samples you took?"

The young doctor throws me a look as cold as the water in the tub.

"Sterile, just as always," she mumbles, without looking me in the eyes.

"And the wound samples?"

"Sterile as well. Why are you so anxious? Come on, calm down. I told you already. It's very bad that you always sleep on your back. You don't eat enough. And then you're constantly depressed. Haven't I told you this already?"

"But why does my index finger look like this? I have scrapes on my hands, bruises on my face, and some skin grafts have been torn off. Did something happen in the O.R.?"

Without answering, she grabs my right hand and stares at my finger. She pokes the joint, then drags a bucket from the corner of the room with her leg. It's the same one the orderlies use to wipe the floor. She places it under me.

"I'll have to open your wound. It looks infected. Iulia, give me a surgical knife."

A dizzying fear takes hold of me, draining me of any courage to face her.

"Please... please numb the area."

"It's not necessary. What? Don't you trust me?"

Before I get to answer, to utter the "No" that I've been holding in for so long, she cuts off the green scab from the swollen and bent joint, and opens the flesh, deeper and deeper, until she's made an ugly wound that she splits open. Its edges spill over, revealing the fat tissue and the tendons. When she pries it apart, it makes a cracking sound that sickens me. She squeezes the cut, rubbing against the bone with her surgical gloves, trying to get the pus to come out. But there isn't any. Clean, thick blood pours from the gash, washing over my hand, flowing down my legs, falling into the bucket. Pat, pat, pat. The sound the drops make when they hit against the plastic is maddening.

Someone cancels the world. A pitch-black curtain falls over my eyes, blinding me. The show is over. My mind erases the cruelty I was subjected to, like deleting a picture. I want to scream, but I can't utter a word. My voice is trapped in my chest. A feeling of numbness flows, like hot lava, down to the tips of my toes, and my legs become useless rags. Tears from my eyes stream down my cheeks, on the wounds on my thighs. Am I crying? I can't tell. I can neither hear nor see a thing. Then Silvia squeezes my finger tighter. The pattering sound made by the blood falling in the bucket intensifies, and its rhythm quickens. Like in a nightmare, I hear Doctor Moldovan's voice.

"What did you do? There was no need to cut the joint open like that."

"I wanted to see if it's infected," she answers.

There's no remorse in her voice. She shrugs when she finally lets go of my hand. So what if the procedure wasn't necessary?

"Iulia, slather some Flamazine over her, all right?"

All the strength I mustered up so that I'd stop being their victim spilled out of me in the filthy bucket that still swallows the big drops of blood that fall from the index finger's mutilated joint. I don't have the strength to confront them. They're debating something with their backs turned. Before they leave, they throw me an indifferent glance and walk out without saying a word. I'm ashamed of myself, of the paralyzing weakness that took hold of me, of how frail I've become. I also understand that none of this abhorrence, this nameless cruelty, is truly my fault, as they'd have me believe. Naked and defeated, I cry bitter tears of pain and help-lessness.

Iulia comes to my side and starts to work.

"Alex, I'll wash you with the German disinfectant. It seems to have helped you a lot! Come on, don't cry. It's over. I'm not going to listen to all the stupid things they say. 'Flamazine, Flamazine, Flamazine.' They're like broken records! If I'd leave everything up to them, you'd never go home! I'll cleanse you with the Pron-tosan. It's something else!"

She finishes and sends me to the ward. There's no one waiting for me in the hallway, so I walk alone. With every step I take, I can feel the fever rising and I begin to shiver and shake. Mother waits for me in the doorway, dressed in a "ster-ile" gown that's torn at the edges. She keeps it on until all the doctors are gone, then returns it to the coat hanger in the hallway. She puts on one that's brand new, from the batch she and Cristina bought from the pharmacy. It's clean and intact. "Single use" here means "used several times by as many people as possible". That's why she doesn't wear the ones the hospital provides for the relatives of the victims. However, bringing your own is frowned upon. It casts a shadow on the supreme competence of the hospital. The staff calls the sterile gowns a formality. The truth is, so is everything else: from the cheap drugs that don't alleviate the pain, to the operations themselves.

When I finally make it to the bed, I sit on the edge and start to cry. I weep until I can't breathe anymore. I bawl until I vomit. I try to fight the tears, but I just can't take it anymore. Like an ocean held captive in a glass bowl for too long, pain shatters my heart into pieces and spills out of my being, washing over me in waves of agony. It's finally happened. I broke. After today's excruciating bath-time, after the pointless mutilation of my finger, after bleeding, like an animal, in the bucket they mop the floors with, after listening, for weeks, to their gaslighting and their lies, I finally lost it. The thing I fought to keep whole all this time – my humanity – couldn't handle the blows it was served today. The strength to withstand the torture spilled out through the cracks in my soul, just like the pieces of my decaying flesh washed over the edges of the green tub, on the dirty linoleum floor. What remained of me was either swallowed by the drain and carried into nothingness or kneaded to death by their merciless hands, while their conniving mouths lied: "you're just too skinny," "you sleep on your back," "you don't have any infections," "you're too sensitive," "we're doing all that we can," "if you were my child, I wouldn't transfer you abroad," "you just have to take it," "everything is sterile," "trust me," "it won't hurt," "you don't need painkillers," "it doesn't hurt," "we're giving you antibiotics prophylactically," "you already had pneumonia," "shut up," "stop crying," "you pissed on yourself like a sow," "your veins are too thin," "your sister is nosy," "stop whining," "why are you always so depressed?" "it's your fault," "it's your fault," "it's your fault." What the fire spared, they murdered in this concentration camp hospital in which "treatment" means "torture," where the ghost of the truth tortures in dirty hallways, dressed in used gowns, smutty with blood and pus, whispering to deaf ears that we're all infected. We're all dying.

"Please, bring someone!"

Mother is shouting for help. She strokes my legs and stares at me with bloodshot eyes, wet with tears. Who knows when she slept last...

"When they wash me, they don't give me anything for the pain, Mom. I feel everything, Mom. I feel everything."

Not long after, the psychologist comes to see me. She's not a permanent employee of the hospital, just a volunteer.

"Tell me what happened," she asks, genuinely concerned.

"I can't take it anymore. I just can't."

She asks me if I'm talking about the traumatic memories related to the fire. I realize that she doesn't know why I broke down. I tell her, in detail, what the "hygiene protocol" consists of at the Hospital for Burns and Plastic Surgery. She gulps and abandons the topic of the club. After a few moments of silence, she comes up with an idea.

"What if I talk to your doctors? There must be something they can give you."

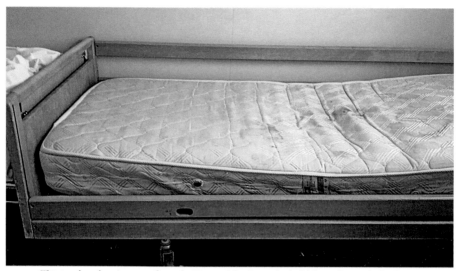

*This is what the mattresses from the Hospital for Burns looked like underneath the sheets:
they were worn-out and stained by the bodily fluids of patients that had laid in them before us.
These were not hospital-grade mattresses, but rather ordinary, store-bought ones.
Burn victims need special, highly technological medical mattresses to heal,
yet this is what we were forced to lay on.*

*These were the blankets that the nurses placed on the threshold of the ward doors, in the evenings
when the personnel performed the formaldehyde disinfection procedure, in an attempt to stop
the vapors from getting into our wards. The same blankets were used to cover us
when we returned from the operating room, riddled with chills because of the escalating fever.*

The broken beds from the Hospital for Burns in Romania.
The position of the mattresses was adjusted using boxes filled with saline flasks for our IVs.

This sponge was given to us at the Hospital for Burns by the medical personnel.
We were told to use it as an improvised support mechanism for our injured hands.
Because it was the only one, we had to take turns with it. Our parents were
not allowed to bring us anything from outside the hospital, like pillows or other devices,
because it made the authorities look bad and contradicted the official narrative that claimed
that they had everything they needed to treat us adequately.

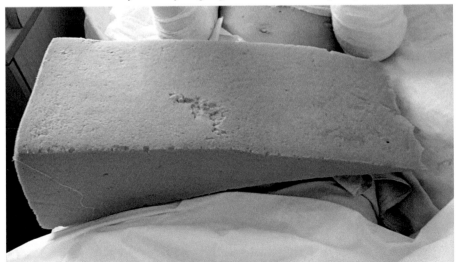

I thank her for her honest desire to help, but I'm reluctant. I doubt that she's going to get through to them. A nurse walks into the ward and brings new Tylenol flasks. I'm feverish again. The world swirls as if I'm on the edge of a vertiginous precipice. I say goodbye to the psychologist and Mom helps me find a less painful position. Under the dressings, my wounds are burning incessantly. Any second now, I'm going to catch fire again. Mom is dabbing my bloodied cheek with a piece of sterile gauze. I fall asleep exhausted. I wake up to screaming voices in the hallway.

"Torturing her like this is unacceptable. The psychologist told you herself. Bath-time without painkillers stops now!"

"Come, now, be reasonable. They give her something every time!"

"What?"

"Ketoprofen!"

"Is an over-the-counter anti-inflammatory drug enough when she doesn't have skin on half of her body?"

"Everyone gets the same thing, lady! She's not an exception!"

"That's horrible! If you don't have drugs, tell us! We'll buy them!"

"It's not that! We have everything we need! How many times do I have to tell you?"

"You do? Then what is this about?"

"Fine! We'll give her Tramadol starting with the next procedure. We'll combine it with another painkiller. Are you satisfied? Is the psychologist pleased?"

"Why do you address me with such arrogance? This is your job! The psychologist was only doing hers."

Silvia walks in, treading heavily. She looks at me with cold, dead eyes.

"I came to tell you that the psychologist informed me about your little breakdown. You really shouldn't have gone so far. We'll ignore the risks and give you a stronger painkiller during bath-time."

"I accept any risk if it means less pain."

"It's your choice."

"Thank you!"

She leaves the ward without saying goodbye to my mother.

"How dare she put this on you? How dare she?"

"It's all right, Mom... It's fine. I'll accept anything if it won't hurt like that anymore."

I receive a gift from my friend Răzvan. It's a nifty little MP3 player. My sister told him that I miss listening to music, so he went to the store, bought me the device, and filled it with songs. Cristina tells me that there's also a surprise tune among them. She puts my earphones in, and presses play. I smile. The boys wrote a piece for me! A few days ago, another friend, Raluca, came to see me too. She greeted me from the door and handed my mother a few presents: a letter that Cristina read aloud, and some DVDs to watch after I leave the hospital. If I leave...

The people I love are striving to keep my spirit intact, but it's a difficult task. I try my best to stay as whole as possible, at least inside. I ask Cristina to put away the MP3 player because I'm in too much pain. I lie in bed, ravaged by it, staring at the walls and counting. In the evening, before going home, my sister leaves the little object on the pillow I rest my hands on. She places the earphones in my ears, just in case. Late at night, unable to sleep, I decide that I'm going to hit the play button.

The tiny phones fell out of my ears meanwhile, because of the thick bandages on my scalp that kept pressing them down. I move my right hand toward the MP3 player, but the pain is too much to bear. The fresh cut on my index finger rubs its spilled edges against the gauze, and the sensation brings tears to my eyes. I give up. I try with my left hand instead. It's in better shape than the right. With difficulty, I manage to grab the elusive earphone, but it takes forever to stick it back in the ear. It keeps falling out. I try again and again. I'm not strong or coordinated enough to push it into the ear canal. The attempts go on and on, to no avail. Enraged and frustrated, I cry, but I refuse to give up. I shove the earphone hard enough to get it to stay put. It doesn't budge. Finally! Now, I have to turn on the device. With my stiff and blackened middle finger, I press the play button a few times in a row until the screen lights up. Then I keep pressing until I find the song I want to listen to. I'm wet with sweat. The melted creams spill out from under the gauze. I'm tired and in pain, but I'm also proud of myself. For the first time in weeks, I managed to do something on my own. The first notes of "Ocean of

Night," by the Editors, sound eerie against the quiet hospital night. A feeling of strangeness comes over me when I realize that the music reaches me from a different life, one that I lost forever.

I used to listen to this song in the hot summer evenings while baking sponge cake in my small apartment. The sweet scent of vanilla filled the kitchen, floating out the open windows, into the street. In the searing heat of July, when Bucharest became molten, there was no other way to cook. I danced holding the plastic bowl to my chest and beating the egg whites to the rhythm of the melody, humming the chorus, either too high or too low, alongside Tom's deep baritone. "I am your hope down the wire, so you can hold back the fire." The neon light in my kitchen had broken down weeks ago and, instead of replacing it, I used the table lamp that Nico, my best friend, gave me for my birthday. I loved the romantic atmosphere created by the solitary yellow bulb and the smell of baked goods that enveloped me. That's why I didn't bother fixing anything. I was having too much fun in my dimly lit kitchen, together with the sugary treats and my favorite bands. Music always managed to chase away the big city loneliness that often engulfed me, threatening to swallow me whole. Will I ever be able to bake sponge cake again? Will I ever regain the ease with which I enjoyed the little things – a broken light that allowed me to transform my apartment into a kaleidoscope? The strange quietness of Bucharest after midnight? Will I ever leave this place?

All of a sudden, I realize where I am. I abandon the memories of my old life and the chimera of the naive girl, with long hair and clear eyes, blind to the great evil of the world. I cry in the silence of the ward, humming the lyrics of the song. The lead singer talks about hope, love, and fire, as if he were reading from a scroll etched deep into my soul, as if he knew how I long to be saved. I use the words as prayers and cling to them with everything I have left inside, to survive yet another night in Hell.

"Gaze at the skyline/ Under the ocean of stars/ This is your slow dance/ And this is your chance to transform/ Lost to a moment/ The moment you confront the storm."

Outside, the snow becomes rain. The drops patter across the windows, making a monotonous sound. Flavia sighs in her sleep, dreaming about the surgery she'll have tomorrow. I close my eyes and I count, because I'm in too much pain to pray: one, two, three, four, five, six, seven, eight, night, ten...

A few hours later, they bring her back from the O.R. on a worn-out metal stretcher with wheels. The orderlies are struggling to put her in her bed, on her tummy. They grab the sheets underneath her to heave her onto the mattress. Just a few inches above it, the fabric tears and the men let out frightened screams. My friend's freshly operated body is heavy and weak because of the anesthetic still coursing through her veins, and she can't defend herself. As she drops, her arms and feet show no resistance, flailing apart. "Be careful not to move too much," they tell us. But look what happens to us when we're unconscious. They manage to grab her last minute before she falls out. Her face sinks into the remnants of the sheet. She moans in pain. It's a miracle that she didn't hit the floor. Finally, they succeed. She's safe now. She's wailing and weeping, still unaware of her surroundings, but deeply aware of how it hurts. After the orderlies leave, she drivels for a while, under the influence of the sedatives. Her breathing is shallow because of the heavy bandages and casts that press on her back as she lies on her abdomen. She can't inhale properly.

"Alex, I can't breathe," she finally manages to utter.

I call the nurse. She comes quickly and throws Flavia a pitiful glance. As best as she can, she adjusts the bed, but it won't really budge. It's broken, just like every single one in the hospital.

Flavia wakes up and falls back into unconsciousness, over and over. She cries in her sleep, crushed by her own weight. She grunts words I can't make out. Mihai swings back and forth in his chair, covering his face with his hands. I told him what the orderlies did, and he's upset. He's not going home tonight. He'll sleep here, his head fallen in his chest, arms crossed, dreaming our nightmares, startling when we startle, burning when we burn.

I open my eyes to the feeling of someone fumbling with the cannula placed on my ankle. I see Miruna unscrewing the tiny stopper and winking at me while holding a big syringe filled with a yellow fluid.

"It's bath-time today. I brought you your painkiller cocktail. They're finally giving you something..."

"I broke down the other day, Miruna. I couldn't take it anymore."

"I believe you, dear. I don't understand why it took them so long to prescribe you a proper drug. We would have given it to you sooner, but we're not allowed to."

I feel drowsy, as if I'm walking on clouds. My heart is racing because of the fear, but I'm also eerily calm. I'm torn between trusting Miruna and doubting the fact that she's really given me painkillers. Her comforting smile brings me solace. She's one of the good ones. She wouldn't lie to me so horribly. On my way to the hygiene ward, the pain caused by the bandages rubbing against my open sores flares up. Once I'm in the tub, the nurse starts washing my feet, my legs, and then finally reaches my thighs, running the shower over the unhealed donor sites, gushing out blood. I close my eyes but open them back up. The feeling is still sickening, but somehow bearable. Is this really happening? Alina drenches the pieces of gauze that stick to my burns, unraveling them gradually. Though the pain is bigger than anything I experienced before the fire, I manage to withstand it and to actually have a conversation with the nurse. I'm talking to her, but I'm very sleepy. I realize, amazed, that I'm not crying anymore. Iulia walks into the room and I show her my index finger.

"It looks like an atomic sausage," I joke.

Her eyes widen and she stares at Alina, surprised.

"I never heard our girl crack jokes before!"

"They gave her painkillers today," Alina whispers.

"Oh... Right."

Silence follows her confession, and I understand its meaning better than a million spoken words. Even though I'm relieved, I'm also ridden with sadness. It was possible all along to give me a stronger drug. They didn't have to slaughterhouse-wash me. They could have just... I don't want to think about it anymore. The truth hurts too much.

In the dressings ward, Iulia grins at me, delighted. I've never seen her so happy before.

"Alex! You look better!"

Silvia walks in, alone. She takes her photos and consults me briefly.

"And? How was it today?"

"It was the first time that I didn't cry."

"So, you're pleased with the drug."

"Yes. Thank you! I hope you'll keep giving it to me."

"I've written it down in your chart. If you want it, you'll have to ask for it."

I realize how easy it could have all been had they wanted it to be. She grabs my right hand and stares at my finger. Ever since she cut it open, it's been getting worse. If, at first, it was only slightly bent toward the palm, now it's completely hunched. She tells me they'll make me a splint that I'll have to wear for a few weeks. I have what she calls a "boutonniere deformity," which means that the tendons are too damaged to keep the finger straight or allow it to bend. They have to immobilize the joint to allow "the lesion" to heal. I'm not sure if by "lesion" she means the pointless gash she made, or the accident that took place in the O.R. Or, rather, didn't take place, according to them. I don't ask. I'm just happy I survived bath-time one more time. Silvia leaves and Iulia starts treating me.

I talk to Cristina and my mother about the new painkiller. After almost eight weeks of hopelessness, today we allow ourselves to believe in the future. Later, they call me to the nurses' office. A young doctor makes a gypsum mold of my right arm and hand. She kneads and presses it down to get it to fit. She puts it on me and fixes it in place with elastic bands. It's very heavy and uncomfortable because it's too long. It extends from my palm to my elbow. I tell her that I only need a splint for my index finger, and she replies that they only have gypsum in the hospital, and she can't make something so small from it. Forced to sit straight, the joint starts to throb and ache, bleeding through the gauze. The pain is torturous, but it's the price I have to pay to keep the finger.

"I'm so sorry. I have to be honest with you. Normally, I'd have used some sort of lightweight plastic, but we don't have anything like that here. Try your best to keep it on as long as you can. I know it hurts…"

I thank her for the honesty with which she admitted that they don't really have everything they need. I take my evening walk with the help of my mother, who holds my hand up. The improvised splint is massive and heavy. I simply can't carry it alone. I grow tired fast and return to bed, just when the nurse walks in the ward, bringing us the last IVs of the day. She attaches the bag to my cannula, but the serum won't drip. The vein is too damaged. She decides she's going to have to find a better one, so she starts tapping the skin near the ankle. She presses here and there a few times, and then I feel a sharp sting. Nothing... Her hands drift across me, feeling me up, desperate to find something. After the catheter incident, when the device became infected only three days after it was inserted, the nurses haven't spared any part of my body in their search to find blood vessels capable of enduring the endless IV flasks that are poured into them. I've become a human pincushion. She pushes the needle in abruptly and drills with it back and forth, looking for blood. It hurts, but I stay quiet, even though tears start streaming down my cheeks. She repeats the procedure again and again, to no avail, pulling the needle out, sticking it back in again someplace else. After eight attempts, she finally finds something behind my knee. She exhales with relief as she glues the cannula to my skin. When she starts the drip, I feel a numbing pain, quickly followed by the formation of a big purple bulge.

"This one broke too. There's no other way. They'll have to insert a new catheter."

Even though I'm lying down, I can feel my knees going soft. I'm shaking because of the fear.

"Please, I'll take the drugs by mouth; I'll do anything to avoid a new insertion procedure. Maybe you can ask another nurse to help? Perhaps four hands are better than two."

She starts to shout at me, annoyed. My suggestion offended her, even though that wasn't my intention.

"After all this time I wasted with you, you still don't want to do anything! Aren't you ashamed of yourself?"

Mom is shocked by her aggressive reaction. The nurse vanishes down the hallway, screaming and threatening. We exchange glances, appalled. We don't understand what caused the escalation. A few minutes later, someone knocks open the ward door. An angry female doctor walks in.

"What's this *bullshit* about not wanting to take your drugs? How dare you threaten us with something like that? You should be ashamed!"

Flavia opens her eyes and looks at me, confused. She had barely managed to fall asleep after a torturous day of having to lie on her belly, constantly in pain and incapable of breathing right. Now she's awake again because of the screaming.

"Please, stop shouting. I don't understand what this is about. I never refused my medication. I only asked if I could take it by mouth. And who are you? You didn't even introduce yourself."

When she sees that I'm calm and collected, she takes a step back.

"I'm the doctor who's on duty tonight. The nurse told me that you're belligerent, and that you refused to take your medication and have a catheter inserted."

"I didn't refuse at all. I had a catheter placed recently, and they had to take it out three days later because I developed extreme swelling. It was a terrible experience for me."

"Oh, I see. I apologize for yelling at you, but that's not what she told me. She said you didn't want to take your drugs anymore, and that made me very upset. It's paramount that you receive your antibiotics."

"Either way, I don't think it's appropriate to shout at a patient like that."

"But Doctor, if her blood and wounds are sterile, why can't she take the drugs orally?"

"Because she can't, and that's that! There's too many of them. The intravenous route is the only viable one."

"All day long, the doctors shout at us in this hospital. How can we possibly deserve it? What mistakes do we keep making to be treated like this? All we can do is lie in bed and suffer."

As usual, Flavia comes to my defense. She can't stand the threats and accusations anymore.

After the doctor leaves, Adina shows up with a new IV kit. Her shift just started. I greet her, relieved, and tell her what happened. She shakes her head.

"Oana probably told her something. A lie to justify her inability. She was upset that you asked her to bring someone else to help her insert the cannula."

"I didn't mean to insult her. I never thought she'd take it like that. She pricked me so many times, Adina. She kept inserting the needle and fumbling with it under the skin, looking for the vein. It really hurt, and when I couldn't take it anymore, I suggested she bring a colleague with her."

"You did nothing wrong! It's her fault. She should have accepted she can't do it. Her pride got the best of her. Who knows what crazy things she told the doctor... And then, it really is critical that you receive your antibiotics. We can't mess around with those..."

All of a sudden, I understand why the doctor on duty was so desperate. She knows that if I stop taking the drugs, I'll die. She's probably scared of what the infections will do to me if they are no longer kept in check by the heavy-duty medication. Adina taps on the skin on my neck, where she's found a vein. She pushes the needle in carefully and smiles, satisfied.

"There you go. We found one! If we take good care of it, it will last at least a few days."

I can feel the cold serum dripping through it, a clear sign the cannula was placed correctly.

"Thank you, Adina..."

"No problem, my dear. I'm just doing my job!"

The nurse checks to see if Flavia needs something. We joke about the silly position the doctors make her lay in. Adina suggests elevating the back of the bed and placing Flavia on the side, supported by the pillows Mihai brought. After a few attempts, they succeed in changing her position, so that she's neither lying on her tummy all the time, nor putting pressure on the fresh skin grafts. Flavia cries with relief. Small things, such as a comfortable sleeping position, have become unattainable. We learned to appreciate everything we took for granted back when we were healthy. Flavia stuffs her face in her own pillow fort and falls asleep immediately. Mihai crashes on the chair next to her bed. His smile fades away and is replaced by an expression of worry.

"Why are you upset?" I whisper.

For the past few weeks, living here together, in the Hospital for Burns, brought us closer. We've become friends. Some nights, when my mother and sister are too tired to sleep next to my bed, he stays behind and helps me. He startles every time we cry out because something hurts. He wakes in the dead of night to give us water, with hands shaking because of the exhaustion. We cling to him and to the jokes he tells us when he tries to comfort us, and he clings to us because he's afraid we might be gone tomorrow. Today, Mihai is sad and burdened. He's lost in the darkness inside himself.

"Ana... she's very unwell."

Ana is his best friend. She's a photographer, just like him. The doctors said they had to intubate her, so she's in the ICU. Mihai speaks often of her, of the concerts they attended together with their group of rock concert photographers. Claudiu and Teo were part of the gang too. They didn't make it and we're still mourning them. Every day we find out that someone we loved died. We were part of the same world, the so-called "underground scene", the preferred exile spot for those who don't share the commercial vision of conventional media outlets, often sold to dirty politicians and press moguls. In the end, a cultural endeavor like any other, scapegoated by angry voices, we hear when the nurses turn up the volume on their TV set: "they were Satanists," "they worshipped the Devil." The press would say anything to hide the Romanian government's fault and mask the corruption that caused the fire in the first place.

I've heard these "theories" even as I lay in the green tub, prey to the most inhumane pain, while praying to God. They spewed out of the little radio in the hallway. In my tired mind, exhausted by the bodily suffering, by the endless ripping of my flesh, as the shower spray tore through me, they sounded the same as what the doctors were saying: "she brought the pneumonia from home," "she sleeps on her back," "she's too skinny," "her veins are thin," "she's too depressed." In Romania, the victim is always guilty of something. "Why did they go to the concert in the first place?" "They had it coming." A gutting sadness comes over me when I listen to these aspersions and understand that people will believe anything to avoid confronting the awful reality. We live in a trap set by years of corruption, and that's hard to accept. To maintain the illusion of normalcy, they grab truth by the neck and mutilate it. They put horns on its head and sully its wet cheeks, from the tears it cries for redemption, until it looks like their demons. "This is the real problem!" they yell over our bodies, turned to ash. In the meanwhile, we're dying in these so-called hospitals, abodes not of healing, but of extermination. We're being punished for the sin of thinking we were safe in our own country. Safe enough to go out one Friday night and come home unscathed.

The Devil... I'm afraid I've seen his face quite often since I've been lying here. He doesn't look like a monster. He's dressed in neat human attire and murmurs deceit with nicely puckered lips: "she's not infected," he sighs, "we're doing everything we can, her body was too weak." Sometimes, he hides in the quivering eyes of a nurse, as she looks away from the cruelty, or in the whispers in the hallway, early in the morning, when everyone thinks we're sleeping. "He's got Pseudomonas, all of his wounds are infected." The Devil hides behind their secrets and behind the lies they tell when they blame us for dying. He rests in the blindness of eyes shut on purpose, to not see the blood, the pus, and the pain. He dwells in this place where we should have found healing but instead encountered death. He doesn't hang out in clubs or nestle in a music genre. Of what I've seen, he prefers hospitals, town halls, schools, and sometimes even churches. Everywhere where people are willing to lie to conceal a truth that could save others.

The other day, we received a special visit. A delegation of priests came to see us, sent from above. No, no. Not by God, but by the leaders of the Romanian Orthodox Church. In red plastic bags imprinted with the cheery face of Santa Claus, they brought us alms: some oranges and a piece of *colivă*, a traditional Romanian funeral cake, to honor our dead friends. They went from ward to ward, without wearing any protective equipment, dropping the gifts on the chairs that our parents sleep on when they keep vigil over us. When they walked into our room, Flavia and I were in deep suffering because of the fever and the pain. They didn't offer to say a prayer to comfort us. They didn't ask us how we were. They didn't bless us. They uttered a muffled "hello," deposited the bags, and then left without saying goodbye. They were in a hurry to fulfill their dreaded assignment and, once they got it over with, they were gone. God didn't walk with them that day. He was nestled within us, staring at them, ashamed. Who, then, trotted along among the sick, bored and sneering?

Such high-profile visits have increased in number lately. Some people from the Ministry of Health showed up a few days ago. The men had rigid faces and wore neatly tailored suits that covered the crookedness of their souls. They put on the green gowns in the hallway, which have become frayed rags. Ignoring the blood, urine, and pus stains, they lay them on top of their expensive ties. It's only a formality, at the end of the day. The protective gear stopped being sterile a long time ago, and they know it very well. Admitting it, however, is out of the question. If I wasn't this sick, I'd laugh at their embarrassing fakeness. Like sextons, they walk in the ward with their ugly shoes, looking at us with empty eyes that mimic pity. They ask us how we feel, while our teeth chatter because of the chills from the fever. They don't really want us to answer. They look around, understanding the decay, but they don't react. In the hallway, they make small talk with the doctors, shake their hands, and disappear. Everything is fine at the Hospital for Burns and Plastic Surgery, where there are no infections, and the hygiene is impeccable. Where the patients don't bawl until they vomit in the dirty tub they're washed in, without being sedated, one after the other, like a slaughterhouse for people. We have everything we need, they tell themselves, while they walk away from us, with the Devil following them, slavish and meek, a dutiful mirror of their tarnished souls.

Other times, starlets make their appearance. They claim they want to see us because they found top-notch plastic surgeons abroad who are willing to treat us after we're discharged. They bring the so-called doctors with them as proof. It's a publicity stunt, of course, but no one seems to realize it except for us.

"Come on, Iulia, get her ready! A. will arrive any second now with the Turkish doctor. I want all of them to be in the wards, freshly washed and bandaged."

Even though she hurries, the nurse doesn't manage to finish my dressings. She wraps gauze around me so that my open wounds are not exposed and asks me to come back after the celebrity visit is over.

"Iulia, I don't want them to see me. Can't you just ignore her and finish your work?"

"Come now, Alex. You heard what the doctor said. I don't want any trouble. Come find me after it's done. She probably just wants to look good in front of them."

Disgusted, I crawl to my bed and sit on the edge. I can't lie down without help, and Mom isn't here. They probably sent her away so that she wouldn't interfere with the "show". I can hear enthusiastic sighs and laughter in the hallway. The medical personnel are starstruck. The celebrity reeks of expensive perfume and she's dressed in a stylish gown. She's wearing heavy makeup, and her hair is bouncy and tousled, like she just came from the hairdresser. She struts in the ward, dragging a short man in an extravagant suit behind her. He has big golden rings on all of his fingers, which is why he's not wearing single-use gloves. He doesn't bother to take off his sunglasses either. I stare at them, wide-eyed, like I'm watching the circus roll into town. Their swishy, pretentious look strikes a nauseating contrast with the obvious ruin of our bodies. The entire scene seems taken from a dark comedy. I ask myself how these chiseled puppets landed in this hell. I can't contain myself. I burst out laughing. The woman mistakes my shock and amusement for delight and introduces herself and her companion with wide, dramatic gestures and words.

"Doctor M.is *the best* reconstructive surgeon in the world. After they discharge you from here, he can take care of you at his private clinic."

The man grabs my shoddily bandaged left hand and stares at the unhealed wounds. The bruise they made when they dropped me in the O.R. peeks, purple and swollen, from under the gauze. He didn't disinfect himself before he touched me. He turns my hand around, showing no real interest. He doesn't say anything. Then, he moves on to Flavia and does the same thing. They get up, say goodbye, and vanish out the door, never to be seen again.

"What was that all about? They just bragged, stared at us, and left without giving us any information. Where is this clinic? How do we get there? What can they do for us? How much would it cost? What sort of assessment was this?"

"Just be grateful that they didn't take any pictures, to show-off in the magazines. Maybe we would have launched a new trend with our mummy look."

We laugh and shake our heads. I'm not sure how often the Devil goes clubbing or what sort of music he listens to. What I know for certain, though, is that he loves dirty hospitals and people willing to sell their souls for something. And in Romania, we've got plenty of both.

I spend my morning watching Flavia, who fell asleep in a strange position. Mihai went home for a few hours to take a shower and cook some food. Her body is dangerously close to the edge of the bed, and I feel like she could fall any minute. I can't use my hands to catch her, so, despite the pain, I stretch my leg forward. If I could push her forehead backwards with my foot each time she veers forward, maybe I can prevent an accident from happening. I whisper her name so as not to startle her. She opens her eyes.

"Oh, Alex! Is this how you want to catch me?"

"I can't let you fall. It's enough that they hurt us all the ways they do."

We crack jokes until Alina shows up in the doorway. She helps Flavia out of bed. It's her first bath-time after the surgery, and we both know what that means. The two vanish in the hallway. I hear Flavia weeping and dragging her legs toward the hygiene ward until she goes silent. I eavesdrop to make sure that my friend's all right, and, after a while, the spray of water bursts out of the shower head, hitting against the rubber tub. Then it moves to the flesh. Helpless, Flavia starts crying. And then she screams.

"George, please, don't! George, those are new grafts!"

"Shut up!"

"George, please, it hurts!"

"I don't care if it hurts! I have to do my job."

"Please, let Alina wash me, please!"

Flavia begs like a child. My heart breaks and my legs start to shake. I call the nurse and ask her to give me the Tramadol. She returns with a syringe filled with the yellow fluid and injects it into my cannula. I want to know what's going on in the hygiene ward. She tells me that Iulia took a few days off. George, the orderly, is replacing her, and he's also helping Alina finish bath-time quicker. Normally, the doctors should make the dressings when the specialized nurse is not on duty, but they're rarely, if ever, up for the task. Flavia never stopped crying. The hallway rings with the desperate echoes of her pain. When she comes back, her eyes are bloodshot and tearful. Her dressings look shoddy and improvised.

"Alex, he destroyed me. It'll be his fault if my grafts don't take. He tore the gauze from me. If it wasn't for Alina, I'd be dead!"

The painkiller is slowly kicking in. It's making me dizzy and numb. I'm sedated enough not to be as scared of what's coming as I usually am. But I'm still ready for the worst. George is waiting for me in the doorway of the hygiene ward. He removes the scarf my mother wrapped around my body to cover me, grabs me by the waist, and hoists me up in the tub. I should be ashamed of my nudity, but I can't feel anything anymore. So many strangers have seen me without my skin, without my humanity, that the nakedness of the body has become meaningless. Often, I'm not even sure if this flesh is my own. It belongs to these people who knead and mold it into the shape of the system that mutilated their souls and our wounds.

Alina is tense. George starts tearing my dry dressings, pulling and pushing them. She stops him and grabs the shower head. She runs water over me until the drenched gauzes fall down on their own. I shiver because of the pain, but I'm not crying. The drug restored my dignity.

"Your only job here today is to hand me the tools that I need. From this moment on, I'm in charge of bath-time."

He doesn't say anything. They had some sort of fight. Impatient, George fidgets, stomps his leg and scolds Alina constantly. The procedure is taking too long. She's unmovable. She does her job without paying any attention to him.

"You're getting better every day, Alex. You still have a few open wounds, but many other skin grafts took."

I ask her about the burns on my scalp.

"Alina, is my hair ever going to grow back?"

Instead of answering, she starts singing. The sad truth lies in the lyrics of the lullaby she wrote for me on the spot. The last few minutes of bath-time hurt almost like before, but not quite. Alina turns off the tap and sends me to the dressing ward with George. My doctors are supposed to bandage me today, but I doubt it's going to happen. Silvia shows up alone. She examines me in a rush, puts her single-use gloves on, and starts dressing the wounds, distracted. She puts everything down, tells George that she has to leave, and urges him to finish alone. Gulping, the orderly accepts. He can't say no. He's not allowed to tell her that it's actually her job, not his. He doesn't have Iulia's light hand, and he doesn't pay attention either. He wraps the gauze too tight and doesn't like separating the fingers. He doesn't have the necessary training to dress a burn victim, but if the doctor told him to do it, he will.

"You can't mess with the boss!" he says.

"George, can you please loosen the bandages? It really hurts when they're so tight."

He stares at me with weary eyes. He does what I asked but, after a while, he forgets about it. I have to remind him all the time not to wrap me up so tight. He talks to me about his wife, his family issues, and his feelings of abandonment. He feels like no one cares about him. He confesses how unhappy he is and sighs, looking out the window while he struggles to fasten the pieces of gauze together. He's distracted and brutal. I feel sorry for him. But then I remember Flavia's ordeal. He's not a bad man, but this is not the job for him. He huffs and puffs, trying to dress the wounds on my scalp. He doesn't know how to. I want to help him, so I tell him what Iulia usually does. He shushes me abruptly.

He unravels an entire bandage roll and twists it around my chin to fix the gauze on my head in place. When he's done, I can't open my mouth. I show him and he becomes furious. It's pointless to fight him. I let it be. He unravels and unravels until he's satisfied with the result, and I can barely speak.

"You're ready!" he thunders.

I look and feel like a mummy that's about to fall apart. I ask him to tie the scarf around my hips, so that I don't have to walk down the hallway naked from the waist down.

"I have a better idea!"

He brings a pile of bandage rolls from the medical cabinet and forces me to sit up. He starts wrapping the dressings around my body. I ask him what he's doing, but he doesn't answer. He wraps and wraps. I gawk at him and realize that he's making a pair of underwear from the gauze.

"But George, I don't need that! Mom will help me with that."

"Shut up and let me work!"

He tapes the pieces together until my privates are covered in bandages. He looks at his work, satisfied. He's very pleased with the boxers he designed for me.

"I can't use the toilet with these, George..."

He stares at me, tired and annoyed. Then he gets it. They need an orifice! He turns me around and starts tearing at them. The fabric makes a loud sound when it rips apart. I look down and see that he's made a hole in the makeshift underpants. Now I won't have any trouble going to the bathroom, he thinks. I don't know how to react.

"Come, now. Hurry up and leave. You're done!"

When I walk into the ward, Flavia and Mihai burst out in laughter.

"Jesus, Alex! He's made you granny panties!"

I told them what happened. We learned to find the funny bits in the painful absurdity that surrounds us.

"Are you still in pain?" I ask Flavia.

"Yes. But I've decided I'll never let him touch me again. I'll just say no."

When Mom arrives and sees how George bandaged me, she cuts off the gauze boxers and throws the dressings away. She wraps a freshly washed scarf around my hips, making it look like a skirt. I'm finally comfortable again. The stiff, improvised underwear was chafing my thighs. Not long after, the shoddy dressings start to unravel, revealing our wounds. One of the nurses walks in with a bandaging kit and patches us up.

It's Alina's turn to take a few days off. Stephanie takes her place, working under Iulia's supervision. At least she's back from her holiday. Ever since they started giving me painkillers and my wounds started to heal, I've gotten better at withstanding bath-time. It's not as hard to remove the gauze from the flesh, and I'm not bleeding as much as before. Pieces of me still wash down the drain, but they're not as many as they used to be. In my prayers, I bless the surgeon from France, the artificial skin he used, and Iulia. The skin grafts started to take after the last surgery.

Stephanie doesn't sing to me, but she's very gentle. With a sweet voice, she talks to me about the amazing things I'll do after I go home. I still shiver because of the pain and the sensation that the spray of water is piercing through my flesh, to the core of my being. I listen to her patiently, focusing on the sweet cadence of her words, to take my mind off the hurt. Her small hands hover over me, barely touching me. She doesn't like to scrub and scratch. She covers me in foam from the antibacterial soap. She doesn't dare use the gruesome toothed sponge. Every once in a while, she gives it a slanted look, but she never reaches for it. I'm grateful beyond words for this kindness. When she's done washing me, she wraps me up in the usual green shroud and takes me to Iulia. I greet her with joy and thank her for returning.

"I hate that I had to leave you, but I was exhausted."

The few good people here are forced to play by the dirty rules of the institution. After a while, in order to survive, they convince themselves that everything is as it should be. They need the job, and they love what they do. They genuinely like helping others. At some point, the boundary between truth and deceit, between good and evil, becomes blurred. How could they change something? They're small. So very small. The strong ones would crush the weak in an instant and then they'd lose everything. When they speak up, no one stands by them. The rest look down, letting them take the hit. Even though they had opinions of their own before, now their lips are sealed. And there they are, standing alone, face to face with the hangmen that tell them that they're imagining things. They have everything they need! The hospital is prosperous. Sure, they don't have enough drugs, so what? The sick will just have to take it. Yes, they don't have special beds for burn victims either, but what's wrong with the old ones, with the broken circuits and the dirty supermarket mattresses? Yeah, yeah, there's no anesthesiologist available for bath-time. Why waste money paying another doctor? You can wash the patients awake. Just tell them that's how they do it everywhere in the world. They'll believe you! Infections? There aren't any. The rockers brought the germs from the club, or from home. Also, let's stop talking about transferring people abroad, all right? Why leave when they have the same conditions here as they would in Germany? "If my own child was in her situation, I wouldn't transfer him."

The Minister of Health himself looked an entire country in the eyes when he said these things out loud. He put the seal of silence over truths that could have saved lives. His lies became torture weapons in the hands of those who should have healed us. The deceit was perpetuated and moved through the ranks, from one minister to the other, from doctor to doctor. They held onto it while they condemned us to those wicked procedures that could only pass for medical treatment in a nightmare. They abandoned us to hide the failures of a ruined medical system, covered their trails by quitting their jobs, then vanished, taking with them the responsibility for their deeds. They let us rot, imprisoned in these extermination wards, devoured by germs and by the fever that won't go down. We lie in these dumps, witnessing our own decomposition while they accuse us that it's our fault we're dying. We don't smile enough. We're not sleeping in the right position. We don't eat what we're supposed to. They have everything they need; don't we get it? We're the ones that lack something.

They sold their souls to corruption to keep their status and to maintain the illusion of their competence. We paid the price for this chimera with our flesh, watching it die in their hands while they denied there was a problem. HAIs? Of course not. Just lazy patients with bad skin. We're lucky to be alive. The antibiotics that coarse through our veins are the last bastion standing in the way of the ravaging multidrug resistant germs. That's why the doctor shouted at me that night. She knew that if I stopped taking the drugs, I wouldn't make it. But what about our friends who weren't as lucky? They died, and they'll keep dying, murdered by the lies spewed out by these people who are supposed to take care of us.

Three silhouettes dressed in black hover in front of my tired eyes. The door of the ward is half-open and, even though I can't see their faces, I can hear their voices. They're crying. I'm not quite sure, but I think I recognize Mihai's voice. Is this a bad dream? I force myself to wake up, but I can't. It's real. The sun has set over the Hospital for Burns, and someone is counting the souls stolen by the darkness. Flavia stares outside through the crack in the door. She starts to cry, and I suddenly understand. When Mihai walks in, he's grief-stricken. He crashes down on the chair next to Flavia's bed and wipes the sweat off his forehead with his hands.

"Ana died…"

The black silhouettes were her parents. They came to the hospital as soon as they heard. They were here every day for her, but in other ways. Her soul was still with them, fighting. Today they only found her body. Ana vanished, and with her, the miracles of her youth, her sweet, childish smile, and her bountiful heart. She only left behind a piece of who she was. The tortured shell of flesh, mutilated by the people who should have saved her, wrung and hurt until she couldn't take it anymore. No wonder I thought her parents were floating. There was nothing left to anchor them in this world that their dear child had departed. Slowly, they climbed after her, only held behind by the materiality of their bodies.

Flavia, Sandra, Mihai, and I cry for her. We weep in vain. Ana is far away now, and our heavy regrets only hold her back. She's off to the Heaven she must have dreamed about; a place of color and joy, filled with the beautiful landscapes she never got to photograph down here on Earth.

We're still mourning when one of the nurses walks in to take our temperature. As always, we're all over 100 degrees. She looks at us with dry, expressionless eyes, and asks why we're upset. We tell her about Ana, and she shrugs. Death is something trivial here. It's such a common occurrence, it no longer holds any meaning.

"She's better off dead, girls," the woman emphasizes. "Had she lived, she'd have been a monster."

She walks out with our thermometers, leaving behind the sharp scent of her floral perfume. Silence falls upon the ward. Within this quietness, her terrible words become the dark dowry of yet another day in Hell. We grab them with our burned, deformed hands and lock them up in the box of horrors that's become our soul. We close the hatch well and guard it fiercely because we never want it to open and release the awfulness of it all into the world. We don't want such cruelty to sully us with its ugliness. We don't want it to infect us with its evil.

Monster... I wonder what the word really means. After each surgery, we lose pieces of ourselves. With our scorched skin and open sores, we've stopped thinking about beauty a long time ago. All we want is to survive, regardless of what we'll look like when we get out of here. We've talked about this resolution for nights on end, and it's become a common decision that gives us the strength to go on, no matter how horrible our wounds are. Our bodies might be "ugly," but our souls strive to remain beautiful and human. Amidst losses, bath-time, botched operations, and nightmares, we fight to stay who we are.

Ana wasn't a monster. She was just an innocent girl, and we'd have loved her just as much, even without her unscathed skin. It's not the face that makes the monster, but its soul, cruel and disgusting, untouched by kindness. Something is rotting behind the smooth cheeks they wear as a mask, filling their entire being with the pestilence of hatred and stupidity. Then, when they speak, they say things that others lock in boxes of horror.

Sandra weeps and sings, sings and weeps while the doctor bends and extends her left hand, which she nearly lost. During the kinesiotherapy sessions, her bandages become drenched in blood, and she has to have them changed. She comes back from the dressings ward exhausted and pale. She lies down and falls asleep immediately, sighing and crying tears she doesn't know she's shedding. Another doctor comes to see me too. She grabs my elbows and pulls on them until she manages to straighten them. The bones and tendons crack because of the effort, and a strange kind of pain takes hold of me, like hot lava coursing through my body. Then she moves on to the fingers. I beg her to stop, but she doesn't. It hurts beyond words.

"There's nothing I can do about it," she says. "This is an ailment specific to burn victims. You become stiff and the only way to fix it is to pull on the limbs."

She gives me a few minutes of reprieve, and then she starts over. She wrings and pulls. I bleed and cry. In the end, she wipes the blood off me with a piece of sterile cloth and leaves. Afterwards, I can't really focus on anything. I try to talk to Mom, but it's useless. I'm so exhausted, all I can do is stare at the walls. Bath-time and kinesiotherapy hurt the worst.

Flavia's skin grafts didn't take properly. She lies in bed in the same tortured position, on her side, at the edge of the mattress, leaning on her forehead. She talks in her sleep, and I can hear her whispering names of people we'll never see again. The days go by in deep suffering, one after the other, in a succession of torments we're forced to relive.

I shiver in the green tub, holding back the tears. Near the end of the procedure, the painkiller wears off, and it hurts almost like before. The wounds are getting smaller, but I still have open sores that sting and burn. Stephanie tries to finish quickly. At the end, she stops the water and runs to get the green shroud. A female doctor I haven't seen before barges into the ward and stares at me with unbridled curiosity. She examines me unashamed to the point where, for the first time in a while, I become aware of my nakedness. She swirls around me awkwardly, prodding and huffing, as if she's looking at something both ghastly and fascinating.

"What the hell is this girl still doing here? Send her home! Do you want her to get infected again?"

"Her doctors think she has to stay with us a while longer. She hasn't healed yet, the poor soul," Stephanie explains humbly.

"I can see that very well. She has a lot of open wounds. But that's precisely what I'm afraid of. Who's taking care of her? Dr. Moldovan and Silvia?"

"Yes..."

The woman shakes her head disapprovingly and heads to the door, shouting over her shoulder:

"Send her home or she'll catch something again! You'll see. If she doesn't leave now, she never will!"

Ever since I arrived here, I learned that the patient is nothing more but an unwilling witness to the cunning observations exchanged between the doctors and their staff. There's no time or interest for real dialogue. Our questions are met with indifference. Things are said over our heads, with words destined for no one in particular, but, at the same time, for everyone. The conversation is rarely personalized, intimate, between the sick person and their caregivers. If you cry, no one soothes you. On the contrary. You're scolded and accused of being weak. Decisions are made without asking for your permission. All you can do is deduce your fate from replies that aren't addressed to you. If you demand answers, you receive a brief explanation, delivered either in overly complicated jargon or so simplistically, it's incomprehensible. Even though I'm standing right here, in front of her, the doctor isn't talking to me, or to Stephanie. Somehow, she's speaking to Dr. Moldovan and to Dr. Preda. Everything that isn't said openly, in an acknowledged fashion, needs third parties to make its point. The medical communication takes place through gossiping, on the grapevine, until it reaches, through whatever crooked means, its real target.

Even so, it's the first time in months that I've heard someone talking about the infections openly. A few nights ago, a nurse, together with my sister, tried to change my position in bed, on the advice of the surgeons. My hands were so stiff it was impossible to lay them beside me. Felicia and Cristina asked me to kneel on the bed, while my sister grabbed my hips and the nurse pulled on my arms to straighten them. They tried everything humanly possible, shoving me, bending me, but nothing worked. As if they were made of stone, my limbs wouldn't budge. In the end, they gave up. Frustrated, sweaty, and bitter, the nurse broke down and confessed.

"Dear, sweet girl! It doesn't matter if you sleep on your tummy. Listen to me, healing has nothing to do with the position you're lying in. These beds are so useless, it would make more sense to hang you upside down!"

After struggling for more than an hour, my sister and I burst into tears. The bandages on my scalp fell off, revealing the big burns underneath, covered in pus. The nurse didn't say that the multidrug resistant bacteria are the reason why I'm not healing. No. Something like that can't be uttered openly in this place. But she did cast a doubt on the honesty of those in charge of treating me. And so, gradually, with every half-confession made in secrecy, the certainty that I'm being eaten alive by germs rises from the ashes of the trust I once had in these people. No one ever told me that I was infected. Not in so many words. If the doctors denied it, their staff couldn't admit it either. It's as if someone holds a hand over their mouths, but loosens its grip every once in a while, letting fragments of words escape. As distorted as they are, they still tell the truth that can't be spoken out aloud.

Stephanie gawks at me, worried after the departure of the "talkative" doctor. She's afraid I'm going to ask questions she's not allowed to answer, but I stay quiet. I'm too tired and in too much pain. I also already know the truth. Or, rather, I feel it in every wound that won't heal. In the dressings ward, I wait for the doctors who are running late again. It's normal to sit here naked, for minutes on end, shivering because of the pain, counting the minutes to their blessed arrival. As soon as they walk in, they start to take pictures.

"Don't dress her wounds anymore. Leave them open," says Silvia.

"But..."

"Leave them open, I said. Exposure to air will help them close," she insists, cutting Iulia off.

The nurse's eyes stay glued to the floor for the entire duration of the conversation. She's lost in thought. After the doctors leave, Iulia looks at me with empty eyes, and stares out the window. She goes to the cabinet and ravages it, looking for something. She takes out a big jar of Prontosan. It's the disinfectant donated by a hospital in Germany. I rarely see it around because she's the only one who uses it. Ever since she started cleaning my wounds with it, defying the doctors' advice to only apply the Flamazine, I've gotten progressively better, and the skin grafts stopped dying.

"I must leave you open, Alex. I can't dress your wounds anymore."

"But.... isn't it dangerous? Can't I catch something?"

"Try not to leave your ward too often. Avoid going out in the hallway as much as you can."

She drenches me in disinfectant, and I nearly bite my tongue because of how it stings. I'm afraid the pain will become a part of my being and I'll never be able to get rid of it. I walk back to the ward alone, with the green shroud wrapped around my naked wounds. The burn on my right wrist, the one they tore the fresh graft from when they dropped me in the O.R. already soaked the sheets. Big drops of blood fall on the floor, leaving a trail behind me. I hurry up. I don't want the orderlies to shout at me because I'm making a mess. I sit on the edge of the bed and wait for Mom. I still can't lie down by myself, so I just stand there, shivering, and drowsy. Mother arrives and stops in the doorway. She grows pale and her hands start to shake. It's the first time she's seen me without any dressings. She's shocked by the big, open wounds that still plague my body.

She crawls to the chair and crashes on it. She forces herself to smile to hide her horror. "Yes, Mom. I know I look bad." Mom contradicts me, but her voice is weak. I don't have any clothes to wear, so she must go home and bring me something. Since I had no idea they planned to remove my bandages, we couldn't properly prepare. Mom leaves and comes back a couple of hours later with clean, sleeveless t-shirts that she washed at 194 degrees and dried over the stovetop. She helps me get dressed, but the fabric sticks to the open wounds on my back. She tries to pry it away from the burns, but it won't budge. I cry because of the pain, and she weeps with me. I soil the sheets and the pillows with blood and pus. Mother changes the bedding and the pillowcases, making sure they're always clean. I spend my day in agony, tortured by the gaping gashes on my body. Unhealed as they are, they stick to everything I come into contact with.

"This is unacceptable," Mom says. "They must dress your wounds. This was a very bad idea."

She leaves to get a doctor. When she comes back, she's sad. Judging by her eyes, I think the answer she received wasn't what she expected.

"Silvia is on duty. She insisted that it's better this way because you'll heal faster. I told her you're in pain, that the clothes keep sticking to your wounds, but she just shrugged."

I wake up in the middle of the night in agony. Mom went home because she was exhausted. Olivia, our friend, offered to stay with us, to allow our folks to rest. She helps me go to the bathroom, washes her hands, and gives me a sip of water. I ask her to pull on the parts of my t-shirt that were stuck to my wounds, to dislodge them. I'm in pain because of how the fabric rubs against the sores. She tries. The clothing makes a nauseating ripping sound but won't move. The sensation is one of tearing, and it reminds me of bath-time. I can't take it.

"Let it go, Oli. They'll just get stuck again, anyway."

She gives up. She fixes my pillow fort and helps me lie down. Then it's Flavia's turn, and Sandra is next. Olivia became the night-shift nurse.

Even if I'm lying on soft pillows, they exert pressure on the open wounds and cling to them. What's worse is that, because of the position of the bed, I keep slipping down and landing on the coarse sheets and hard mattress. Now, not only the t-shirt is digging into my sores, but the bed dressing as well. I can't do anything about it, and I'm too ashamed to wake Olivia up again. I look at her dozing intermittently on the rudimentary chair next to Flavia's bed. Her youthful face is riddled with worry, and she frowns and twitches in her sleep. When dawn breaks, she opens her eyes and I close mine to pretend, once again, that I'm resting. She comes to our side and looks at us, making sure we're all right, then she walks out of the room. Once she's gone, I get up and stare at the bed. It's dirty with dried blood and pus, just like the bandages once were. My wounds left undeniable clues regarding the true state of my body. I'm nowhere near healed. The pain is unbearable. The sharp cold in the ward pinches the wounds that are agony under the stuck clothing.

I make slow, gentle movements, in an attempt to dislodge the t-shirt from the flesh, but it keeps clinging to me. As the cotton rubs against my deep sores, fresh drops of crimson blood fall from under the once loose-fitting garment. In a last-ditch effort, I grab the margins of the clothing item with my weak, stiff fingers, and pull as hard as I can. I scream. I pull until I remove the fabric from a wound on my shoulder blade. I keep going, tearing, and crying, until the whole garment comes off. I sob quietly, trying not to wake the girls up. When my mother arrives, I'm shivering because of the pain. She finds me lying in a pool of blood. She strips me naked and changes the linen. I'm afraid to lie down, so I just sit on the edge of the bed until I'm drowsy. There's no bath-time today, so I can rest a little. I refuse to go out in the hallway for my usual walks. I have to put clothing on, and right now, that's unacceptable. And then there's also the risk of catching something. When I don't have the strength to sit up anymore, my mother lays me on the clean pillows that smell like home. I miss normality so much. I miss the days when I was able to take a shower without crying. I forgot what it's like to live without pain.

Flavia's cannula broke today, and it's her turn to be probed. Oana walks in and gives me a blunt stare. She gropes my friend's ankles, disinfects the skin, and throws the used cotton pad in the "sterile" tray with fresh, unopened cannulas.

She pushes the needle in, but she doesn't find the vein. She wiggles it right and left, pushes it in deeper, but nothing comes out. She removes it, then inserts it someplace else. Nothing. She repeats the procedure a few more times, without any success. She removes it, and inserts it, removes it, and inserts it, without bothering to change it. She finally grabs a new kit because the old one had become blunt. She keeps at it for seventeen more attempts. I count every attempt and I can't believe Flavia isn't saying something. Is she all right?

"Please, stop. Enough. Stop!"

My friend finally lost it. The nurse pulls out the needle, throws it directly in the tray, over the sterile kits, and leaves the ward angry. Flavia's breathing becomes shallow, and she starts to wheeze. I shout after a nurse and Sonia comes. She calms Flavia down. She's having a panic attack. When she feels better, the nurse starts to search for a new viable vein and finds one immediately, without much effort. While she fixes the cannula with tape, Flavia sobs, prey to a desperation I know all too well.

"I can't take this anymore. I just can't. I can't, I can't..."

She repeats the words over and over until they become the mantra of her suffering. When Mihai arrives with fresh food, she's still weeping. I tell him what happened, and anger clouds his eyes. He clenches his fist and grabs the doorknob.

"Please, don't! Stay with me," Flavia whispers. "Stay here, I need you."

Broken, he sits next to her and caresses her. He tells her stories about all the things they'll do once she gets out of the hospital. He describes the trips they'll take, the concerts they'll attend, the beautiful dreams that await them beyond this hell. Flavia sighs and listens, feeding her soul with these illusions to help her body make it through another day of torture. Slowly, a soft, shy smile lights up her face. She's holding Mihai's hand as best she can, with her bandaged, injured fingers that she can't intertwine with his because of the wounds. She has to make do with this incomplete touch. Even if it's imperfect, it's strong enough to fill the void inside her. After a while, she falls asleep. Mihai is wearing black and there are deep, dark circles under his swollen eyes. He's pale from all the crying. I remember that today was Ana's funeral. I remain quiet. I watch the antibiotics drip through my IV line and start to count, hoping that I'll fall asleep too, but nothing happens. My wounds are stuck to the bed linen again, and the nightly suffering begins. The pillow I rest my right hand on is soaked in blood. I'm so cold that I think I'll never be warm again. When Mihai turns the lights off and leaves, the horror of it all takes hold of me.

I'm afraid of death, and I cling to the strip of light that makes its way to us from the illuminated hallway.

When I'm this troubled, I imagine that there, beyond the cracked door, my guardian angel spies on me with his serene, blue eyes. His wings are ruffled from flying in to see me tonight, and so is his blond, curly hair. He sighs when I sigh. He cries when I cry. The nurses pass him by without noticing him, whispering words that they only utter when no one is listening. Sometimes, he follows them to their office or to the emergency room. They keep talking and, even though he's innocent and doesn't understand the ways of this wicked world, he realizes what's going on. A shiver runs down his spine as he comprehends. He runs back to me, frightened. His big, otherworldly heart races with worry, but when he sees me, he calms down. He prays for me because he knows that God will listen to him. Every once in a while, when I'm actually asleep, he walks in the ward and sits on my mom's chair. I like to think that he weaves beautiful dreams there. He sends them to me to protect me from the darkness and the fear, the fire and the shadows that agonize the canvas of my mind, repeating, over and over, the macabre spectacle of burning alive. He tells me stories like this one. In the deep silence of the hospital night, my wandering angel watches over me and, no matter if he's real or just a figment of my imagination, he's the hope I need to survive until dawn.

Silvia informs us that a medical team consisting of physiotherapists from the Elias Hospital will come to see us. We'll need burn rehabilitation procedures after we're discharged, and they offered to help. They want to meet us beforehand to assess us. It's the first time that I hear the word "discharge" being uttered around me. The idea of going home gives me hope, even if I know it won't happen very soon.

The doctors arrive after lunch. They're dressed in sterile gear. A tall man with gray hair smiles at us from the door. He's accompanied by a shy, brunette woman. She has a pleasant, soothing voice. They don't want to touch us. Instead, they examine us from a distance. They tell us that we'll receive outpatient care in their physical rehabilitation ward at the Elias Hospital. They ask us a few questions, and then they're off.

"They seem to be nice people," Flavia says.

"Yes. I really hope they're able to help us."

Iris is the first one to be discharged. Her sisters come to pick her up. Before she leaves, she comes to see us. She sits in Mihai's chair and sighs. Because of the dressings, her clothes don't sit right on her body. There's gauze peeking out from under her sleeves and neckline. Her collar is already drenched in blood from the wounds on her ears. She doesn't say a word. She just sits there, staring at us with her sad green eyes. She feels like she's abandoning us but, at the same time, she's happy she's going home.

"We have to go out together some day. Now that we're friends, we must keep in touch," she whispers.

"That's the only good part of this ordeal. That we made new friends."

Before she vanishes in the hallway, among busy nurses and frowning doctors, she looks behind with tears in her eyes. Iris, the girl who went out to have fun on the night of October 30th, is not the same person as the one who comes home today. That happy, easy-going redhead will never return. She stayed behind, haunting the ashen streets of Bucharest, calling for someone who can't answer back. For this Iris, with her scarred body and maimed heart, a new life begins once she steps out of the Hospital for Burns. A future she could only imagine in a nightmare.

Shortly after, it's Sandra's turn to leave. Her doctors discharge her because the holidays are coming. But in January, after the New Year festivities, she's coming back for more surgery.

"We won't drift apart, all right?"

"Of course not. You can't get away from us!"

Flavia uses her happy voice to comfort our friend. She smiles and winks with joy. As Sandra's voice becomes fainter amidst the "thank-yous" and "goodbyes" she utters to the nurses, so does Flavia's grin. Once silence falls upon the hallway, she begins to cry. The wounds on her back haven't made any progress in days. They stay open in spite of all the new grafting attempts. Some areas have even gotten worse. They keep telling her the same thing: her skin is too white and too thin, but we already know the truth. Her body isn't reacting to the antibiotics anymore.

"What if I stay here forever? What if I never leave?"

I try to calm her down, but I've thought about it too. We comfort each other as best as we can to endure this inferno some more, while it spits out the souls that it's tormented. We're left behind to satiate it as it empties itself of victims. Identically, the days go by nameless, dateless, numberless, endlessly repeating the same routine, as if we're stuck in a time loop, condemned to relive the torture forever. The painful baths, the cannulas that break down, the IV drips pouring through our scarred veins, the pillow forts, built and torn down over and over again, the fever, the wounds that stick to the dirty sheets, the nightmares, the tears cried in the middle of the dark night. We can't shake off the feeling that the suffering is eternal. We count the hours that pass with the burns that don't heal. In an upside-down world, time is not measured in minutes, but in the wounds that won't close.

One evening, Dr. Preda walks in the ward while Mother is busy erecting the pillow fort. Afraid that she'll get scolded, she stops and greets her, hiding her hands behind her back.

"You're going home tomorrow. Flavia will stay behind a little longer but, before Christmas, we'll discharge her as well."

I have a hard time understanding the words coming out of her mouth. I'm not sure if what's happening is real or I'm just dreaming.

"You're... discharging me?"

"Yes. You still have open wounds, but your mom will wash you in your tub at home until they close on their own. There's nothing more we can do for you in this hospital."

"Thank you," Mom answers in a haste.

After Silvia leaves, I stay quiet. I don't know what I'm feeling. I'm happy, but I'm also terrified. I'm not sure if my mom can take care of me all alone. I've lost the use of my hands and I'm totally helpless because of the unhealed burns. I'm a baby trapped in the body of a 27-year-old woman. Won't something bad happen to me at home? "She'll catch something again if you don't send her home." I can still hear the words that doctor shouted over her shoulder the day she barged in the hygiene ward. A cold shiver runs down my spine. They're not discharging me because I'm ready to go, but because they're afraid I'll get worse if I stay.

"You're leaving me all alone," Flavia sighs. "I'm happy you're leaving, but I'm terrified of the loneliness. What will I do at night when the nightmares and the fear overwhelm me?"

She cries and breaks my heart. I want to comfort her, but there's nothing meaningful I can say. I'm going home and she's staying here. She's staying behind to suffer. But aren't I leaving to do the same? We'll be together in the pain even if we're not close physically. I promise her all the things in the world to comfort her. Mihai tells her about the preparations he's made for her discharge. Her favorite plush toys are waiting for her on the new bed he bought. Flavia calms down while he describes a future that's bright enough to chase away the shadow of fear. We crack jokes about surprising our friends with our new look once we leave this place, and we remember funny things that happened during the shows we attended together. We talk and talk, until Flavia falls asleep, and Mihai lays his head on her bed, exhausted.

I open my eyes at six o'clock in the morning. Alina is watching me from the door.

"Alex, today is your last bath-time."

I never thought I'd hear these words. Today, I don't only feel terror, but also elation. I'm leaving this place! But then the doubt sets in. How can this be the "last" bath-time when I'll have to have countless others at home? I hope that they'll stop being as painful once all the wounds are closed. I still can't walk right because of the donor sites on my thighs. They haven't healed either, so I drag my legs on my way toward the hygiene ward, supported by Alina. She's unusually quiet. She doesn't offer to hum me one of her lullabies. After a while, she opens up.

"I never wanted a daughter because I think that women have a harder life than men. But ever since I met you, I've had a change of heart. I would have liked to have a little girl like you."

My eyes well up with tears. She helps me up in the tub and waits for the nurse to bring the painkillers. Once I'm numb, she starts to wash me. There are no more bandages left to unravel from the wounds. Even so, the water still hurts. I don't cry anymore. I just shiver, trying to take my mind off the nausea, like always. For one last time, I ask her to sing to me. She picks a happier song, and, in our own way, we celebrate my discharge. I watch the water going down the drain, noticing that it's not as bloody as it used to be. Scabs, dead pieces of skin grafts, and blue stitches that the surgeons forgot to remove cling to the margins of the tub, sullying it. I stare at my right hand. It's getting harder and harder to remember how I looked before the fire. I don't know if my mind blurred the image of my unscathed body to protect me or if I'm simply forgetting who I was before the fire.

My left shoulder is still filled with deep gashes. They throb and ache under the pressure of the water spray. Now, the water becomes bloodier and fatter. I've still got dressings on my head, where the new skin didn't take well. The gauze is drenched in pus, and it's clung to the infected burns and the tiny hairs that grow around the bald patches. I've made peace with the fact that I will always have visible scars on my scalp. The stinging is merciless, and I shut my eyelids tight, as if to stop the hurt from blinding me.

I remember fragments from my old life. In one memory, I'm combing my long, dark hair and smiling in the mirror. In another, I'm painting my nails bright red. There I am, bathing in the sea, under the blistering summer sun. Such small things that I never paid attention to. Now, they've become impossible. I'll never be able to do them again. Not like before. They're testimonies of the irreversible nature of the tragedy. Alina sings as the foam from the surgical soap gets richer and soaks my burns, turning pink in the process. As the effect of the painkiller fades, the pain grows. Before it becomes unbearable, she turns the water off.

"You're done, Alex."

I open my eyes and take a good look at her. She's holding the green shroud that she'll cover me with. Tears fall down her cheeks, but she's smiling. She's happy that I'm finally leaving this place. There were days when neither of us thought I was going to survive. I imagined they'd take my body away in the quietness of the night, while the girls were asleep, just like they once took Delia. I still don't understand why I lived, and she died. And now I'm also walking out of here, out of this Hell that claimed her, while sparing me. I stifle the heartbreak I feel and grin, winking. Shivering and naked, I thank her for all that she's done for me. She clenches the sheet tight, as if surprised by my gratitude.

"I'd hug you if I could. Maybe we'll try later."

She covers me and helps me out of the tub, then takes me to Iulia.

"Alex, see? You've made it!"

"Thank you... I don't know what I would have done without you and Alina!"

After she sits me on the bed, she takes the sheet off and the doctors walk into the room. They take turns looking at me. As usual, they exchange words, whispers, and telling nods. Silvia gives Iulia a metallic object that looks like a bent metal plate.

"What is it?"

"Use it as a splint for the index finger. It's lighter than the cast."

"But... how? It's not built for that."

"Come now, we'll manage somehow. That finger has to be immobilized."

"What about the wound?"

"It'll heal."

Silvia grabs my hand just like she did that day, when she cut my joint open with the surgical blade, without warning or numbing me. She throws some bandages on the bleeding gash and presses the finger down hard on the metal blade. I hear it crack. It hurts very bad and I sigh.

"I can't believe this... Are you going to cry on your last day here?"

While she squeezes my index finger, Iulia wraps layers upon layers of elastic gauze onto it until it's completely extended and straight. She fixes the margins together with tape, to make sure they're not going to come apart. The bandage is soaked in blood already. Silvia looks at it and shrugs. She explains, emotionless, that it was to be expected.

"Are you happy you're leaving?"

"Yes," I answer, dizzy from the pain. "I was afraid. I thought I wasn't ready..."

"You'll come back a few times a week outpatient so that we can check on you."

"How should I care for myself at home?"

"Ask your mother to wash you in the tub every second day."

"What products should I use?"

"Some hydrating cream where your wounds are closed."

"What sort of hydrating cream?"

"Any hydrating cream..."

I try to get her to be more specific.

"Isn't there a special product for burn scars?"

"What can I say... Marigold ointment, Nivea, something like that."

"And over the wounds?"

"Nothing. Just leave them out in the open to dry up."

The dialogue ends abruptly. Silvia shifts her attention to Iulia and gives her instructions. I'd like to ask more questions, but I know it's useless. This is all she's willing to tell me. I can't help wondering how we're going to manage at home, just me and my mother. How is an elderly woman going to be able to wash me? What soap will she use? Sandra spoke to her doctor, and he made several great recommendations. I'll just get the stuff that he mentioned. He also told her that marigold ointment is useless for such deep burns like ours. Before she leaves, Silvia says she'll bring me the discharge papers later, in the ward. Iulia sighs and approaches me.

"I have to dress your wounds. I can't let you leave like this. Your mom is going to remove the bandages at home and then you can sit 'out in the air' for as long as you like."

She drenches a few compresses in the Colistin solution she prepared and washes me gently. It stings really bad, but I stay quiet. She soaks me in the liquid, insisting on the open sores. She wraps me up in gauze, just like before, paying close attention to the burns on my scalp. She comes up with a sort of gauze helmet that will protect the oozing wounds from the environment.

"You'll have to be careful with these, Alex. Please, always keep them clean. Many wounds on your body can become reinfected."

Now that I'm leaving, the word "infections" isn't as gatekept as it once was. They speak it more freely. It's not completely forbidden anymore. I'm scared that the grime I carry in my wounds is going to seep out into the home I share with mother and taint it. I'm afraid I'll infect her too.

"Darling, your mother would have to have open wounds of her own for the germs to get into her system. Rest assured. She's safe."

Her words comfort me. I've waited for this day for so long and, now that it's arrived, I don't know what to do with it. After she finishes her work, she looks at me for a long time, with a cryptic expression on her face. I don't know how to interpret it. It's as if she's not convinced that I'm really getting out of here. If I think about it, that's just the way it is. I'm not leaving here alone. I take a piece of this hell with me, in my flesh. The anonymous bacteria whose name they can't utter.

In the ward, Mother holds a bag of clothes to her chest. She's brought a large hoodie and loose-fitting lounge pants that won't cling to my bandages. Cristina is here too. Daniel, her brother-in-law, drove all night so that she could be with me today. She shows me the brand-new pair of rock'n'roll boots that she got me.

"Come, let me help you put these on. They're your discharge present, so that you can walk out of here proudly. I knew you'd like them from the moment I set eyes on them. Florin sends you a hug. He's sorry he couldn't be here, but he'll wait for you at home."

Flavia forces herself to smile and be funny. After the two months I spent naked, I feel like the clothing is too heavy to carry. Its weight is painful against the wounds that throb under the pressure of the dressings. After tens of minutes of torment, Cristina and Mom finally manage to get me dressed. I realize how much weight I lost. The wide clothing makes my emaciated frame look skeletal.

"You'll plump back up in no time, don't worry."

Cristina notices that I'm troubled and tries to comfort me.

"You're about twenty pounds lighter, but we'll feed you some great meals and you'll be all right."

Mother takes the pillows off the bed and throws them into a black plastic bag. She empties the drawers, making sure we don't leave something behind. I sit on the hard mattress for one last time. I'm tired. I'm shocked to discover that standing up with clothes on is a difficult task. Flavia is anxious. We talk and make plans for when she'll be discharged. I invite her and Mihai to my place and we promise we'll call each other often. When Silvia arrives, we're both sulking.

"What? Aren't you happy you're going home?"

"If only Flavia could join me..."

"Come, now. We won't keep her long either. I brought you your papers. I wrote that you have to come to us three times a week, so that we can assess your progress. We're good, right? You know what you have to do. Now you're entering the rehabilitation phase."

"Yes. Thank you... for everything. See you soon!"

"Of course. Every second day, at the bottom floor of the hospital, in the out-patient ward. After the 20th, go to the Elias Hospital. Have them take a look at you and schedule you for physiotherapy. They don't normally work with burn patients. It's not a specialized clinic, but they'll help you as best they can."

"They haven't worked with burn patients before?"

"Who do you think has, except for us? We only have one therapist, and she can't take care of all of you. Her office is too small."

She gives Mom the papers and vanishes before we get to ask any questions. Cristina shakes her head and closes her eyes.

"God, I'm so happy we got rid of her..."

Before we leave, we say goodbye to Iulia and Alina, who left their wards to greet me. Mama exchanges phone numbers with them and we thank them for their kindness and care. We visit the nurses too. Miruna, Adina, and Felicia are on duty today, and they hug me clumsily, barely touching me. I look around and register everything I see in the hallway. The white doors of the wards, the green linoleum, and the sober walls whisper things without meaning. They're playing back memories of the torments I endured in this abode of suffering. There's a bitter taste in my mouth and I start to shiver. I turn my back to everything and head toward the door. When I hear the heavy gates closing behind me, I lean on the railing. Cristina grabs me and asks if I'm okay. I burst into tears.

"Help me down the stairs, please."

Step by step, I leave behind the first floor of the Hospital for Burns and Plastic Surgery. I stop in the yard and take a few deep breaths. The air is fragrant with the frozen smell of winter. Two months ago, in October, the ambulance driver put my stretcher down right on this spot. It's hard to believe that I'm standing on it today. I try to shake away the terror.

"The car is here," Cristina tells me.

She helps me climb on the seat next to the driver. Daniel greets me without looking me in the eye. He doesn't want to offend me by staring at me, so he focuses on the GPS map. Cristina shuts the door and joins Mom in the backseat. The engine roars as the car starts.

"Say goodbye to hell. I hope we don't ever have to come back here."

We leave behind the dreary building. I remember listening to the noise made by the cars passing by our windows in the nights I couldn't sleep. Overwhelmed by the loneliness, the fever, the pain, and the fear, I used to latch onto their murmur because it summoned images of warm homes and loving families waiting for the drivers to return. I eavesdropped on the sounds made by the freeway, clinging to them like to a promise that something else exists beyond the walls of suffering I was trapped behind. Something better than the torture I was made to endure in the Hospital of Neverhealing. Now, I'm a passenger in one of those cars. I find it hard to believe that it's real. Did I leave? Did I survive? I smile bitterly and wonder if it's true. Maybe I died, and this is my journey to another life.

That's accurate in a way... Because I'm not the same girl who was brought here on the night of October 30th, 2015. This isn't my old existence, but a new one. I'm a different person in a new life. I'm fully aware that this isn't over yet, that other aches and torments wait for me at home, other fears about my devastated body. For the moment, however, I allow myself to be happy and sad at the same time. I escaped, but Delia didn't. Neither did Ana, Alex, and countless others like them. Like me. My thoughts fall apart, and I look up at the cold and silent sky with teary eyes. Daniel turns the stereo on, and Cristina strokes my cheek.

"One day, it'll all be okay, you'll see."

On the radio, through some sort of odd coincidence, the lead singer of the band Soul Asylum hums a story about lost smiles.

Can you help me remember how to smile/Make it somehow all seem worthwhile.

Yes, one day it'll all be okay, I tell myself. One day, I'll smile without flames burning in my heart or ashes smoldering in my soul. Someday, maybe, I'll even understand the meaning of it all. But no matter how hard I struggle to find it, I realize that, in the end, my quest is purposeless. Meaning only exists for those who are alive to seek it. For the rest, it died when their heart stopped beating.

III
A Series of Abandonments

"We prepared everything for you. We sterilized the sheets, bought new pillowcases, and cleaned the whole place; we disinfected the bathroom and the kitchen. The apartment is as good as new!"

I look around my home as if I was staring at a foreign place. It's only been two months since I've set foot here, but I feel like entire years have passed. Everything seems so unreal. For a moment, I wonder if I'm dreaming. The whitewashed wall and the humble furniture tell stories about a life that I lost too soon. It makes me sad to think that I'll taint this place, this effigy of my past, with the dark turmoil I hold within my soul and the dirtiness I carry in my flesh. I freeze in the hallway for a few seconds, and then I come to. I sit on the bench in front of my large mirror and Mom takes my shoes off. I should refrain from doing it, but I stare at myself, hungry after my reflection, which has been hidden from me in the hospital.

The wound on my left cheek is still open. My forehead, nose, and chin are red and swollen. The thin skin that has grown over the burns is fragile and awkward like it doesn't belong there. I'm wearing a hood made out of gauze that covers the deep injuries on my scalp. It makes me look funny, like an injured cartoon character. "You were beautiful once." I remember the words uttered that night by the supposedly isolated patient who roamed about the hospital as if he wasn't carrying deadly germs. Cristina holds me up as I walk into the room and takes my clothes off.

"I don't want you to keep anything that you wore or used in that place. Everything in the house is new and has been freshly washed and ironed."

Mom dresses me in a pair of loose lounge pants and stares at the bandages that cover my trunk. She's in doubt.

"What should we do? Perhaps it's wisest to leave them on, at least for today?"

"I'm not sure if that's such a good idea. Iulia said that we should take them all off to let the wounds breathe."

"Then let's do it."

She tears the adhesive off and starts unraveling the dressing. The pressure put on the wounds by the gauze is released, but instead of soothing me, it wakes up the pain that had laid dormant until now. With every piece of bandage removed by Mom, the hurt grows in intensity until I'm in agony again. In the end, all that's left is a layer of light gauze lying directly on top of the wounds. Cristina grabs one end and pulls on it gently. It won't budge. She looks at me, worried, and tries again. I beg her to stop.

"Give me some time," I ask her.

Unfortunately, she has to go home to Târgu-Mureș. My nephews need her, and she can't stay with me any longer.

"I'll come back as soon as I can. I must take care of some things, and I'll return."

One of the reasons why I'm happy I was finally discharged is that, now, my mother and my sister will finally be able to relax and rest. I encourage Cristina to leave and try to soothe her. I ask her to give the little ones a hug from Auntie Alex. She doesn't want to go. She just sits there, in front of the bed, in doubt, unable to move. Her phone keeps ringing, but she's ignoring it. It's Daniel. He's waiting for her downstairs, in the car. She rejects the call and spends a few more minutes with me. She kisses me clumsily on a patch of healed skin and heads for the door, looking back at least ten times. Then she walks out of the apartment, and I hear the sound of the elevator descending.

"Poor Cristina," Mother says. "Imagine that the internal medicine doctor told her that she didn't think you'd make it. She took her aside one day and whispered to her that your body was too weak to endure the suffering. That's why she brought you the eyeshadow palette and the perfume. We cried in the store when we bought them for you because we weren't sure you'd get to use them."

Mom chokes up. She runs to the kitchen so that I don't see her crying. At first, I feel heart-wrenching pity for the emotional torture they had to go through, but after a while, it's replaced with anger. I'm angry with the damned doctors. These

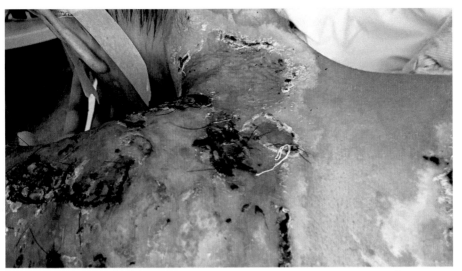

December 2015: This picture was taken by my mother in the Hospital for Burns, a few days before I was discharged. The new skin grafts had failed to heal on the left side of my body because of the HAIs, and the blue stitches were hanging on to necrotized tissue that was no longer viable.

March 2016: The state of my scars five months after the fire.

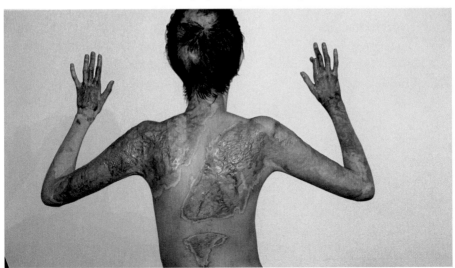

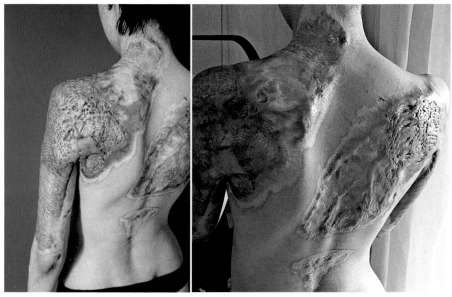

Left: Picture taken in April 2016 at the burn rehabilitation clinic in Germany.
Right: Picture taken in July 2016, showcasing the strange shape taken by the scars,
which looked like wings made of fire.

August 2016: My hands before I had the surgery to reconstruct my index finger.

people didn't only play with my life, but they also toyed with my family's health, and that's something I can't forgive.

"She took her aside and told her you're going to die." My body was to blame, of course, not the inadequate conditions in the hospital and the lies told to hide the infections I had acquired. Then it dawns on me. That's why my sister was so unraveled the day she brought me the gifts she had gotten me. She thought it was her last chance to talk to me.

Anger grows inside my heart. I take advantage of it to garner the strength necessary to try to remove my bandages. I can only use my left hand because my right is stuck in the wannabe metal splint. If I'm not careful, I can cut myself with its sharp edges. They didn't bother to polish them. There isn't much of a difference between this odd object and the blade of an old knife. I don't know what it was before they turned it into a splint, but I'm certain it wasn't used as a medical device. I grab the bandages with the tips of my fingers and tug at them gently. They won't move. It's hard for me to understand how it's possible for the gauze to be this stuck to the wounds already. The pain is terrible. It feels like my skin is being ripped off every time I pull on the compresses. I try and try, but I just can't remove the dressing. I call Mom.

It's bath-time again. I step into the tub and look at it, amazed. It's as if I'd forgotten what a normal one looks like. Mine is white and hard, made from ceramic material. It shines with cleanliness and smells like disinfectant. Mom helps me sit in it and turns the water on. I have an adjustable shower head and she picks the lowest setting for the spray. She opens a pack of sterile gloves and puts them on. After she drenches the bandages in water, they become heavy and start to fall off. She manages to remove them one by one. The pain makes me shiver. I suddenly realize that they didn't prescribe any painkillers that I could use at home and there's nothing I can take to lessen the sensation that I'm being skinned alive. I'm back to enduring drugless bath-time and it's killing me.

"Jesus, dear. I don't understand why they sent you home like this. You're bleeding profusely. You're an open sore."

My teeth chatter because of the shaking, but I refuse to cry. I clench my jaw shut. I don't want Mom to worry about me. After she removes all the remaining compresses, she helps me out of the tub and pat dries me using sterile gauze she bought from the pharmacy. My apartment has become a hospital ward. She lays me down in bed and tucks me in. My shivering has gotten worse, but I find solace in the warmth of my home and in my fluffy blanket. I'd like to go to sleep, but I don't know what position to take. If I lie on my back, my wounds will stick to the bedsheets. Lying on my stomach is impossible because I can't stretch my arms. I sit up for a while, rummaging through my brain in search of an answer to this predicament, until I'm too tired to think. I do the only thing that's possible. I lie down on my back. The cotton sheets stick to my wounds immediately. Soon, they'll start to sting. My first day at home passes by slowly, as if time itself has changed after the accident. I watch the light sink into darkness, exhausted. I twitch and sigh every time I move, trying to pry the sheets off my wounds as best as I can. I hide the chills and the nausea, even though I'm feeling feverish again. I refuse to say a word about them. I don't want to go back to the hospital. I'd do anything to avoid that hellish place. I'm just as horrified by it as I am by the container that I burned in. I count again, as far as I can, hoping that I'll fall asleep. I don't know what new life will start tomorrow and I'm too tired to think about it. One, two, three, four, five, six, seven, eight, nine, ten...

It's already been a week since they released me. I have to go back to the hospital every second day so that they can assess the healing process. Tens of patients wait in the hallways for hours on end until the doctors show up. We arrive at 7:00 A.M. and leave five or six hours later. I'm still very weak and when I can't stand anymore, Mother helps me sit on the stairs that lead to the doctors' offices. She's the one who brings me here every time. She gets up early, washes me, changes my bandages, dresses me, and gets me to every appointment on time. I can't do anything on my own. My hands are a far from healed, so I can't use them at all. Every joint of every finger and those in my wrists are locked in an unnatural, fixed position, and no matter what I do, they won't budge. I keep cutting myself with the improvised metallic splint. I can't even hold cutlery. Mom feeds me as if I were a baby.

When it's finally my turn, the surgeons remove the dressings that Mother worked on diligently, but without any knowledge of what she was doing. They look at the wounds underneath and exchange cryptic glances, while putting their gloves on. I show them that, in certain areas that seemed to be healing well previously, especially around the fresh skin grafts, greenish scabs and crusts that become moist during bath-time have appeared. They ooze an odd-smelling fluid. They dismiss me and tell me that it's all part of the "natural healing process." I should leave them alone. I ask them if there's something I could use, some cream, some drug that would make things at least a little bit better. I always receive the same answer: something from Nivea or marigold ointment.

Silvia digs into my wounds with a pair of large tweezers, then rubs my bleeding flesh with a compress doused in disinfectant. I can't stop the chills.

"Seriously? I hope you're not going to cry again..."

I remain silent. Anger grows within me, in the quiet, like a malformed tree with roots set deep in the entrails of trauma. Now she's assessing my right hand. When she removes the bandages from my index finger, blood begins to pour freely from the wound, which is no longer protected by the gauze. The pain is throbbing, acute. She disinfects the cut and wrings it. Pushes it down and squeezes, as if she wants to extract something from it. I well up with tears, but I swallow my cries. I don't want to give her the chance to roll her eyes at my suffering again. Every time she does that, something inside me breaks. Blood drips on the floor like it's nothing, staining the floor, making a dull, patting sound.

"Your index finger isn't doing so great. You have to wear the splint we made you for a little longer than anticipated."

I nod. She places a sheet of Atrauman on the gash, but the blood soaks through it right away. She puts the splint back on, pushes my finger down again, and wraps it with elastic gauze. Doctor Moldovan supervises the procedure, gazing lifelessly ahead, as if through me. I remember his words: "There was no need to cut the joint open like that." If only they hadn't dropped me when they brought me back from the O.R., then they wouldn't have needed to conceal the deed with a useless procedure, and perhaps my index finger would have been all right now. Hurt, but whole, just like the others.

After they're done with me, they send me home. While I'm getting ready to leave, an older patient barges in, visibly displeased and shouting.

"My wounds are infected again, Doctor! What should I do?"

I shudder when I hear about his infections. Silvia wipes my blood off the floor while the man sits on the bed I just got out of. They didn't change the "sterile" sheet where I lay, so he rubs against it, not knowing I too might still harbor germs. I feel nauseous and try to leave faster, clumsily grabbing the door handle with my sleeve, so as not to touch it with my burned skin. In the hallway, I'm greeted by a myriad of sad faces. Countless strangers peer at me, envious that I've escaped the room of terror and am free to go home to continue suffering in a less threatening setting. Feverish eyes follow me out, wanting desperately to join me. The eyes of those who have burned alive and have returned to the Hospital of Neverhealing.

The days pass at a monotonous pace, marked by the ever-growing pain. The once healing skin around the grafts becomes more and more afflicted by the strange, green scabs, which spread like some sort of flesh-eating plague. None of the wounds have healed, even though Mom washes me diligently every day. Bathtime doesn't seem to be helping. I'm worried about the state I'm in, especially since I keep getting the chills every once in a while. Silvia wasn't there when I had my last appointment, so Larisa, her colleague, did my checkup. She's the doctor Alice and I had physiotherapy with. I showed her the green scales and told her that they're multiplying, that they hurt and itch, as if the wounds are alive underneath the crusts. I asked her too if she can recommend some medicated ointment, or anything for that matter, which might bring me some relief.

"Oh, come on! Even if you rub shit all over, you'll still heal at this point."

Then, she produced a mysterious container from the medicine cabinet, grabbed a sterile glove and a spatula, and put a few globs of cream *in* the glove. She tied a knot on the whole thing and threw the gummy blob in my lap.

"Here, take this. Slather it all over. But don't tell anyone I gave you some! Hide it somewhere."

"What sort of cream is it?"

"Something special!"

I showed her the pockets on my hoodie and asked her to grab the glove and put it there because I can't do it myself. She shoved it in and bid me farewell. I left the hospital with a fat pocket, filled with "contraband" cream, given to me secretly, as if a crime was being committed. I can't help wondering why she didn't just write a prescription. I could have simply taken it to the pharmacist, who would have been happy to make a batch for me to use at home. The way things function here, at this hospital, remains a mystery to me.

Still full of open wounds, bandaged scarcely at home by my mother, I go in for my first appointment with the physiotherapy department at Elias Hospital. I'm sent there by Silvia, who recommends I start the rehabilitation procedures. Because it's so early in the morning, Mom and I decide to grab a cab. The driver gawks at me but remains silent. Occasionally, he looks my way, examining my bandages with curiosity. He can't keep quiet. He must say something. In the end, he bursts out:

"Hey, listen. You look like something really bad happened to you? What was it?"

"I was injured in the Colectiv Club fire."

"Jesus Christ! And? Was it like they showed on TV? Did everything really burn down so quickly?"

"Sadly, yes."

It's the cue he's been waiting for to go on a rant about complicated conspiracy theories.

"Listen here, miss! That there wasn't just an accident. They set you on fire on purpose to sabotage the government."

It's not the first time I've heard this wayward interpretation given to a tragedy that occurred because of negligence and recklessness. It shares the same semantic universe of shallow compensatory narratives as the so-called Satanism they accused us of, so that Romanian society would feel better about what happened to us. Somehow, in that upside-down world, we deserved it. People simply can't accept the fact that the world we're living in is utterly unsafe, and the pillars upon which lay our certainties are made of foam. The highly flammable kind. They'd rather believe the manipulative discourse being spit out by the media these days instead of acknowledging that we've all failed, as a nation, to live up to our potential. For thirty years, we've been tolerating the corruption that led to the inhumane hospital conditions I endured and to the absurd risks we expose ourselves to every time we do something as simple as walking down the street. Of course, it's more convenient to always find a scapegoat.

I have a flashback to my favorite childhood cartoon: Scooby Doo. A gang of pesky teenagers and their talking dog, Scooby, spent their time catching bad guys who pretended to be monsters just so that they could scare people and steal from them. Time and time again, the ghastly ghoul proved to be just an ordinary person, made of flesh and blood. One of the key moments was the unmasking, when everyone gathered round the villain and revealed his identity. Usually, it was a character that had been introduced to us previously in the episode. It was never an actual supernatural creature. The moral of the story? The truth is always much simpler than it seems, and because of this, we don't really like it. I smile to myself and shake my head. If we tore off the flamboyant mask of conspiracy theories from Romania's face, we'd be surprised to find our own eyes and the eyes of our elected officials staring back at us, as if from a mirror. They're the real bad guys, and they've condemned us to this precarious, uncertain, and dangerous reality we seem to be oblivious to.

"Why are you laughing, miss?"

"No one 'set us on fire'. What happened was that thirty years of unacceptable choices, thirty years of refusing to vote, thirty years of making friends with corruption finally had some consequences. That's why we burned alive that night."

The driver raises his eyebrows and peers at me through the rear-view mirror. He doesn't answer. He stays quiet for the rest of the trip. He drops us off in front of the hospital, wishes me well, and darts off.

"He didn't like what you said."

"Nobody likes the truth, I guess..."

After searching for the rehabilitation center for a while, we finally find a nurse who can explain where it is. From there, we're taken to Professor Ionescu's room. He's the head of the physiotherapy department. My mother joins me for the consultation because I need her help to take my clothes off. The tall, gray-haired man who visited us in the Hospital for Burns sits at a majestic wooden desk. He gets up, greets us, and invites us to sit down. He asks me to take off my hoodie. Mom helps me undress until I'm only wearing a baggy sleeveless shirt she bought for me recently. She picked it because it's wide and it doesn't stick to my wounds. The doctor can't really assess me because I still have a lot of bandages on.

"She still has a lot of open wounds. I can't let her leave the house without dressing them."

"Of course, that's very wise of you. It's just that, since she hasn't healed yet, it's going to be difficult to start the procedures. Ours is not a sterile environment. We can begin slowly and progress gradually until she's in a better state."

Professor Ionescu asks me to move my fingers, but I can't. He wants to see if I can bend my wrists, but they're stuck. He tells me to lift my arms up, but I can't raise them beyond a few measly centimeters. I can't turn my head from side to side either because of the grafts on my neck.

"The burn sequelae are severe. Your range of motion is almost zero. I am very sorry that this happened to you. You're going to need long-term care. Let's see what we can do about that."

While he talks to my mother, I look around. Professor Ionescu has an immense library filled with books. He's decorated the shelves with a rich variety of crystals, and he's placed religious paintings of various shapes and sizes here and there. What looks like a big quartz pyramid embellishes his massive desk as a sort of *pièce de résistance*. I must admit that I'm a bit taken aback by the plethora of trinkets.

"You may put your clothes on."

I get up and Mom starts to fumble with the baggy sleeves of the hoodie, trying to widen them so that my hands can pass through them seamlessly. I haven't dressed in anything pretty for a long time. My fancy slim tops have been lying in the wardrobe, wondering, as am I, if I'll ever wear them again. Right now, I doubt it will be the case. My aching body can barely handle any fabric touching it. And even if there was a way for me to dress up, I'd ruin every single outfit. I bleed through all my clothes.

"What's that pattern on your shirt?"

I can't stretch my neck enough to look down. I try, but it's useless. Suddenly, I realize that I haven't given much thought to my appearance lately. The only reason I picked certain clothes was because they were wide enough to allow me to move in them without sticking to my wounds. Mom looks at my shirt, squinting, trying to make out what the print depicts. She pushes her glasses up, stares, and eventually shrugs.

"I have no idea what that is. I bought it for her because it's very large and it can't hurt her." She's slightly amused by the whole situation. She doesn't understand where this is going.

"It's a cow's skull!" Professor Ionescu emphasizes, outraged, pointing at my chest with a shaky finger. "Why would you wear a design like that, especially after... what happened to you?"

Mother and I are livid.

"You know what I mean. All these symbols, and that music you were listening to. You're a smart girl. I'm sure you get what I'm saying. Just let it be, leave it behind. Stop wearing such awful clothes, don't listen to that noise anymore. You'll see that it'll all change for the better. You'll never experience anything like... that, ever again."

He utters the last phrase with disgust. He's never stopped pointing at me, and now he makes an encompassing movement with his hand, as if he's showcasing me to someone. I feel like a hideous museum exhibit, maybe a species of dangerous tarantula that's being presented during a talk about pests.

I'm too astonished to reply. My feelings are all over the place. I'd walk out of here swearing, but I can't even take a few steps without feeling exhausted. And then, even if I'd get to the door, I'd have a hard time pressing down on the knob, which most certainly means I'd fumble with it for a while. That's not exactly what I call a dramatic exit... And then, I also really need his help with the burn rehab. I know very well that if you upset a Professor of Medicine in Romania, a lot of doors are going to close for you, and I can't afford that right now. Now I'm angry with myself for my pettiness. It's not in my nature to allow someone, no matter who they are, to sully the memory of the band members, who died so tragically on stage, giving their hearts to the audience. Even if he's the only person who can treat me, I won't tolerate his disrespect. When I open my mouth to tell him what I really think about his opinions, Mom grabs me by the left forearm – the only part of my body that isn't sore – and squeezes me. There's desperation in her eyes. I swallow my words and my tears. I stay quiet, fixing my gaze on random artifacts in the professor's enchanted room. Countless crystals, in different shapes and sizes, emit a dainty glow from every corner of the ward. The glass icons depicting the Virgin Mary reflect their gleams, creating a bizarre, eclectic atmosphere. Then it dawns on me. The kaleidoscopic richness of this phantasmagoria is proof of a deep inner inconsistency. I'd like to ask him how an Orthodox Christian reconciles his faith – renowned for its condemnation of mysticism - with an obvious love for crystal therapy.

"Your collection is quite eclectic," I interject, as I look around, seemingly fascinated, and ultimately point at the large quartz pyramid on his desk.

"Oh, yes. These are my beautiful little things."

I nod and Mom breathes a sigh of relief. We sit down again. The professor ends the appointment and schedules me for rehabilitative procedures. For starters, I'll come to the hospital every second day. We'll begin slowly and work our way up to a more intense program, as my wounds heal. Aside from the scar massage, he recommends that I undergo electrotherapy, using ultrasounds, a form of laser therapy, and light therapy sessions with a machine called "Bioptron." I ask if it isn't too early for laser and he dismisses me, displeased.

"I have a special laser here. It heals with the power of light, instead of burning the skin."

I'd like to know what the device is called so that I can read about it, but he doesn't answer my question. He sends us away, telling us we must go downstairs, to the basement, where the rehabilitation wards are located, to meet the team that's going to handle my case. He hands me a document where he wrote down all the recommendations he made for my treatment and instructs me to give it to the therapists. We say our goodbyes, thank him, and leave.

"God, what an odd and tactless man. Did you see how much stuff he had in there? Crystals and pyramids alongside icons and crosses."

Still shocked by what she saw in the professor's room, Mom rolls her eyes, checking to see if I'm all right after the encounter. If I was still angry before and had been getting ready to tell her what I really thought about the whole thing, the genuine expression of surprise on her usually stern face makes me smile. I calm down as we discuss what just happened. We laugh at how similar our thoughts are.

We're waiting for the elevator that will take us to the basement. I hope that the therapists are less eccentric. The ward is spacious and filled with older patients who are being treated by a handful of young specialists. I'm greeted by the woman who accompanied Professor Ionescu during his visit to the Hospital for Burns back in December.

"I'm Adela, really nice to meet you!"

We talk a little about the accident and my injuries. She proceeds to consult me. Mom shows her where I still have large open wounds, without removing the dressings.

"What did the boss say?"

"He suggested we start slowly, taking it one day at a time."

"I think that's the wisest approach. Alex, you'll come to see us as often as you can, and we'll increase the frequency of the treatments gradually as you heal."

She helps me get on the stationary bike and asks me to ride it for ten minutes. I can't. I tire quickly, and then the pain starts. I'm so disappointed I could cry. My body is so weak I can't even finish a basic exercise like this. Adela notices the tears in my eyes and comforts me. She reassures me that one day, I'll be strong again. She sends me to the electro-therapy ward. It's at the other end of the hallway. Mom and I leave and, as we're walking toward the room, I stare at the exposed technical ceiling, filled with winding pipes. I shudder at the thought of the scalding water passing through them. If just one of them were to burst, I'd get burned again. My knees begin to shake. I can barely put one leg in front of the other, but I push myself to keep going. We make it to our destination somehow and we stop in front of the door of the electro-therapy ward. A nurse stares at me, confused. She reads the paperwork written by the professor and scratches her head.

"Miss, I hate to say it, but our laser hasn't been working properly for some time now. It heats up and then it shuts down."

She checks my dressings and asks what area she could use the device on.

"Maybe we can remove the bandages from a small wound and try there."

I look around the ward. It's filled with beds that are separated from one another by some sort of curtain that's supposed to ensure the patients' privacy. Just one of them is free, the rest are already taken. It seems to be clean, but I doubt the environment is sterile. We're wearing the same shoes we walked down the street with. I don't feel safe removing my dressings here. I don't think these people really know what they're doing. I ask if they've ever worked with burn patients before. She's honest. No, they haven't. We're the first.

"Sweetheart, I have an idea. Perhaps she can use the machine on that small wound on your right shoulder blade."

The nurse helps me lie on the free bed, takes my clothes off, and leaves to bring the machine. Mom puts sterile gloves on and removes the compresses from the oozing sore she mentioned to the nurse. The gauze comes off with difficulty and leaves behind a deep red gash surrounded by green scabs. Meanwhile, the laser makes its appearance. It looks like a huge table lamp with red glass. The nurse plugs it in, but it won't start. She pushes all its buttons one by one, slaps its large dome, and swears. She repeats the procedure a few more times and, at some point, the machine makes a loud "Ping!" and comes to life. She directs the thing at my back and keeps making disapproving noises while she tries to position it accurately. She pushes and slaps the laser like a little child trying to fix a broken toy. "Ouch!" she shouts, cussing with even more intensity.

"What happened? Are you okay?"

"It's this damn laser! Lately, it heats up so badly we can't even touch it."

"Isn't it...dangerous?"

She clears her throat and denies that there's a real problem. Then she adds:

"However, if you feel it's too hot on the skin, please tell me."

I can sense my heart racing. The fear of the device exploding on my burned skin overpowers me. I close my eyes and count to ten again. The laser starts and makes a buzzing sound. I feel a strange kind of warmth that scalds and stings. My wound seems to be boiling on the inside, grinding, oozing. The nurse keeps making little sounds to show how displeased she is. After a sequence of acute pinging sounds, the laser shakes and stops altogether.

"To hell with this piece of crap!" she bursts out. "It broke down again. I'm sorry. We won't be able to use it anymore today. Let's try with the Bioptron."

She drags the now useless whopper outside, on wheels that screech loudly, filling the hallway with sounds of decrepitude. It jolts and hitches until it reaches the other end of the ward, where the noise suddenly stops, only to be replaced with similar screeches, jolts, and hitches, made by the other device that she's bringing over. It too looks like a huge table lamp.

"This one still works," she says, visibly proud.

She turns it on and directs the yellow light it makes toward the same wound on my back. The heat is not as scorching, but it's still unpleasant. She draws the curtains as she walks out, leaving me alone with the machine. When she's gone for good, I move away from under it. The sore calms down immediately. If I hear her steps drawing near, I move back. The pain and stinging return.

"We're done," she proclaims. "See you again next time. Maybe we'll fix the laser by then."

I feel relieved as I'm saying my goodbyes. I'm secretly glad the first machine broke down and I hope they won't ever repair it. The wound on my back throbs, aches, and oozes. I call Mom and she puts on a new pair of gloves, and then does my dressing. Her purse has become something akin to a surgeon's kit.

As soon as I arrive home, I lie down in bed, exhausted, too weak to pay attention to the hurt. I fall asleep right away and wake up a couple of hours later, sweaty and ridden with chills. I don't tell my mother. She's cooking in the kitchen, and I listen to the comforting, domestic sounds, latching onto them to forget the pinging, buzzing, and jolting from before. I'm struggling to learn to eat on my own again, but I tire quickly, so she's always there, within arm's reach, ready to feed me herself, as if I'd become a small child again. She cuts my food into small pieces and places it in my mouth. It would be endearing if I didn't feel so ashamed. Ashamed of my childish needs when she's only getting older. I muster up a fake smile so as not to sadden her further. After I'm full, she sighs.

"Come on, darling. It's bath-time."

She helps me sit in the tub. When she douses me with water and it reaches the wound treated by Professor Ionescu's machine, I scream. The stinging is unbearable. Mom wants to remove the compress from the sore, but it's stuck to it. This hasn't happened in a while. The gauze has grown thick from the secretions, and it's soaked in sticky yellowish fluid. It simply won't move regardless of the water.

"What should I do?" she asks. Her voice is shaky.

"Tear it off."

"Are you... are you sure?"

"No, but we can't just leave it there."

She grabs the gauze with her fingers and holds her breath. She tears it right off. I howl with a voice I don't recognize as my own, just like Flavia once did when they stripped her of her dressings in the green tub of the Hospital for Burns. Mom drops the shower head in shock.

"It's all an open, oozing wound. It looked a lot better before the procedures. It's turned into mush."

She takes my dressings off one by one. Pink suds gather near the drain, together with green and brown scabs and crusts. I'm cold and nauseous. I can't hide the

chills anymore. The water stops and Mom takes me back to my room. She drops
the clothes she wants to dress me in. She grabs others.

"What is it, Mom?"

"Sweetheart, I think you're getting worse..."

She rubs the cream Larisa gave me all over my burns and lets the wounds air
out a little.

"What did you have today?"

"Some sort of laser treatment."

"Don't let them do that to you again. That sore... it oozed and bled so much."

The wound on my shoulder blade, the one they treated today, sullies the sheets
with abundant exudate. I feel like it's writhing and boiling, as if something is alive
within it and wants to get out at any cost. The day unravels in a splitting migraine
that takes away my eyesight and replaces it with bright flashes of light. I go back
to bed and fall into a deep sleep, interrupted by confusing nightmares about grotesque machines that catch fire and burn me. "To hell with this piece of crap!"
someone shouts and starts to run. I hear their muffled steps. They're stomping
toward me, as if they're behind a door somewhere in my mind's basement. I wake
up in the middle of the night feeling ill. The sheets are wet with blood. I cry quietly, not wanting to wake Mom up. What will become of us?

Even though my wounds are becoming larger instead of smaller and they're
increasingly painful, I hear the same thing every time I go in for my weekly check-
up: the process is normal and to be expected. I'm doing great. The chills don't
mean anything. They're just my body's reaction to the cold. I don't have enough
healthy skin to keep myself warm. A little bit of a fever is nothing to worry about.
If it's not above 100.4, it's meaningless. "Even if you rub shit all over, you'll still
heal." Larisa's words are stuck on a loop in my head while I'm unraveling physically
and emotionally. "But it hurts," "They smell bad," "They're bigger and bigger," I
tell them. Every time their replies baffle me: "Just stop paying attention to them
and be done with it. It's a natural phase in the evolution of the scarring process.
The scabs will fall off and you'll be like new."

I'm standing in the bathroom, looking in the mirror at the new thick green
plaques that appeared on my right arm almost overnight. At some point, the healing process was hijacked by these horrors. No matter how much they insist that

they're normal, I find that hard to believe. Mom is at the store, so I take advantage of her absence to examine myself thoroughly. With my left hand, I grab the scabs and pull on them. It hurts, but I keep going until I manage to tear a piece off. As I suspected, there's no scar tissue underneath, just an oozing, yellowish wet wound that smells weird, sweetish. I struggle to pump out a dollop of soap and rub the area until the whole thing becomes a mucilaginous mess, and I can't stand the pain anymore. No matter how hard I try, I can't wash this dirtiness out. It's stuck to me, and it melts in the wounds, consuming them. The already nasty smell has become stronger, pungent. When Mom returns, she finds me crying over the sink, bleeding. Abundant festering secretions ooze from my arm, mixing with the pink suds tainted with blood and pus.

"That's it. I'm calling Iulia."

Later that evening, after having spoken on the phone with Mom, Iulia comes over, carrying a large bag filled with surgical utensils, creams, and vials. She takes one look at me and shakes her head.

"I don't usually do this, Mrs. Furnea," she tells my mother. "My job is at stake. But I really want to help you. Come, Alex. From now on, you're going to heal, you'll see. It's bath-time."

I'm in the tub again and she's dousing me in water. She uses the dreaded pair of tweezers to remove each and every scab and crust from my wounds. My teeth are chattering because of the pain, but I shut up. I know how badly I need this. Mom is watching us from the door, wringing her hands, then holding them up, as if in prayer.

"I'm not capable of taking care of her. Maybe it's my fault she got worse. Maybe I did this to her."

"There's absolutely no way that you could have done that. She needs a specialist, a place where she can be taken care of professionally. Shame on this country, shame on the system for not having built anything for her and people like her. At least the doctors could have told you what products to use."

She takes out a bottle of surgical soap and pours some on the horrendous sponge with silicone bristles that I hate so much. Tonight, it'll be my friend. She rubs the wounds on my body and on my scalp. Scrub, scratch, scrub. Scrub, scratch, scrub. I choke on my tears, bawling. She comforts me.

"Hush now, child. I'm ridding you of this filth. You'll heal in no time. Hush."

She helps me up and washes my entire body. I'm utterly helpless and ashamed of what I've become. Once she's done with bath-time, she pat dries me with sterile gauze and sits me on the bed, where she continues her work. She takes out a couple of vials of Colistin from her bag and dilutes their contents.

"Please go to the pharmacy and buy her at least twenty more," she instructs my mother.

"But I don't have a prescription."

"Tell them she's one of the Colectiv Club victims. They're going to sell you the drug when they hear about that. They know how badly she needs it."

Mom leaves and Iulia toils away at my broken body. She pours the antibiotic solution on the compresses, drenching them in it. Then she squeezes them all over my wounds, washing me with Colistin. When she's done, she grabs a different container and sprays me with disinfectant. After the wounds have dried, she applies neatly cut sheets of Atrauman on the sores, with surgical precision.

"This was it for today."

She sits on the chair next to the bed and waits for Mom to return. She walks in with a big bag.

"Did they give you the drugs?"

"Yes, when they heard about Colectiv, they stopped asking questions."

Iulia pats me on the back gently and says goodbye. She closes the living room door behind her and talks to Mom in the hallway. I eavesdrop. They're making a deal. They decide that Iulia is going to come over every other day and treat me until I get better.

"She probably has some sort of streptococcus and who knows what else," she tells my mother, lowering her voice.

It saddens me to hear such a thing. My worst fear came true. I didn't get rid of the infections. After she leaves, Mother walks back in and we talk about the news. Even though we're scared, it's also the first time when we feel relieved. We know I'm in good hands. We can trust Iulia.

"I told you there was something wrong with my skin, Mom. I told you."

"Those bastards... Every time you went to the hospital for the check-ups, they'd deny you were sick. What did they think was going to happen? Did they think that if you died at home, then they could accuse us of not taking proper care of you?"

I stop attending the physiotherapy sessions at the Elias Hospital for a while. My wounds have become too deep again, and I'm scared to expose them there, in the unsterile environment of the rehab wards. Every night, Iulia washes my body and douses my injuries with antibiotics. She wastes two hours with me, caring for me as if I were her daughter. Neatly, like a surgeon, she picks off every infected scab, cleansing the pus underneath.

"Please don't tell them about this at the check-ups, Alex," she asks me.

"I promise!"

With the help of her treatment, the wounds become smaller, and the scabs disappear, healed by Colistin, the antibiotic she's washing my wounds with. The sweetish, disgusting smell goes away too. Bath-time stops being so painful, and I often laugh and joke around with Iulia. She washes my shaved head with my favorite shampoo, and we're delighted by the luxurious foam it makes.

"Your hair is going to grow back beautiful! You'll be able to hide the bald patches eventually. You still have open wounds on your scalp now, but they will heal."

She tries her best to comfort me, but I know they're all white lies. However, her words bring me solace, and I choose to believe her, despite the obvious.

A few days later, I'm back at the Hospital for Burns, where Silvia does my check-up. Larisa joins her. They remove the dressings and exchange incredulous glances while they stare at my arms. The neatly cut stripes of Grasolind and Atrauman lie on top of the wounds, that neither smell nor ooze. Thin skin covers the once open gashes left behind by the disgusting scabs. It's clear that what they're looking at is the work of a professional, but they don't say a word, they don't acknowledge it whatsoever. They notice that the index finger is now straight, and the ugly and unnecessary cut made by Silvia is almost closed.

"See? I told you that you didn't have to do anything special because you'd heal eventually!"

I laugh out loud, thinking about Iulia's titanic efforts to mend me. Thinking about the surgical procedures she performed on me in the small ceramic tub from my apartment and the Colistin wound baths, with drugs bought from the pharmacy without a prescription. About all the nights Iulia spent with me, trying to cure the infections they sent me home with. This woman, who they thought was "just" a nurse, demeaning her, was so much better than them, more honest and competent than the doctors in this hospital, some as arrogant and self-satisfied as to believe that I healed without any help. Just like that. On my own.

"You're finally smiling for a change? How come?"

"I'm just glad I'm doing a bit better."

I made a promise to Iulia, and I intend to keep it. I don't know if this makes me a liar too, just like these people. I'm not sure if protecting her doesn't mean that I'm contributing to the medical system's ruin by covering up its shortcomings. The thought makes me sad. There's no real reason to smile. The fleeting happiness is replaced by a feeling of profound grief that I can't seem to shake off. It's as if God has turned the lights off inside me and has shut the door, leaving me alone in the darkness.

I'm standing in front of a new building, someplace near University Square. It's so cold that I'm shivering. The downside of wearing large clothes is that they can't keep me as warm as they should in the freezing Bucharest winter. I'm here because Silvia sent me. I must buy a new splint to replace the improvised metallic one. I hurt myself with it a couple of times and they decided it was time for a professional one. Silvia gave me a flyer describing the device and an address where I could get it from. Mom checks the intercom number and rings.

The employees of the medical company stare at me, confused. One of the women looks away when I notice her examining my hands, frightened. I understand her reaction. I look terrible so skinny, with my warped, mutilated hands, that I try to hide under the wide sleeves of my ill-fitting jacket. My burned face is still swollen and the dark circles under my eyes have turned a deep shade of purple, in stark contrast with the paleness of my tumefied cheeks. A loose beanie hat barely covers the ragged dressings on my skull. From the corner of my eye, I see their frayed edges making their way out of the fabric.

Clearing his throat beforehand, a man with a colorful badge asks us what he can do for us. Mom gives him the flyer we received from Silvia and tells him that I need a splint that looks like that.

"Um, well, do you still have open wounds underneath the bandages? I mean, um... Please excuse me. You were injured in the Colectiv Club fire, right?"

"Unfortunately, yes. And I also still have open wounds."

"In that case, I really don't know what to say... We have that splint here, but the instructions of use state clearly that it shouldn't be worn on injured skin."

"Oh, I see. But the doctor recommended it." Mom sighs, saddened.

"I can sell it to you, and if it's no good, you can bring it back and I'll give you a refund."

He grabs a box off a shelf and takes the device out. It has something akin to a black button in the middle, and tiny metallic rods all around.

"You place the round plastic part right over the sick joint, and it will force it down, correcting the boutonniere deformity. That's why I think it's not adequate for you. My advice is that you talk to the doctor and tell her that she should bandage the finger with some manner of soft dressing if she really insists you wear this type of splint. In the hospitals, they should have various types of wound dressings, made from special sponges."

I smile at the man's suggestion. Judging by the splint I'm wearing right now, I'm almost certain that they don't have any special dressings in the Hospital for Burns. Mom and I talk it through and decide that we're going to buy the splint, regardless. At home, I read the tiny instructions manual that came with the device. I keep going over the warning on the last page: "Do not use on damaged skin or open wounds." I sigh, rub my eyes, and lie down in bed. It was a long day. Actually, it hasn't even ended yet. I doze off, but Iulia's happy voice wakes me up a few minutes later.

"Hey, sleepy-head, it's bath-time!"

I go to the next check-up with the new splint in my pocket. Silvia reads the instructions manual and after she's done, she plays with it carelessly, turning it on all sides. She takes the dressings off my right hand, removes the old splint, and throws it in a metal tray. It makes a shrill chink that fills the ward with acute reverberations.

"I read that the new one isn't supposed to be used on damaged skin," I suggest. She doesn't reply. "Maybe it would be best if we waited until the finger was completely healed?" Nothing.

I follow her every gesture. She's already removed the dressings from the joint. The wound isn't fully closed. A thin streak of blood emerges from the middle of the gash that extends from the top of the finger to the bottom. She pats it out with a fresh compress and, before I realize what she's doing, she pulls the splint over the joint and releases the knob. The finger is pushed down forcefully, making an odd, clicking sound. The pain is so overwhelming, I feel like I'm going to lose consciousness. The doctor holds a thick compress under the finger, absorbing the blood that is now pouring out of the wound she made herself a few weeks before.

"Don't even think about removing the splint! You must wear it day and night. You'll only remove it to cleanse the wound, and then you'll put it right back. You wash your finger in the sink, it's as simple as that."

There's a sharp ringing in my ears, making it hard for me to understand what she's saying. I hear her cold, careless voice, drilling through my skull, like an ice pick. I'm so drained, I can't even ask her anything. I exit the ward staggering. In the hallway, Mom helps me sit down and gives me a few sips of water. On our taxi ride home, I cry because of how bad it hurts and because of the humiliation. Yet again, I couldn't stand up for myself. I sat there and allowed her to mutilate me.

Two days later, pus forms under the black knob. The finger doubled in size and, no matter what I take for the pain, it doesn't work. When Iulia arrives, she shakes her head. The joint has split open, and it's become infected.

"This splint is made for people with healthy skin, not for burn victims. I don't understand why they recommended such a thing to you."

She cleans the wound and squeezes Colistin into it. Then, she places a sheet of Atrauman over the finger and creates a sort of padding for it, using compresses. She puts the splint over the padding.

"Do I really have to wear it all the time?"

"Unfortunately, yes. Otherwise, your index finger will bend until its tip will rest inside the palm of your hand. When the pain becomes unbearable, take it off for a short while, but don't do this too often."

Late at night, I wake up and rush to the bathroom. I vomit because of the pain. My right hand is shaking uncontrollably, and I have a hard time recognizing my index finger. It's so swollen, it engulfed the sides of the splint. I grab the device and manage to remove it after a few excruciating attempts. With the pressure gone, blood squirts out of the freed wound, sullying the sink and the floor. I press on the finger as hard as I can to stop the hemorrhage. My knees feel weak because of the pain, so I sit on the edge of the tub. I rock back and forth, holding my right hand next to my chest. Blood drips from the finger onto my clothes, staining my pajamas. It stops after a while, but the pain won't go away. It's throbbing, intense, gut-wrenching. When I finally go back to bed, it's almost morning. Mom hasn't woken up. She's exhausted. She's been complaining about backaches that come and go. I'm not surprised. Taking care of me is hard work and she's much too old for it. She cleans the house, cooks, and carries heavy grocery bags back and forth. She also dresses and undresses me, feeds me, and does everything I can't do on my own. She's aged much faster than normal these past few months. She's almost unrecognizable because of the gauntness of her face and the new wrinkles. A bad thought crosses my mind, and I have to shake it off. I close my eyes and wish it away. I don't want her to become a collateral victim of the fire, although she already has turned into that, in more ways than one. I put the splint on the bedside and lie back in bed. I'm still nesting my right hand next to my chest, to both soothe and protect my finger. Every once in a while, a drop of blood forms in the middle of the ugly, tumefied slit. The compress is full, but I'm too tired to get up and find a new one. I let the blood flow. I let it stain me. I cry myself to sleep. I've run out of faith in tomorrows.

Not long after, Mom falls ill. She wakes up one morning with a horrible backache that soon becomes unbearable. She calls the ambulance in the afternoon, scared that she can't get out of bed anymore. She can't even go to the bathroom alone. I sit by her side, utterly helpless. I try to grab the corner of the blanket to cover her, but I can't. She's crying and wailing like a child. When the paramedics arrive, I shout at them through the door, asking them to press the knob down, because I can't use my hands. They walk in and stare at me, confused. Then they look at Mom. They don't know who needs their help.

"Who are we here for? Who is the sick person?"

I tell them it's Mom, but they can't take their eyes off me. With my ragged bandages and open wounds, I seem to be the ill one. Dana, one of the doctors, is friends with Flavia, and she recognizes me. She came to see us at the hospital back in November. She tells the other doctors that I was injured in the Colectiv Club fire. The pain makes Mom delirious, so they put her on an intravenous sedative. There's nothing more they can do for us. They leave, and I'm once again alone with her. After she wakes up from the drug-induced sleep, she asks me to make her some tea. She realizes that what she's asking is absurd, so she apologizes. She's still confused because of the high dose of painkillers. Later, she grabs the phone and calls my sister. She starts to cry while she talks to her.

"I don't know what to do, we're alone here, and I can't move," she says.

Desperation creeps over me and I leave the room. I go to the kitchen and decide that I'm going to try to boil some water for mom's tea. My hands are almost completely useless. I can't make the tap run. I must use my left forearm to push it up, but when I finally succeed, the pressure is too high, and the water splashes me from head to toe. I can't grab the pot either. I shove it in the sink, and it collapses inside it, making a racket. When it's half full, I want to lift it, but the fingers of my left hand are too stiff and weak. I try to involve my right hand somehow. The pot slips and its handle hits my index finger. I start to bleed again, painting the water in the pot a bright red. There goes Mom's tea. I finally give up. I sit down on the floor and sigh, feeling defeated. I can't believe this is real. I can't believe I can't even perform a simple task like putting water to boil. Like a sick ocean tide, hopelessness washes over me, drowning me. I'm so afraid. What will become of us?

Cristina arrives the next day from Târgu-Mureş. She has a heavy heart and dark circles under her eyes. She left her two young children at home with their dad and came to help us. The eldest is autistic and needs her. She takes Mom to the bathroom, washes her, cooks, and then feeds us. The day goes by fast, with her caring for the both of us. In the evening, she walks from one corner of the apartment to the other. She's agitated and exhausted. She looks out the window, fidgets, and examines me and Mom with troubled eyes.

"I really can't stay for more than two days. There's no way I can do that. I must take care of the kids too."

"And what am I supposed to do?" Mom bursts out in anger. "What am I supposed to do? I can't even get up to use the bathroom, and your sister isn't doing any better either. She's completely helpless!"

"Why didn't you take better care of yourself? How would you like me to fix this?"

They're fighting desperately, overwhelmed by the severity of the situation. Their words become uglier and more aggressive as the evening progresses.

"I can't take care of her right now! I just can't! I want to go home!"

"What do you mean, you want to go home? What about her? You'll leave her here, all alone? Have you gone mad?"

They don't notice me leaving the room. They're blinded by the fight. I go to the bathroom and start the water as if I was washing my hands. I sit on the laundry basket and cry, muffling my wails with the sleeves of my pajamas. I've become a burden to the people I love. A heavy weight that drags down everyone around me. From the bed she can't get out of, Mom screams at my sister, accusing her of not caring about us. Angry and hurt, Cristina tells her that she's fallen ill out of negligence and that she's abandoning me when I need her the most. Reproaches fly from one corner of the room to the other.

"I can't! Don't you understand? I can't!"

Their screams fall apart around me, and a sudden silence cloaks the painful uproar. It's gotten dead quiet inside my head. From the darkness of this eerie peace, a thought emerges, organizing the chaos, finding a solution that only desperation could come up with. I don't like it. However, it does offer me a way out of it all. What if I just died? Maybe if I stopped breathing, things would get better for them. It would be so much easier for everyone if I just disappeared. With my mind's eyes, I see the balcony of my sixth-floor apartment. The doors are wide open. How long would the fall last? A few seconds, and then nothing. My heart starts racing and I feel nauseous, as if I was staring down a precipice. Staring at my death. I'm still crying when Cristina finds me and takes me into her arms.

"See what you've done? Al doesn't need this right now! I'm calling Iulia."

She takes me back to the bedroom and helps me lie down on my side of the bed. The balcony door is open, and I can smell the cold winter air. I stare through the window at the dark January night, freezing inside. I listen to Cristina's phone conversation with Iulia. Her mother is currently unemployed, and she could, theoretically, help us during weekdays. Starting from tomorrow, they'll both come over. Iulia will take care of my wounds and her mom, Mrs. Daniela, will do house chores. Later that night, Cristina and our mother reconcile. My sister improvises a bed out of two armchairs and falls asleep instantly. I listen to their steady breathing, prey to an overwhelming sadness. Two people I love atone for my suffering through their exhaustion and unraveling.

I pull myself up and lean on the pillows, staring out the window again. The lights on the Nerva Traian boulevard flash like incandescent specters in the frosted night, forming yellowish halos around their misty cores. Brassy snowflakes furrow the deep violet sky, like orange veins on a bruise. The thoughts of death come back, and both appall and relieve me. As tired as they are, they wouldn't realize I jumped. They'd wake up because they'd hear a muffled thud and someone screaming on the street. The sirens would wail in the distance, letting everyone know that something happened. I close my eyes and press down on my chest with my left hand, as if to stop myself from getting up. "It would be better for everyone," I tell myself. "They'd be free of the burden, and I'd get rid of the pain." Out of nowhere, I remember the lyrics of a song. They come to the surface from beyond the threshold of my conscious mind.

Felt it coming/ The only choice was forgive and forget/ And I found comfort/ In that it hasn't happened yet/ Something inside me was calling/ But all I could see was a threat/ 'Cause I was sure it would cost me/ Another lifetime to repent.[2]

They're taken from the song "Atonement," the third single from Goodbye to Gravity's second album, Mantras of War. Memories of the band members on stage, having fun, and giving their hearts to the audience flash before my eyes. Until recently, the boys were alive and well. Now, they're just shadows on the

---

[2] Goodbye to Gravity's single "Atonement," taken from the band's second record, *Mantras of War*.

canvas of my troubled mind. Bogdan, Mihai, Vlad, and Alex. Andrei is still alive, but it's uncertain whether he'll survive. Their joy when they performed onstage haunts me; a ghost of happiness lost. We were so alike in the pure love we had for music. Theirs died when they closed their eyes forever. Mine lies buried somewhere inside me, underneath darkness and ashes, trying to recover, trying to get up and move forward from the tragedy of it all. What would they do if they were here? Would they think of jumping too? I feel a gutting shame. How dare I dishonor them with such thoughts? I grab the new phone Cristina bought me. I shove it in my lap and use my left index finger to search for Goodbye to Gravity's YouTube account. Like that night in the Hospital for Burns, when I listened to music for the first time in a long while, I struggle to put my earphones in and press play. The song goes straight to my heart. It frees and heals me. It's like a hug that's tight enough to seal all my broken pieces together. I look out the window at the big snowflakes, imagining that the boys are out there somewhere, looking over me, looking over us. The tears in my eyes blur out the balcony door and wash away the desperation.

In the freezing night, as the world succumbs to the somber darkness of winter, I decide that I'm going to face the pain and defeat it. I decide that I'm going to live. That I'm going to finally leave the molten container I burned in, the Hospital for Burns, all the circles of hell that I've walked through, stripped of skin, prey to horrors I cannot yet name. I decide that I'm going to honor my body's struggle, so innocent in its attempt to keep me alive. I smile through the tears. Utterly helpless and surrounded by the ruined lives of those I love, I surrender my heart to music and ask it to save me. Like it always did before the fire. Like it always did before bath-time. "Thank you," I whisper, thinking of the boys. From afar, through the notes laid down in song by their beautiful souls, they convinced me I must survive.

It's time for me to return to Elias Hospital for my burn rehab procedures. My goal is to become more independent so that I can help Mom. Taking a cab alone every morning is very difficult because I'm still severely disabled, but somehow, I manage to pull through. Most of the wounds, except those on my scalp and my right index finger, have closed as a result of Iulia's amazing work. She still visits me a few times a week to wash me professionally, and to maintain the progress I've made. My finger, however, didn't react well to the new splint. The infection forced me to remove the device, and, without support, I developed a permanent bouton-niere deformity. Yet another medical mistake I pay for with my health. Mrs. Daniela does all our house chores, which gives Mom time to heal. She went to a few appointments, and the doctors found a benign cyst lodged between her lumbar vertebrae. It developed as a result of the physical effort she's made these past few months and because she slept too many uncomfortable nights on the chair next to my bed in the hospital. It's an injury caused by wear, and it has no cure. Things have settled down after the terrible night she fell apart. But without Iulia and her mom, I don't know what would have become of us.

The system abandoned us the moment we walked out the hospital door. They discharged me unhealed, covered in large, open wounds, totally helpless. They sent me away to die at home. The burden of my care fell on my sick, elderly mother's shoulders. I should have been committed in a specialized stationary center right after leaving the acute care ward. A place where professionals would have washed me, bandaged me, fed me, something they were trained to do. But no such place exists in Romania. Here, you're all alone. How can they even imagine that a mother, a father, a brother, or a sister could possibly help someone with wounds such as mine? Someone who isn't a doctor or a nurse, just an ordinary person. Both of us could have lost our lives. I could have died because of the infections and my mother because of the exhaustion. We wouldn't have even become numbers for their statistics. Nobody counts the dead who perish outside corrupted institutions.

At the Elias Hospital, I have a new therapist, K., who is replacing my old one, A. I'm happy with the change. I liked K. from the first moment I set foot in the ward. She's very good at her job and she has a special kind of warmth. She learned to work with burn victims from her superiors, who were sent by the Romanian Ministry of Health to Belgium, to train with experts. A few handpicked therapists from various hospitals in Bucharest were chosen to take part in the program and traveled to Brussels to learn scar massage and kinesiotherapy techniques. They came back with new skills, but also with lots of opinions about the menus, the hotels, and the restaurants. I heard them complain on more than one occasion about how displeased they were that the accommodation provided was too far away from the city center, in neighborhoods they disliked. They didn't talk nearly as much about what they learned.

K. is not like them. She avoids useless conversations and focuses on her work. She massages my rigid and tumefied scars. She straightens my increasingly crooked finger. The pain is so bad, I grind my teeth. When she's working on my back and shoulders, she sits me down on a chair and lifts my arms up gradually. Sometimes it's too much to bear, and we both cry. The treatment session with her lasts for a few hours, depending on how many other patients she must care for. We're not the only ones who need help. Other people, with different types of injuries, also have to undergo procedures. Many times, K. runs from one patient to another, in an attempt to treat everybody. She disinfects her hands incessantly until she bleeds.

"Alex, we don't have any real-life experience with burn victims. I must be honest with you. I'm often scared that I'm going to hurt you without realizing it. And then I'm afraid that I won't know what to do to cure you because I don't have any reference. You're the first burn patients we ever worked with."

The fact that she's so honest with me makes me like her even more. She doesn't hide the truth. She explains the hardships she endures because she has to care for so many patients. I like to think of her as an exception to the rule of disinterest and cruelty that governs the Romanian medical system – an *exceptional* if you wish. She, and those like her, keep things afloat. You can still find *exceptionals* everywhere. They're usually hidden among the others, who are committed to dysfunctionality because it's what allows them to keep their stations and thrive. These special people are often dismissed or even downright persecuted. When they speak out, they're silenced or ignored. However, where they really make a difference is in the relationships they build with those who need them the most. If you're lucky enough to be assigned to one of them, you'll be forever grateful. I learned the hard way that in Romania the success of the medical act is a lottery, a question of luck. If you end up in the right hands, you're saved. If not, you die or you're going to be mutilated for life.

I had a different therapist for a while, before K. She used to knead my scars with carelessness, never paying attention, while she spoke on the phone with her boyfriend. She was set to leave the country for good in a few days, and she didn't care about the patients anymore, even though they still needed her help. I was very happy when I heard that she quit earlier, and I was assigned to K. In her, I found a soulmate who saw from the very first moment how immense my need for healing was. She puts all her skills into my service. Every day, she toils away at my scars, and, in her free time, she reads articles about burn scars and watches massage tutorials. She shares her discoveries with me.

I've stopped going to electro-therapy, despite Professor Ionescu's reproaches. The old and broken machines scare me. The scorching pain, the bleeding, and the oozing I experienced after the laser treatments convinced me that it was too risky to undergo more procedures. Every time I asked for information about the devices, I was met with silence. I don't trust that the therapists really know what they're doing, since it's so hard to extract an answer from them. I've undergone too many improvisations and experiments during my time at the Hospital for Burns, most of them with awful consequences, and I'm no longer willing to be a guinea pig.

Sandra and Iris have also been assigned to the Elias Hospital for their procedures. We get to meet almost every day. Sandra underwent a new surgery on her left hand, so she's still bandaged. Her surgeons placed metal rods inside her fingers to fix her burned joints. She must be careful not to exert herself. Even so, she's in so much pain that she often goes to sit on a chair in the corner of the ward, cradling her injured hand to her chest. She closes her eyes and rocks back and forth, waiting for the spasm to pass. Iris's left hand isn't doing much better either. Because of the botched skin grafts, she has multiple subluxations that have led to severe deformities. Some of her fingers are permanently bent in the palm of her hand, just like my index finger, and there's nothing she can do to change their position. When the therapists try to straighten them using sheer force, Iris rests her head on her arm and cries, so that no one can see her. Amidst sighs, she recites poems or lyrics, trying to think of anything else but the horrible pain. Sometimes she screams, vanquished by the hurt. It reminds me of bath-time at the Hospital for Burns.

I've been having nightmares more often lately. They're comprised of a dreadful combination of scenes from the night of the fire and moments from my days at the hospital. Sometimes, in complete darkness, the ceiling starts to burn, and I notice I'm lying in a dirty rubber tub. There's something on its edges and even though I can't see clearly, I know it's human skin, torn to pieces of various shapes and sizes. Someone is praying behind me, and their voice is neither male nor female. When they finish, they grab the burned flesh on my back and rip it off. Fragments of it fall into the water that's filled the tub, making a disgusting plopping sound. Some of them are eaten by the drain, swallowed whole, going down in fast swirls, disappearing into the nothingness below. I beg them, whoever they are, to stop, but they won't. Now they're praying again, praying, and tearing, praying, and tearing until they hit bone and I scream. But I don't wake up. Not yet. Not until the fire from the ceiling engulfs the entire room, and I start to suffocate. Other times, I'm still in the container, lying on the hot floor. Many people sit on top of me, holding me down, and I can't move. The place is burning like a pyre, but my executioners don't seem to care. "Shove the needle in here, right here!" one of them shouts. "I can't! She has too many scars!" It feels like a thousand needles are going in and out of my skin, all over my maimed body, numbing me. Then, we all catch fire.

I wake up drenched in sweat and overwhelmed. My brain isn't wrong to concoct such stories. The fire itself and everything that happened in the hospital afterward are chapters of the same book. One about corruption and recklessness. One in which the ultimate consequence is death.

But the nightmares are nothing compared to the pretty dreams in which my friends are still alive. They're far more painful because I have to mourn them every time I open my eyes to the reality that they're no longer a part of. I bury them again and again, each morning after and it tears me apart.

Sandra, Iris, and I talk about our sorrows and, when the confessions are too hard to bear, we stare at the scars on our hands. We've made a haven out of this tic, a safe gesture that allows us to protect ourselves from the heavy emotions that might overwhelm us. It's as if, by staring at the sick lace that has replaced our skin, we seek to find an answer to our suffering, some sort of release, which never comes. But at least we can escape from it all for a while. Every day, at Elias Hospital, through the pain and the tears, we also share a still fragile hope in the future, building ourselves up, taking turns holding each other's hand when the kinesiotherapy hurts too much, when the therapists pull on the stiff skin and joints a little too hard. A deep friendship is born out of these trials, an unexpected gift in the aftermath of the tragedy that tore our lives apart.

Flavia and Mihai come to see me every once in a while. We talk until late in the night and eat pizza. Flavia goes to therapy at the Military Hospital and she's very pleased with Mrs. C., her therapist, who also treats other people injured in the fire. She's "adopted" a few of us and takes care of us single-handedly, a daunting task for just one specialist.

"Why didn't you come to Elias, Flavia? We really miss you over there."

"I had an appointment with them and they told me that they can't take new patients at the moment. That there's no room for me there. I didn't really like the way they talked to me. Their attitude made me sad, so I started looking for alternatives. That's how I found Mrs. C. I was really lucky she took me in."

What she describes sounds familiar. Our lives have become a series of abandonments. The medical system can't wait for its next occasion to turn its back on us.

"Also, Silvia and Dr. Moldovan ignored me when I asked them about the reconstruction surgeries. They're always looking for reasons to postpone them."

The same thing happened to me. I tell her and she becomes upset.

"After all they've done to us... They discharged us filled with germs! It's written point blank in the medical letter."

"What medical letter?"

"They didn't give it to you?"

"I don't think so. All I have is the discharge paper."

"No, dearest. Look."

She shows me a screenshot of the document on her mobile phone.

"You have to ask them to give it to you. Did they give you the photos?"

"No, I don't have those either."

"They kept saying that they were photographing us so that they could attach the pictures to our medical record. Now they claim they never said that."

We decide that we're going to demand our papers the next time we go for our check-up. Ever since I started healing "miraculously," I haven't gone to the Hospital for Burns as often as I used to. They told me I should only go once every second week.

At my appointment, Silvia and Dr. Moldovan are very pleased with my progress. They talk about how important it is to have patience and "let time do its work" and "allow the body to become stronger." I despise their willful blindness, but I stay quiet for Iulia's sake. They're so self-absorbed that they can't see that it wasn't time that cured me, but the superhuman efforts of a nurse, who still comes over to offer me professional attention. Some of the other people who were burned in the fire came back to the hospital to have their wounds regrafted. I didn't have to. Because of Iulia.

I don't utter a word, even though I want to shout the truth out loud, revealing their murderous incompetence. I care about Iulia too much. I don't want her to get in trouble. I know it's not right; I know I should just tell them everything, but something doesn't let me. I'm disgusted by my own pettiness. Here I am, putting on a show, lying, just like them. The similarity between our acts appalls me.

I finally speak up and tell them I want my medical letter and the photos they took of me during my stay in the hospital. Silvia clears her throat and tells me that I can obtain my medical record from the secretary's office, at the first floor of the building. I'll file a written request and, after it's approved, they'll call me to come get the papers. She changes the topic and starts talking about my scars again, as if she ever really cared about my progress, lying to my face about my outstanding recovery.

She and Dr. Moldovan stare at my index finger, making disapproving noises and blaming me because I didn't wear the splint enough. They never mention the fact that they prescribed a device that wasn't supposed to be used by burn victims, on damaged skin. They fail to acknowledge that placing it directly over my skin resulted in an infection that destroyed my chances of healing forever. Each time I ask them if they can't perform a surgery like the one their colleagues did on Sandra, to straighten her fingers, they scratch their heads and talk nonsense. They claim my issues are far more severe than Sandra's. I need to wait. It's paramount I show even more patience. Meanwhile, the finger keeps bending, and the pain is excruciating. In the end, I give up. It's pointless. They're never going to help me. I say goodbye and head to the secretary's office, where she hands me a piece of paper and a pen. I haven't written by hand since the fire, and I discover that it's almost impossible to do it. When I'm finished scribbling, I'm drenched in sweat. Not once did the secretary offer to help me. She grabs the request from my hand, rolling her eyes. She yawns while she files it.

"Call us in two weeks."

I don't bother to ask why it takes so long to make copies of an already existing file. I thank her and leave. On my way home, I decide that I'm going to seek help in the private sector. I'm going to look for a competent surgeon who is willing to treat me. I talk to my sister, who has heard great things about Professor Pavel. Hopeful for the first time in months, I call his clinic. The nurse who answers the phone makes a long pause when she hears that I was injured in the Colectiv Club fire. She puts me on hold. It takes a while until she picks up again. She's probably talking to the surgeon.

"Well, what can I say... Come tomorrow at around 6:00 P.M.," she sighs.

She hangs up without saying goodbye. I have a bad feeling after our conversation, but I try to chase away the negativity. Mom is still bed-ridden, so she can't go with me. Two of my friends will join me instead. Meanwhile, I go to a clinic nearby and get an x-ray of my hand, so that I'm well prepared for my appointment tomorrow.

The next day, Andreea and Nico help me put my clothes on and call a cab. We decide we're going to wait for it outside. It's been a long time since I've had a heart-to-heart conversation with my friends. It's hard for me to open up to them. I still can't find the words to describe what I'm going through. We take advantage of the fact that Mom isn't around and try to chat and gossip like back in the day, like before the fire, but I often feel like I can't tap into that part of me anymore, or at least not completely.

It's already dark outside and huge, endearingly puffy snowflakes embellish the sky with their silver innocence. I haven't gone out in the evening since October 30th. Nostalgia washes over me as I watch the bodies of agitated passers-by rush toward their warm homes. I've lost some of the hopefulness I had yesterday. I didn't like the way Professor Pavel's nurse spoke to me. It left a bitter taste in my mouth. We arrive at the clinic and my friends decide to wait for me outside. I talk to the receptionist and tell her my name and the reason I came to see the professor. She examines me from head to toe and vanishes behind a door on my right. When she returns, she asks me to go inside. The tone of her voice is chilled, and she's visibly displeased.

"So, I understand you were injured in that fire, right?"

The professor doesn't waste any time on introductions.

"Good evening, Doctor. Yes, I was hurt there. I came to see you because..."

"Save it. I can't help you. I don't want to get involved in this whole Colectiv situation. It's a political thing, and I'd make a bad impression."

I stare at him, confused. What does politics have to do with my appointment? He interrupted me so abruptly I lost my train of thought. I try to steer the conversation back to my medical needs.

"But Professor, I... I just want your opinion about my index finger. I don't care about politics at all. I'm in a lot of pain because of my deformity and I keep bleeding, and..."

"So? What? Aren't you well taken care of by those people at the Hospital for Burns? What do you want from me? Why don't you just go back to them?"

"I did, but..."

"And? It's not my business to fix what others broke. Just go back to them. There's nothing I can do for you."

I feel humiliated. I don't understand why he agreed to set up the appointment if he knew he didn't want anything to do with me. He could have simply sent word through his nurse that his schedule is full, or any other excuse for that matter. Anything would have been better than a scene like this. In this heavy winter jacket, much too large for how emaciated I've become, with blood-sullied bandages peeping from under my clothing, incapable of doing something as simple as opening a door on my own, I stand there, with my heart racing because of the shame, fighting back tears. I freeze in front of the professor, with my x-ray tucked under my right arm. I'm not sure if there's any point in insisting or if I'd be better off leaving without saying a word. Suddenly, nausea comes over me and I feel weak to my knees. It's very warm in here for how I'm dressed. Big drops of sweat trickle down my tumefied cheeks. I can't take my jacket off without help and I don't dare ask the doctor to lend me a hand. As for his nurse, she walked out of the room when I came in, and she hasn't come back. No witnesses. Yet again I'm alone and helpless, amidst people whose sole purpose is to help their kind. But they do no such thing. On the contrary.

A deafening silence falls between me and the professor. He's playing with a pen on his desk and examining me from under his glasses. I gulp and make one last attempt.

"Please, if I'm here, just allow me to show you my x-ray."

"If you insist..."

I sit down uninvited on the chair in front of his desk and start to fumble with the envelope. Because of the effort to open it, my disabled hands are shaking, which only worsens the outcome. I finally manage to pull it out and I push it clumsily in front of the doctor. He looks at it for a split second, then gestures at me to take it away.

"Yes. Looks like arthritis. Anything else?"

I struggle to put the x-ray back in the envelope and Professor Pavel looks at me detached, unmoved by my difficulties. He doesn't offer to help me this time either. My maimed fingers won't listen to me, prolonging the awkwardness, which lasts for minutes on end, as I fumble and stagger. When I've finally succeeded, I'm wet with sweat. I'm so drenched that the wounds on my scalp sting underneath the thick beanie hat. Still, I ask him.

"What do you advise me to do?"

"Go back to those people at the Hospital for Burns. Let them tell you what to do."

I've lost all will to react, so I say goodbye and open the door with my elbows. The nurse looks at me sideways and tells me, with a hint of superiority in her voice, that I don't have to pay for the appointment. I run out, disgusted, and reunite with Nico and Andreea.

"Let's get out of here."

"So soon? What did he say?"

On the ride back home, I tell them what happened. After I've finished, we fall silent. I stare at the headlights of the cars that pass us by, trying to fight back the tears. The same big snowflakes stud the sky, committed to never leaving their beloved winter vault. I have lost all hope and faith in getting better. "It's a political thing," "Why don't you just go back to them?" I can't help asking myself how a well-renowned and greatly respected surgeon can speak like that to a traumatized girl, who came to see him from the other side of town, still wounded and bandaged. I shake my head and feel Nico's hand slip into mine.

"Al, don't be so sad. It'll be all right. This surgeon... he's not even a human being, let alone a doctor. People worship him for nothing."

I rest my head on her shoulder and thank her. In my dark book of sorrows, I write down another defeat. I remember what that nurse said, back at the Hospital for Burns, the night poor Ana died: "She's better off dead. Had she lived, she'd have been a monster." Once again, I realize what a shallow understanding of the word "monster" we have. We often use it to describe physical ugliness. But the real monsters are those who walk among us unscathed, whole physically, yet utterly broken inside. They humiliate and torture others, hiding behind positions of power: doctor, mayor, minister, and whichever other mask of vapidness and corruption. Here lies the true ugliness of people, not in the imperfection of their bodies.

I arrive home and call Cristina. She sighs on the other end of the line.

"There's no other choice. You have to leave the country and seek help abroad. They won't take care of you here. They're afraid of something or someone bigger than them, and they'd rather let you die."

"How is that even possible, Cristina? We don't have the money for something like that."

"Don't worry. We'll figure something out."

I now understand that, for us, the survivors of the Colectiv Club fire, things are far more complicated than they seem. "It's political." If, at first, I had no idea what politics had to do with my mutilated body, in desperate need of medical attention, I'm starting to see that, for them, the people in charge, we're not just ordinary burn victims, but problem-patients. We humiliated the system when our suffering and death revealed the corruption that renders it incapable of doing what it's meant to do: saving lives. They don't want anything to do with us, that's why they tell us lies about how we'll heal effortlessly, refusing to operate on us. They keep postponing our surgeries, hoping we'll eventually disappear. Hoping that our wounds will vanish spontaneously, without any involvement of theirs. Actually, all they want is to get rid of us. They don't care that we'll end up with permanent disabilities. What's of paramount importance is that they keep their pristine reputation untouched. Which is exactly why they despise us. We ruined their image with our bleeding burns. Such wounds are not adequate mirrors to reflect the illusion of their competence. Neither are they the anchor to fix their position in place. On the contrary. They are the nauseating abyss that truth has fallen into and screams to escape. Our bodies burned by the fire, mutilated by the infections, devastated further by the torture we endured in the hospitals are a testimony of the monstrous reality they've been trying to hide for decades, with the price of countless avoidable deaths.

Until Colectiv, people didn't know that the rot had spread so far, but our tragedy revealed the true extent of the gangrene. The many bosses, ministers, professors, and system hangmen, who would give anything to keep bathing in adulation, dislike this status quo and would sell their souls to go back to how things were before, even if their patients are still dying because of the multi-resistant strains of bacteria that haunt their ORs, because of the worms that often nestle, in the hot seasons, in the wounds of the burn victims from the ICU. So, they made a choice: they abandoned us. They decided that they simply wouldn't take care of us. Just like that. The ones who died are dead. The ones who are still alive, well, they can go to Hell. "What do you want with me?" "Go back to them!" "You'll heal, eventually." We're just a sensitive topic in the Romanian medical system's archive of tragedies. We're no longer human beings, young people, vulnerable and mutilated, in need of all the help we can get. Life after the Colectiv Club fire is nothing but a series of abandonments, as Flavia pointed out so wisely. They've left us to fend for ourselves for the sake of "politics."

I received my first compression suit from a foreign company that agreed to help us after being contacted by volunteers from Romanian NGOs. I'll have to wear it 23 hours a day, taking a one-hour break for hygiene purposes. The costs of the garments are covered by a handful of organizations and foundations that fundraised money for us, through donations made by ordinary people, touched by our suffering. The producers told us that, in Western Europe, all the costs for a burn patient's medical needs are covered by the health insurance plan. We were too ashamed to tell them that, unfortunately, this isn't Western Europe. Here, we're at the mercy of kindred spirits, everyday people who know better than anyone what it's like to be failed by the system. That's why we can afford to buy, every once in a while, at least a few of the special creams and dressings we need. Marigold ointment doesn't really do the job, contrary to Silvia's opinion.

The compression suit is made from a special kind of fabric. I touch it, curious about what it feels like. I'm taken aback by its rigidity. Even with all the weight I've lost, I'm not sure how I'll be able to fit in it. Iulia uses the plastic applicator I received together with the garments to help with the dressing process. It looks slightly like a green, soft funnel. She helps me put my arms through it, then pulls the sleeves of the suit over, one by one. It's like I'm getting into an armor. Because of the pressure of the garments, my hands turn blue. It hurts really bad, but I know I need this, so I don't complain. The gloves are next. The right one won't get past the deformed index finger. Iulia tries a couple of times, but the fragile skin tears open, so she gives up. She manages to pull the glove on the left hand, and claps, relieved that she finally got me completely dressed. I stand there, next to the edge of the bed, feeling like a swollen knight, unaccustomed to the weight of the metal. Every move I make is painful and I realize that wearing this as long as they say is necessary is going to be very difficult. I'm committed to doing it, though. I don't want to develop more complications. Normally, I should have received a compression suit right after I was discharged from the hospital, but that didn't happen in Romania. In the time that it took me to get the garments, my scars have grown and become thick and painful, like a hard shell, as if my body built a sick shield to protect me. The squeezing from the suit only makes the sensation of tightness worse.

A few weeks later, Silvia and Dr. Moldovan summon Iris to the hospital for surgery. They're going to regraft her left hand, to try to release her joints and fingers. Sandra and I go to pay her a visit. Iris is lying in one of the broken beds we know so well. She's pale, and she's rocking back and forth, holding her hand up next to her chest. Her bandages look strange, shabby, as if done in a hurry. Bloodied compresses fall from under the dressings, into her lap. When she sees us, she sighs. It's cold in the ward because they still haven't fixed the heating system. I can feel anger building up in me. I struggle to keep it at bay.

"I don't know why I let them operate on me again. It was horrible. They only gave me local anesthesia, and it didn't take properly, so I was in pain most of the surgery. I felt them working on my tendons! After they were done, they sent me to the ward. They sat me up and showed me the O.R. door. I walked out on my own and came here on my two feet. The hallway was empty. I could have collapsed, and no one would have noticed me."

Iris cries and covers her face with her right arm. I remember her sitting on the edge of the bed, on the night of October 30th, right after the fire. Black ash covered her face, and all I could see were two pink streaks of clean skin, left behind by her tears. A few hours later, she was vomiting darkness in the metal tray the nurses left on her lap, trying to cleanse herself of the molten tar that had stuck to her insides when she tried to breathe in the container, unaware that the air itself was scorching. I feel an overwhelming sense of pity wash over me. Pity for her, pity for Sandra. Self-pity, too. They abandoned us and condemned us to seek healing alone after we lost everything. Everything but our lives. We're completely on our own. No one has our back over here. It's as if they'd have preferred that we died.

A desire to overcome this grows inside me, replacing the anger. I decide that I'm going to find a way out of the Hell of helplessness that they've laid out in front of us. A way out of this impoverished, inhumane medical system, in which saviors become executioners, for the sake of politics. They care about it far more than they do about their patients. We never really left the Hospital of Neverhealing. We're still here, wasting our health, waiting for a miracle. But it doesn't come. And it never will. Dirty hands and sold souls can't mend us.

My wounds have finally healed because of Iulia's devotion and love. With her help, and K's, I've become stronger. My left hand is doing much better, and I recovered some of the mobility I lost. Unfortunately, I can't say the same thing about my right hand. My disability has become severe as a result of the deformity in my index finger and the stiffness of my joint. I still can't raise my arms above my head as I should. I can't stretch them forward adequately either. Living alone is out of the question. I'm happy that Mom has recovered to a certain extent and can handle some of the house chores. For everything else, there's Mrs. Daniela. Iulia thinks that I'm going to need a few years of physical therapy to get back in shape. The so-called "contractures" have started to form. They're stripes of rope-like tissue that stretch between scars. I can't move because of them, and sometimes they bleed, staining my compression garments and clothes.

I should have surgery to remove them, but no one wants to help me. I had my last check-up at the Hospital for Burns. After Iris's botched surgery, I stopped asking about my procedures. Dr. Moldovan told me he wants to see me again in the summer. On second thought, fall is even better. He'll decide then, together with Silvia, if and where they should start with the reconstructive surgeries. Winter turned into spring, spring turned into summer, summer turned into autumn, and autumn will turn into never. It's clear as day that they don't actually want to help. They're hoping I'll go away "on my own," just like my wounds did. If they wanted to treat me, they'd have done so already, just like Sandra's surgeons, who operated on her in January.

I nod and thank them. We say goodbye. After I leave, I pray to God and beg him to help me find a kind-hearted doctor, who can undo at least some of the harm they caused.

I arrive at Elias Hospital a little late, because of the delay with the check-up. K. called me at 10:00 A.M. sharp, and it's a little over 10:15. When I walk into the treatment ward, I'm panting. It's as if I walked in on someone doing something I wasn't meant to see. When they see me, the therapists end their lively conversations and become silent. They stare at the floor or around, ignoring my hello. K. stands next to our desk, in the corner of the room, wringing her hands and fiddling with her glasses.

"Alex, the professor wants to see you upstairs. He wants to have a chat with you."

"Did something happen?" I ask, scared that I did something wrong without realizing it.

"Oh, no... Don't worry. He just wants to talk."

My hands shake as I press the elevator button. Proud of its majestic station, the pink quartz pyramid dominates the professor's large desk. Austere faces of saints, painted on glass or sculpted in wood, look down at me, from the bookcase. Doctor Ionescu gets up and asks to see my scars. I start the tiresome process of taking my clothes off and, when I'm done, he walks round me, examining my body. He grabs my arms, pushes, and pulls them, assessing the range of motion. They won't go all the way up or turn to the sides as they should. He demands I make a fist with both my hands, but I can't. My fingers won't bend. He pinches the scar on my neck, to test the elasticity of the skin, but the tissue is fixed and won't budge. He shrugs.

"Well, I think you're doing pretty well. I don't see why you should come for therapy daily. We'll have to spread out your appointments. I suggest you come once, or a maximum of twice a week for a while, and then no more."

The news hits me like a punch in the gut. I haven't managed to put my clothes back on yet, and I grab them randomly, to cover myself.

"You mean... I should stop doing physical rehabilitation?"

"Yes. You and your friends have had too many sessions as it is. The CAS[3] only pays for two weeks of therapy, and you've been here two or three months already. I don't want any trouble."

"But... I can't lift my arms. I still can't move very well..."

"Yes, but come now. You're doing a bit better, aren't you? Well, this is all. K. already knows. I informed her about my decision. I'll talk to the rest of your friends today. This is all we can do for you right now. Time to move on."

The professor's last words reach me as if passing through a thick curtain. My heartbeat has become louder, and it's making it hard for me to hear the environment around. All of a sudden, a paralyzing fear grasps me. I pray that I won't have a panic attack here, in front of him. "There's nothing I can do for you." Professor Pavel's dismissal rings in my ears, over and over. There's a racket in my soul, and I wish I could go back to the quiet from before. "We have everything we need," "It's your fault," "Stop crying," "It doesn't hurt." All the voices of abandonment I've heard so far come together as one and scream the same thing: "We don't want to help you. You're on your own." I sit in the chair in front of his desk to avoid toppling over. I pretend it's easier for me to put my clothes back on that way. I fumble with the zipper of my hoodie until my knees stop shaking. After a while, I get up. A million questions that I want to ask the professor come to mind. For example, how does he reconcile kicking me out with the kindness preached by the many saints in his icons? Doesn't he kill the positive vibes that his crystals and pyramids emit when he breaks my heart, leaving me to fend for myself?

He's right. I am doing better. Better than a dying girl, riddled with infections, who couldn't even wash herself on her own. But I'm worse than I've ever been in my life. I need K. more than ever. I look into his eyes, and he holds my gaze, unashamed, remorseless. The sight of his mercilessness is appalling. I gulp and blabber a "thank you" I don't mean. After a few moments of awkward silence, I nod, say my goodbyes, and leave.

---

[3] Casa Națională de Asigurări de Sănătate, in short CAS, roughly translated as "The National House of Health Insurance," is Romania's national medical insurance fund. Every Romanian citizen is obliged to contribute a fixed percentage of their income to this fund, in exchange for medical care in the public hospitals.

K. is waiting for me at our worktable. She has a heavy heart, but there's nothing she can do about the whole situation. The decision has been made by those who hold the power in the hospital, so none of the therapists have a word to say. I thank her for everything she's done for me. The rest of our time together is burdened by sorrow. I know that this is the end. I'm no longer welcome here and I'm aware of what Professor Ionescu's once or twice a week actually means: time to stop for good. After Sandra and Iris arrive, they're also sent upstairs to "the big man." When they return, they're just as upset as I was. They haven't healed either. They still need help. A few hours later, we're standing in front of the hospital, talking, trying to find solutions.

"We have to do something about this. There's no way we're stopping our treatments."

We agree and we go home, motivated to discover an alternative. I tell my mother and my sister what happened. Cristina is seething. Even Iulia and Mrs. Daniela are disappointed. They try to comfort me, but to no avail. I'm too hopeless. I spend the rest of the day searching the internet for clinics and hospitals that offer burn rehabilitation for those with severe injuries who are no longer in acute care. I can't help wondering what happened to the rest of the therapists who were sent to Belgium by the Ministry of Health to learn new skills. I remember the conversation I had with Flavia about Mrs. C., her therapist at the Military Hospital. I call there, but they tell me they're full. They can't accept new patients. I sigh, thank them, and lie down. I'm completely discouraged. I turn my back to the door so that Mom won't see that I'm crying when she walks in. Eventually, I fall asleep. I wake up an hour later because my phone is ringing. It's Cristina, and she's enthusiastic.

"I talked to V. again. Two of the people who were injured in the club are in Germany right now, at a specialized burn rehabilitation clinic. He said he could help you go there too. It's called M. Klinik. Look it up on the internet. He'll talk to the people from the NGOs that have been helping you. They'll provide the payment."

I shake the dizziness off and open my computer. I Google-search the name of the clinic and click on the first link. It takes me to a dark green webpage that has as a background a picture of a lavish forest. In the middle, a pristine white building, with an entrance shaped like a rotunda, opens its virtual gates to me. The words "M. Klinik" are written with elegant, golden letters on the front. At first sight, it looks more like something from a fairy tale book. It's nothing like a hospital. At least not like the ones I've come to be familiar with. I hit the translate button and read about the clinic's over two decades of experience in burn rehabilitation. My fascination grows with every new piece of information. This place seems to be exactly what I'm looking for, yet it's as if it's from another world, one I haven't had access to. I take a deep breath and count to ten. "I must do this," I tell myself. "No matter how hard it is to get there, I must do it." I give myself a few days to think, but the image of the beautiful clinic set deep in the heart of the forest follows my every moment, like a fate one can't escape.

The therapy sessions at Elias Hospital following my conversation with Professor Ionescu take place in a cold and unwelcoming atmosphere. K. is the same devoted therapist as before, but I notice that there's pressure being put on her to get rid of me faster. I'm fully aware now that I'm expected to leave for good. I talk to Sandra and Iris about M. Klinik. We promise each other that we'll reunite there soon. We make a pact that we'll always support one another, even if our time at Elias has come to an end. No matter how hard it is to say goodbye to Mom and Cristina, I can't afford to hesitate once again, like I did before. Now I finally know better. I'm convinced that something more wholesome waits for me across the border.

The specialists at the clinic in Germany reply to my e-mail almost immediately. They ask me to send them my medical record. They want to learn more about my case. It's already been a few weeks since I filed the request to obtain it at the secretary's office at the Hospital for Burns. Every time I called to ask if I could pick it up, they told me it wasn't ready yet. I can't wait anymore. I've run out of time. Mom and I go to the hospital in person to explain that I need the record as fast as possible. The future of my treatment depends on it. The secretary huffs and puffs, rolls her eyes, makes a few disparaging comments, opens a PDF document, and hits "print." When the printing is done, she hands me a pile of messy papers, some of them in random order, makes me sign for them, and sends me away displeased. What stood between me, and my record wasn't any complicated process that needed time. It was a secretary's lack of disposition to press the print button.

We walk out of the office, sit on a chair, and try to arrange the papers, to give them a semblance of tidiness. With a few exceptions, they're unreadable. Some of them are copies made from documents written by hand, with a pencil. My photos are nowhere to be found. The results of the numerous lab tests they made to check for infections are gone too. My medical "record" is a pile of worthless, randomly scribbled papers. I search diligently for the letter that Flavia showed me when she visited me a few months ago. It's missing. I knock and return to the secretary's office to ask what happened to it. She seems surprised by the fact that I know about it in the first place.

"Oh, yes... That document is with the chief nurse. You have to ask her to give it to you."

"And my photos?"

"If they're not in the record I just gave you, they don't exist."

"But I explicitly gave my consent to be photographed under the condition that they attach the pictures to my record. I'm very certain that they exist."

"I don't know. I'm not the one who took them, am I? Talk to whoever photographed you."

I'm too tired to deal with this kind of attitude anymore, so I just leave. I'm still not well and the constant walking from one building to the other is exhausting. All of this was just to obtain paperwork that could have easily been sent online. However, the difficult nature of the process is deliberate. The hospital management wants to discourage the patients from trying to obtain their records. The hope is that we'll give up, go home, and forget about it.

I make it to the other building and climb the stairs, prey to a feeling of utter disgust, to the first floor. I walk in and the strong smell of surgical soap and oozing burn wounds hits me like a punch in the gut. I'm back in these hallways again, next to the wards with half-open doors, where I lay, dying, for more than two months, begging for medication that was never given, no matter how bad the pain got. I'm fighting the urge to vomit. My legs are shaking, so I want to sit down in one of the armchairs. I stop myself. I remember the patient with the Clostridium infection who was supposed to be isolated but who actually walked free, perusing the hallways, and making awkward comments. He sat in that chair. And so did we, with our bloodied bandages and torn-open flesh. Who knows what filth lies in the crevices of the worn-out furniture... I don't want to risk it. I've healed hard enough as it is. I stand up, swaying on my feet, trying to avoid collapsing. The chief nurse makes her appearance. Memories of how she used to lock the medical items we received as donations in her office, denying us access to them, come back to me. She's annoyed that I'm asking her about the medical letter. At first, she says that no such document exists and that I must be mistaken. I show her a scan of Flavia's paper and she pretends to suddenly remember what I'm talking about. Oh, yes, *that* medical letter! Too bad it hasn't been issued yet. I have to go back to the secretary's office and file another request. I can't stand this anymore, so I interrupt her. That's exactly where I've come from and the secretary herself told me that she already has it. She gives me a vile look and starts to tap on the counter between us nervously. I force myself to smile and demand the letter. I tell her that I'm all out of niceties and that I'm not leaving without it. She fumbles through a drawer, takes out a big dossier, and, as if by miracle, discovers my document inside it. She hands it over to me and walks away, upset. I don't even get to thank her. Not that I would have really meant it anyway. We say goodbye to the other nurses and walk out. We stop on the staircase at my request. I want to take another look at the medical letter, to make sure it's what I requested. I read through the various abbreviations of the procedures performed on me, arranged in chronological order, from the moment I arrived at the hospital, to the moment they discharged me. I stop on November 5th and stare at the lab results of the wound samples collected during the first surgeries.

Among the clutter of biomarkers, spelled out in small letters, the word ANTI-BIOGRAM 1 RESISTANT GERM, in capitals, stands out. "Sensitive only to Colistin." Resistant to everything else. In parentheses lies written, like it's nothing, (Pseudomonas spp.). There it is. The renowned hospital-acquired bug everyone dreaded, yet no one carried. The feared infection Călin caught, for which we avoided him, scared he'd give it to us somehow. In reality, we were all infected, and this piece of paper proves it. My labs came out positive continuously, day after day. On November 14th, the lab result of the sample collected from the tip of my central venous catheter, the piece from inside my body, comes out: "POSITIVE for Pseudomonas spp." You don't have to be a doctor to know what that means. I was one step away from developing sepsis. Until December 8th, all my samples came out positive for various bugs, some multi-resistant, others "sensitive" to various antibiotics. The names of all these other germs are not featured in the letter. They're gone, just like my photos.

That's why they were giving me so many antibiotics. Not because they wanted to prevent the infections like they always claimed, but because they were trying to treat them. They were sewing dirt into my wounds instead of skin. I falter and sit down on the stairs. Scared, Mom takes the papers away from me and starts to read them. Her eyes widen and she gasps as she goes through the sequence of abbreviated horrors. Her hand is shaking and her mouth twitches, as if she's crying silently. Even though she hasn't healed from her back injury, she sits beside me on the cold concrete. Like lightning, the truth passes through the core of our being, shattering us. I was never "sterile" or "outside of any danger." Death had always chased after me, like a famished beast, lured by their lies. "She's not infected! She's just too skinny."

"Murderers! Child killers! Bastards!"

Mom shudders and shakes, bawling. I comfort her as best as I can, trying to raise my left arm enough to hug her.

"You could have died any moment. You were always one step away from... And we just stood there, listening to their lies, believing them. Cristina was right from the start. And the photos? Where are the photos? They know that the pictures don't lie, that's why they 'lost' them."

The sharp midday light coming through the tall windows hurts my eyes. Indeed, what is most troubling is that they refused to give me the photos. They're a part of my story that I deserve to know, a missing piece from my puzzle of suffering, and the void left behind by their absence pains me like a rejection. Like I'm denied access to absolution. It's my body! It's my right to see it in the state it was really in back then: burned to smithereens and sullied by the infections they denied existed. My mother is right. They're afraid of the pictures because the infections are obvious there. Words can be misinterpreted but photos, especially those like mine, can't. I'll talk to Silvia. She has some explaining to do. I'm filled with bitterness. All I want to do is leave. I want to go home, take off the clothes I wore in this place, replete with disease, and throw them off.

	PLAGA(POZITIV); GERMENI 1(b.Pseudomonas spp); ZONA RECOLTARII(sc.fata);
49070/ 07/11/2015	CREATININA SERICA(0.67mg/dl); EO#(C.2710^3/ul); EO%(1.80%); GLUCOZA SERICA (93mg/dl); INR(0.90); LY#(3.1710^3/ul); LY%(21.20%); MCH(30.10pg); MCHC(34.89g/dl); MCV (86.25fL); MPV(7.04fL); NE%(53.90%); PCT(0.251%); PLT(35610^3/ul); Potasiu(3.6mmol/L); PT (12.9s); RDW(12.45%); s(6.20AUTOMATIC); TGO(29U/l); TGP(35U/l);
49105/ 09/11/2015	AP(116%); BA#(0.0810^3/ul); Clor(100.8mmol/L); CREATININA SERICA(0.62mg/dl); EO# (0.2710^3/ul); EO%(2.30%); GLUCOZA SERICA(76mg/dl); INR(0.92); LY#(3.0810^3/ul); LY% (26.10%); MCH(30.96pg); MCV(85.93fL); MPV(6.91fL); NE#(7.0010^3/ul); NE%(59.40%); PCT (0.219%); PLT(31710^3/ul); Potasiu(3.6mmol/L); PT(13.2s); RDW(12.36%); s(7.00AUTOMATIC); TGO(26U/l); TGP(36U/l);
49133/ 09/11/2015	COMENTARII(vezi rezultatele); EXAMEN SECRETIE PLAGA(POZITIV); GERMENI 1 (b.Pseudomonas spp); ZONA RECOLTARII(sc.brat);
49188/ 12/11/2015	AP(94%); BA#(0.0610^3/ul); Clor(104.1mmol/L); CREATININA SERICA(0.69mg/dl); EO# (0.1910^3/ul); EO%(2.10%); FIER THERM (SIDEREMIE)(50); GLUCOZA SERICA(80mg/dl); IMM# (0.18%); INR(1.04); LY#(2.5210^3/ul); LY%(27.90%); MCH(29.93pg); MCHC(34.21g/dl); MCV (87.47fL); MPV(6.40fL); NE#(5.3010^3/ul); NE%(58.70%); PCT(0.294%); Potasiu(4.3mmol/L); PT (14.6s); RDW(12.36%); Sodiu(140mmol/L); TGO(20U/l); TGP(15U/l); WBC(9.0410^3/ul);
49234/ 14/11/2015	ANTIBIOGRAMA 1 REZISTENT(Amikacina(11);Amox+ac. Clavulanic;Cefotaxime;CEFPIROM;Ceftazidime;Ceftriaxone (Rocephine);Ciprofloxacin;Gentamicin;Imipenem;Levofloxacin;Piperacillin / tazobactam;Sulperazona(12);); ANTIBIOGRAMA 1 SENSIBIL(Colistin(14);); EXAMEN SECRETIE VARF CATETER(POZITIV); GERMENI 1(b.Pseudomonas spp);
49247/ 15/11/2015	ALBUMINA BCG(48.2g/l); AP(94%); BA#(0.0710^3/ul); Clor(100.9mmol/L); CREATININA SERICA(0.76mg/dl); EO#(0.1610^3/ul); EO%(1.90%); GLUCOZA SERICA(76mg/dl); INR(1.04); LY#(2.3310^3/ul); LY%(28.50%); MCH(30.17pg); MCHC(34.08g/dl); MCV(88.52fL); MPV(6.14fL); NE#(4.4210^3/ul); NE%(54.10%); PCT(0.333%); Potasiu(4.9mmol/L); PROTEINE TOTALE(7g/dl); PT(14.6s); RDW(12.70%); TGO(20U/l); TGP(24U/l); UREE SERICA(20mg/dl); WBC(8.1810^3/ul);
49304/ 16/11/2015	ANTIBIOGRAMA 1 REZISTENT(Amikacina(11);Amox+ac. Clavulanic;Cefotaxime;CEFPIROM;Ceftazidime;Ceftriaxone (Rocephine);Ciprofloxacin;Gentamicin;Imipenem;Levofloxacin;Piperacillin / tazobactam (11);Sulperazona(15);); ANTIBIOGRAMA 1 SENSIBIL(Colistin(13);); EXAMEN SECRETIE PLAGA(POZITIV); GERMENI 1(b.Pseudomonas spp); ZONA RECOLTARII(sc.axila);

Excerpt from my medical letter, confirming what the doctors at the Hospital for Burns denied: I was indeed infected with various multi-resistant bacteria, and I was one step away from septicemia.

"If my own child was in her situation, I wouldn't transfer him," "Your lab results came back sterile," "You don't heal because you sleep on your back," "You didn't catch pneumonia from here," "We have everything we need," "Even if you rub shit all over, you'll still heal at this point," "Stop crying," "It's your fault you're not healing." It's your fault if you die here. My fault. Our fault.

I'll never understand why they played God like this with us. Why they lied. Why they tortured me during bath-time. Why they refused to give me painkillers. Why they infected me with the contaminated central venous catheter? Why they didn't let Cristina find a place for me in a hospital abroad? Why they most likely lied to the German doctors who had come to help us, telling them we were receiving the best treatment possible. Why they risked my life to hide the squalor that prevents them from being real doctors, good human beings. Why did keeping their positions matter more than saving young people's lives? Who are they protecting by condemning us and all the others who seek their help to death?

I'm shaking because of the anger, but I don't have the strength to do something about it. I feel like I could walk back in and destroy them, but I'm exhausted. I'm tired and sick. My hideous scars are stuck to my bones, and each day they grow bigger and become thicker, as if they're spreading, like some sort of disease. They are the testimony of the evil that was sown into my flesh by the dirtiness in this hospital, by the superbugs that etched their work onto my body forever. I hate them, and I'm ashamed of it. I'm tainting my soul with the disgust I feel when I remember them walking arrogantly among us, like gods among pigs, bullying us, lying to us, photographing our wounds, knowing full well we'll never see the pictures. In their neat scrubs, with their perfect skin, clean and whole, yet utterly abject on the inside, they sowed death wherever they touched. Prancing about in the hallways, thriving and greedy, while we died so that they could climb higher and higher on the ladder of success. If monsters ever wore human faces to disguise their true nature, theirs would be the ones they'd choose.

"Mom, let's leave this hellhole. Now."

"But aren't we going to demand an explanation? Aren't we going to hold them accountable?"

"I'll have to leave this one to God, Mom. And to the justice system. I can't breathe because of the hate I feel. I think I'm going to be sick. All I want is to get out of here."

After I arrive home, I sit down in front of the computer, distraught. I write to Silvia and ask her to give me the photos she took of me. Her answer is cold and relentless: "The pictures are not official, therefore I can't send them to you. They were taken for the sole purpose of following your progress." I insist, reminding her that I agreed to the photographs because she promised she'd attach them to my medical records. I tell her that I need them, first and foremost for myself, for my own peace of mind. She refuses, arguing that she doesn't want to breach confidentiality rules. I explain that I have the right to my own image and that I only consented to being photographed under very specific conditions, which she's breaching. Those pictures are mine by law, because it's me in them, at my worst and most vulnerable. They're deeply mine and no one else's, let alone hers. She leaves me on "seen," ending the conversation. It's over. She's probably deleting the photos as we speak.

The medical letter makes it clear why she won't give me the photos. She's afraid of what the wounds show so clearly, of the terrible truth of the infections that lays bare in those images. Devoured by bacteria, tortured by their ineptitude, the burns reveal what they sold their souls to conceal, and they won't have it. Those pictures will never see the light of day. Even now, when she can't lie to me anymore, she still tries to do it. I need to see those photographs for closure so that I can look upon the true extent of my ruin and let go of it. It's an inner necessity that is paramount to my psychological healing. However, I must accept that I'll never gaze upon that image, because she's made the decision for me, and it both hurts and angers me. A chapter from the book of my suffering will forever remain unknown, and the void that's left behind frustrates me, making it difficult to move on.

After a while, I stifle the trembling of my hands and open my mailbox. I must write to the German clinic and send the doctors the newly received medical letter. Fear grips me as I think about the dreaded revelations it brings forth. What if the clinic won't receive me? What if, after they see how many dangerous germs I was infected with, they won't want anything to do with me? I don't want to be dishonest, so I go ahead and attach the terrible letter to the rest of the folder, completing my record. I refuse to hide reality from them. Such shameful and cowardly behavior once maimed and killed us, and I refuse to be a part of it. I press the "send" button and freeze in front of the screen. It doesn't take long, and I receive a reply from Doctor Z., the head of the burn rehabilitation station himself. He writes to me in English: "Don't worry about anything. You're welcome here. We'll be expecting you in two weeks."

I hadn't realized I was holding my breath the entire time I was reading the letter until I exhale, relieved, and start to cry. These people... Even if they don't know me, they want me there. They're opening their doors to me when my own countrymen have abandoned me. I can't think about anything else apart from this certainty. This has been a hard day. The things I discovered are shocking, nauseating, but I feel a strange kind of peace. A weight has been lifted from my troubled heart, made heavy by doubt. It turns out that, in the end, it wasn't me. It wasn't my fault that I was dying. It wasn't because of how I slept or because of how much I cried. My flesh was neither bad nor lazy. It turns out that they actually didn't have everything they needed. It was them all along. I fall asleep hopeful, and my mind weaves intricate dreams about a beautiful white house in a lush green garden, far away from all this tragedy. The letter "M," written in gold with a graceful font, oversees everything like a beacon of salvation.

The morning I leave for Germany, I am overwhelmed by emotion. Because of how fragile her health is, my mother won't be accompanying me. I am secretly happy. Some time away from me will give her the chance to recover. My sister too will benefit. She'll finally be able to focus on her children and husband. These past few months I have often felt like a burden to those I love, and even though they denied it and went out of their way to make me feel good about myself, I know caring for me was very hard on them. My helplessness was destroying their lives. I saw this clearly when they fought that night. They didn't know what to do with someone who was too sick to be cared for at home. Someone who had been left behind by the experts who had a duty to treat her. They were just as helpless and vulnerable as me. My leaving will finally allow them to sew back together the torn fabric of their existence. I'm going to a place where they really have everything they need.

I'm traveling with two of my brother-in-law's friends. Adi and T. have known Florin for years and they agreed to drive me to Germany. I can't fly yet because it would be very difficult for me to carry my bags. They're very joyful and they share funny stories with me from their many journeys abroad. I sometimes catch them looking at me with a mixture of curiosity and pity, but they never pry or say inappropriate things. I'm grateful for their kindness and discretion. It's a two-day drive, and I quickly became exhausted because of the pain caused by the movement. I'm still unwell and the long road ahead is not something I look forward to. Before we arrive at the border with Hungary, we make a pit stop at a gas station, and I ask them to give me some time for myself. I need to be alone for a bit. I walk in and buy myself a bottle of Coke and a chicken sandwich. I sit down at a small table and make sure that no one can see me. I take a small bite out of the sandwich and sip on my cold, fizzy drink. My legs are shaking and I'm having second thoughts. Tears well up in my eyes. I can still change my mind and go back home, be with my family.

But, like dark waterfalls, memories of all the humiliations, abandonments, nasty words, barbaric treatments, and unendurable pain flush over me, drowning me in sorrow. Then, from behind the black curtain of disdain, I see Professor Ionescu and Professor Pavel's sneering faces. They're rejecting me with their harsh, disparaging comments, sending me away, back where I came from, to the nothingness. I see Doctor Moldovan, postponing my surgery dates, telling me he'll operate on me in summer, in autumn, next year, never. I see Silvia rolling her eyes, shrugging, taking out her tools, cutting my flesh, telling me I'll heal eventually, on my own, just like I have to do everything else. They're all saying the same thing, with different lips and different words: "You're alone. We don't want you."

I grin and chew, focusing on getting something in my stomach to ease the ever-present nausea. I don't know if it's the caffeine or some inner force I had no idea existed, but I start to feel better. This time I won't be a coward. If they won't have me, I'll find someone else that will, even if I have to look for them at the end of the world. I won't heal at home. In Romania, the gates of salvation closed in my face, and I was left outside, knocking with bleeding hands, begging someone to open them and let me in. By the time I get back to the car, I'm a different person: a stronger, more decisive one.

"I'm all right now. Let's keep going. I can't wait to get there!"

IV
FOREVER PATIENTS, SOMETIMES PEOPLE

When I open my eyes, the sun has already risen. In the distance, the rich green crowns of majestic trees appear over the horizon, like promises of lushness made by nature. It's the heart of spring and cruel green is the color of the season. The beautiful forest that greeted me when I first opened the clinic's website is no longer a dream. It lays in front of me real, ready to reveal its beauty to me.

"We're almost there, sleepy-head!"

Adi teases me for sleeping like a baby and I smile. I try to stretch but I stop quickly because of the pain that has awoken too. My scars have hardened overnight, and the feeling of tightness is unbearable. If I don't move constantly, the thick shells that have replaced my skin become immobile and rigid.

"Look, there it is!"

He shows me a big white building on a small hill, hiding behind a beautiful park decorated with extravagant flowers, arranged in elaborate decorative patterns. The clinic is larger than I thought.

"Wow, Alex! This place is gorgeous!"

Adi parks the car and takes my suitcases out of the trunk. He walks me to the reception desk, where I'm greeted by two smiling ladies in uniform. They ask me if I speak German and I answer that I do, but just a little. They hand me a metal key with a big keychain, which has the number "1020" engraved on it. Then they give me two coupons for coffee and lunch. They encourage me to eat something at the cafeteria since I must be famished after such a long journey. Adi joins me and, after we've finished, he hugs me and wishes me good luck. He's emotional. He tells me he's certain I'm in great hands after everything he's seen so far. We say our goodbyes and he leaves. I watch as he departs and become nostalgic and anxious. He's going home to see his loved ones, but I'm staying behind to protect myself and the people I care about. Our lives are worlds apart, and so am I from any semblance of normality, from the person I used to be.

One of the receptionists takes me to my ward. The department nurses arrive as soon as I step foot in the room and take me on a tour of the first floor, which belongs to the burn unit. They're set on cheering me up, so they laugh and joke with me, while they show me around. Their names are G. and E., and they tell me that they're here for me, no matter what I need.

"We're more than just *schwesters*, we're your sisters!"

The play on words amuses them. In German, *schwester* also means sister, aside from nurse. I smile and blush. It's been a long time since I've been shown such cheery kindness, and it does my worn heart good. As we walk, I try not to stare at everything, so as not to show how amazed I am. It doesn't feel like I'm in a regular hospital. My ward is more like a nice, comfortable room that could very well be part of a beautiful house. The simple domestic furniture creates an atmosphere of warmth. Everything is extremely clean and well organized. There's a big table lamp in the voluminous study. Its pretty yellow lampshade spreads a cozy light around the ward. I adore table lamps. They remind me of home.

"It's beautiful, isn't it? It's not like a normal sanatorium or clinic, where everything is white and scary."

After they leave, I sit down on the bed and gaze out the window. They gave me a room with a view. It overlooks the gorgeous forest. It also has a small terrace with chairs and a coffee table. They thought of everything here. I walk out on the balcony and lose myself in contemplation. When the doctor comes to meet me, he finds me staring at the lush wilderness with tears in my eyes. He doesn't just barge in, like I'm used to. He knocks politely on the door and waits for me to answer. He shakes my hand and introduces himself.

"Hello, Ms. Furnea! Welcome to M. Klinik. I'm Z., your doctor."

His manner is terribly modest and, at first, I feel taken aback by it. I'm used to a different approach. The one practiced by the almighty professors from the Romanian hospitals, who need to be greeted with their full title, lest they admonish you for being disrespectful. Even if he's the "big boss," the head of the department, he didn't precede his introduction with an elaborate list of all his achievements. He called himself "my doctor," and that was enough. He's a middle-aged man with a handsome face and a straight, neat posture. There's something fatherly about his countenance. With his kind blue eyes and calm presence, I can tell that, beyond anything else he might be, he's first and foremost a good man. He asks me if I can show him my scars and helps me remove my compression garment. When he sees the full extent of my burn sequelae, he makes an almost imperceptible gesture with his lips, as if he's in pain. He examines me and asks permission again and again to touch the scars. He doesn't feel like he's the master of my body. He doesn't feel like he's entitled to knead, probe, and pinch. He palpates me discretely, making sure that he's not causing any pain. After a while, he takes out a small voice recorder.

"Do I have your permission to record your appointment? The final report will contain all my observations in written format."

"Yes, of course. I trust you."

He assesses my sick skin at length, without rushing the process. I don't understand everything he's saying in German as he's speaking into the device for reference, but I realize that he's talking about the severe hypertrophy of the tissue: "The scars have a plaque-like appearance and feel." He's talking about this thick armor of flesh that covers me, choking me, making it hard to breathe. The skin grafts, instead of being thin and elastic, have turned into a compact mass of ill fibers, stuck together as if by mistake, yet relentlessly. He mentions the movement issues I'm facing and makes recommendations about the types of therapies I might benefit from. When he's done, he shuts the recorder off. He leans on the desk and takes off his glasses. He closes his eyes, sighs, and rubs his eyelids with his thumb and index finger. He stays quiet for a while, pondering what to say. Then he addresses me in English.

"Let me help you put your compression garments back on. I have to confess that your sequelae are unusual. Normally, with the right care received in the hospital and adequate prophylactic measures, we wouldn't see such advanced hypertrophy. I read the medical documents you sent us. You too struggled with infections, just like the other patients from your group. Unfortunately, bacteria sabotage the healing process, and the resulting scars are harder to treat than they normally would be. You will need a lot of care, but please don't be sad. You are young and strong, and we're very involved in each one of our cases. We love what we do, and I'm sure we can help you a great deal."

He asks permission to photograph me, and I allow him to. I'm convinced these pictures will indeed be attached to my medical record, unlike those taken by Silvia. He explains what my treatment course will look like, and I listen to him, fascinated.

"I am going to prescribe daily scar therapy baths and lots of scar massages and kinesiotherapy. You will also work out in the gym with our trainers to gain back the muscle mass you lost. I also recommend that you attend the one-on-one physiotherapy procedures with our specialists. It is very important that you take some psychotherapy sessions as well, because it is paramount that you address the trauma you experienced. I will arrange for a surgeon to see you because you need reconstructive surgery. There are also our motion coordination exercise groups. I'll enroll you so that you can learn to use your limbs again, in a normal way. The treatment plan is pretty intensive, but it's worth it. You'll start every day at 7:00 A.M., and you'll finish at 4 P.M. All of your meals are included, and you will have breaks for breakfast, lunch, and dinner. Getting better is going to be your full-time job. As for the compression garments, what is your situation?"

"I own a suit, but it's already worn out."

"Then I will also talk to our specialists and send them to take your measurements. They will make you a new, personalized pair."

"Doctor, may I ask you something?"

"Of course."

"Do the scar baths you mentioned... hurt?"

"Not at all! All you have to do is sit in a ceramic tub, filled with warm water. The nurses will pour various moisturizing substances in it to make sure your scars are nice and soft, so that the rest of the procedures, which can be quite unpleasant at times, seem a little less uncomfortable."

"You know, back in the hospital in Romania, they washed us... They washed our open wounds in a green rubber tub, and they didn't give us anything for the pain."

At first, Doctor Z. looks at me, confused, not sure what I'm talking about. Then it dawns on him, and he gulps.

"In the acute care phase, when the burn victim is still immensely vulnerable, all baths are conducted either anesthetized, sedated, or under serious analgesic medication, not when they're awake. The shock of the pain is not something the patient should experience over and over again, let alone because of the medical procedures. They're in horrendous pain as it is. It's inconceivable that we make any contribution to their torment at all."

I don't insist. I understand everything now. He bows respectfully and says goodbye. Shortly after, Nurse G. walks in and hands me the therapy schedule for the week. I have a different therapist for every procedure. My case is handled by several specialists, each an expert in their field. I'm amazed by how many therapies I'll attend and by how long the sessions are. It makes me really happy. Since every treatment is going to take place in a different ward, the nurses advise me to take a stroll through the clinic so that I can become familiar with the location of each room. But first, they take samples for the tests they're going to perform, to make sure I'm free of hospital-acquired bacteria. They swab me and draw blood. Later, another doctor pays me a visit. This time, it's an internal medicine expert. He does a routine check-up on me and lets me know that, in case I have any health concerns or symptoms, I can reach out to him no matter what. Before he leaves, he tells me that I'm done for the day, so I'm free to inspect the building and its surroundings as I please.

I take my schedule with me, and I go looking for the wards where starting from tomorrow, I'm going to spend most of my time. The building is huge, and each department has its own wards. There's a small courtyard in the middle of the clinic, and its highlight is the artificial pond, home to turtles and species of small koi fish. The ground floor is equipped with a big therapeutic pool, where patients with neurological conditions benefit from aqua-gym sessions. The circular hallway has two entrances to accommodate the many people in wheelchairs. It hosts an exhibit featuring paintings done by local artists, some depicting various parts of the clinic, like the beautiful crimson staircase that leads to the massage therapy wards. It takes me an hour to discover the location of every therapy room in my schedule but, at the end of my exploration, I'm happy. A few more excursions like this and I'll learn the place by heart.

In the evening, I go out to the big park in front of the clinic. I don't like exaggerated words, but I can only describe it as enchanting. The vegetation is lush, with many trees and elaborately cultivated flowers, which form beautiful decorative patterns, in a variety of colors, of which the most impressive is the vivid green, proof of how clean and healthy the air is in this small east German town. The leaves shudder under the sweet touch of the April wind. I sit down on a bench and close my eyes. A gentle breeze caresses my burned cheeks, scarred by the scorching fire. "I'm safe here," I whisper to myself. I'm finally safe.

I go back to my room late when it's already dark. I turn on the table lamp and a beautiful warm light floods the room, flowing from the yellow lampshade I love so much. I leave the curtains open and gaze at the pitch-black vault that spreads across the horizon, utterly clear, with no clouds in sight. Big, luminous stars speckle it, making me feel like I'm trapped in a kaleidoscope, giving me a sense of unreality. At first, I feel joy. But then, sadness comes over me. The truth hits me hard, shattering the world I knew. So, this is the normality that they denied us, the salvation they hid from us. I cry, shaking, at the revelation of the atrocities that I was made to endure to protect the rotten system that almost killed me. The stark contrast between the cruelty I experienced at the Hospital for Burns and the kindness that was shown to me here unravels me. Just thinking that right now, at this very moment, other people are going through the same thing, that bath-time is happening right now for someone, makes me nauseous. My heart bleeds for all those who will follow us in the green tub and in the Hospital of Neverhealing, in those nests of horrors that will continue to birth monsters. Patients will keep dying there, prey to the same lies that mangled us. I manage to fall asleep only at dawn, when the sky turns purple, dismantling the blackness of the night, casting some of the shadows away. My first day at M. Klinik begins in a few hours.

It's really quiet. Big flames lick the edge of the ceiling, spreading all over with an eerie speed, yet without any noise or smoke. We're standing there watching the fire, unable to move, hypnotized, like resigned spectators attending a show they've seen before. I look around and my eyes lock with Alex's. He's pale and tired. My troubled mind has summoned him here again, in the same place as always, making him part of the wry reenactment of the tragedy that mutilated me and killed him. All of a sudden, the fire is extinguished. Darkness replaces the intense shimmer of the flames, drowning them in soft shadows. It's over. We're free to move around now, so I walk from one group of people to the other, hugging old friends I thought I had lost forever. Alex hasn't budged, and he continues to look at me, peering into my eyes, to the very bottom of my soul. He asks me how I'm doing, and I answer fast, as if afraid that I won't get the chance to speak to him: "Good, and you?" Our voices are odd, muddled, like they're traveling to one another from a large distance, trying to meet in the middle. He smiles, but before he manages to answer, the scene unravels.

The table lamp that I always leave on, like a lighthouse that can guide my soul back home from the darkness, illuminates the comfortable ward of the burn rehab clinic. As I wake up from the dream, I see it and realize that it wasn't real. The grief I feel is gut-wrenching and I cry in silence so that the night shift nurses won't hear me. They'd want to comfort me, and right now, I just want to be alone. I don't dare call these strange dreams "nightmares." They're the only theaters where the beloved shadows of my friends still act out parts of their lost lives, cut short with such brutality. Sometimes, we get to talk at length. We smile and we embrace. Other times, there are fewer of us and we're sad. Often, it's just dark and there's nothing there to cast a light, but on most occasions, something is burning. Sometimes it's us. Then, I struggle to wake up sooner, desperate to return to reality.

I breathe a sigh of relief when I open my eyes wide and perceive the safety of the room. I get up and open the window. The cool German spring washes over me, drowning the blistering heat that the dream left behind. I sit there, inhaling the freshness of the scented air, trying to quiet the loud thumps of my heart. I want to go back to sleep, but I can't. Not for a while. I writhe in bed, I get up again, I walk around the room, and, in the end, I take off my compression garments, tearing at them, desperate to remove them. The scar on my left shoulder is purple and numb because of the tightness. It's flatter right now but, in just a few minutes, it will swell and expand, going back to its hypertrophic state. I massage it, trying to alleviate the budding pain, but my thoughts are elsewhere. It gnaws at me that I left them behind in the dream, prey to the fire. That I escaped, and maybe they're burning somewhere, locked in a place in my mind, incapable of breaking out. I latch onto the pretty light shining in my room. Its warm glow reminds me of my apartment, back in Bucharest. One autumn night, I walked out the door and, in a way, never really came back. When I was a child, my mom used to leave the lights on in the small hallway in front of the bedroom because the stories I read came back to haunt me. In the darkness of the night, their shadows grew longer, and assumed different forms, until they became something to be afraid of. I never thought that I'd need a night light again, so many years later.

The morning starts with a lot of pain. My body hasn't gotten used to its new frame, with the scars shaped like mutilated wings that furrow my back. The young flesh that has grown over the deep burns is suffering. It doesn't know what to do with the weight and movements of my body. There's not enough of it to cover my bones and muscles without clinging to them. So, it tortures me, like a punishment. The nights are still hard, even though I don't have any open sores left. But even so, the sick tissue swells and burns, as if I had embers under my skin as if the scars were nothing but thick scabs covering gaping wounds, interspersed by the living matrix of my nerves.

I'm still nauseous in the morning sometimes, remembering how I used to wake up in the Hospital for Burns, with humid, festering bandages, stuck to my infected burns, afraid of what was to come: bath-time. They used to throw us in a green rubber tub and wash us, without numbing us, with silicone-bristled sponges, doused in soap. When they tore the necrotized tissue from me, it made a grotesque sound I often still hear, even in silence: scrub, scratch, scrub. Even now, months after that ordeal, I still feel like vomiting when I open my eyes on a new day, unsure of where I am, whether I'm back in Romania, waiting for Alina to walk in with her wheelchair. I take a few sips of the sweet hot tea the nurses brought me, and the nausea subsides. I calm down, knowing for certain that nobody is going to hurt me like that here. I get in the shower and adjust the spray to the lightest setting. I smile as the warm mist flows down my scars, soothing them. Now, here, water doesn't hurt anymore. For me, it's nothing short of a miracle.

It's breakfast time and I go down to the cantina, where the girls are waiting for me. There are four of us in total. Sandra and Iris have joined me recently, and Anda was already here when I arrived. She told me about how, after she was transferred to Germany, the doctors put her in a medically induced coma so that she wouldn't feel distress while her body was healing. She had bizarre nightmares because of the altered state she was in, but she only felt some of the pain while they were bathing and changing her bandages. Because of the infections she acquired in the Romanian hospital she was in, the German surgeons had to amputate her index and middle fingers. Even if she often jokes about her handicap, I've seen her hiding her hand in her sleeve when she's overwhelmed. Maybe it's not the missing limbs that hurt her so, but the fact that she feels less whole overall. Sometimes she doesn't want strangers to see the inner void left behind by all of this. Her stumps are testimonies of fire and death. They tell onlookers a terrible story that she doesn't want to utter, that she'd rather forget.

She's holding Iris's hand and they haven't touched the food on their plates. I sit next to them, unsure whether to ask what happened. I give up when I see how sad they both are. My eyes well up with tears. I stay quiet because I know how useless questions are in such moments.

"I dreamed of Theo last night," Iris whispers.

Her voice quivers when she says her boyfriend's name. He died on the night of October 30th. They were together, and then, suddenly, they were apart, and she fainted. She doesn't know who pulled her out of the club. Those few minutes when her body broke down and she lost him haunt her like a mystery that could have meant something, had it been solved on time. Even though she couldn't keep her eyes open when the smoke choked her and the fire burned her skin, she's tormented by the thought that maybe things would have ended differently had she managed to stay conscious. After the catastrophe in the ward we shared, for a long time Iris couldn't stop vomiting ashes. She cried and heaved all the darkness that had gathered inside her into a dirty metal tray. She wanted to get rid of the cinders so badly. She wanted to cleanse the evil that had been done to her.

"He was laughing. He was so handsome... I miss him so much..."

She grabs a napkin from the table and tries to wipe her tears away, with clumsy gestures that her hands are yet to relearn. She's far from healed herself. The little finger on her left is perpetually bent in her palm, suffering from what is called a boutonniere deformity, the same thing I have, but on my index finger. Her thick and hard scars force it into that unnatural position because they're stuck to her tendons. It's as if it's caught in a vise. The surgery that Doctor Moldovan and Doctor Preda performed on her didn't bring any relief. On the contrary, it worsened her condition. When the therapists here try to straighten her finger, she screams and frees herself, but the pain she's experiencing now is not physical. There is no physiotherapy for the heart, no exercises, no splints, and when it hurts, it hurts without relief.

Neither one of us can say anything meaningful to her. There are no words capable of bringing any real comfort. We stroke her back while she stifles her sighs. The rest of the patients look at us with sympathy. Most of them already know our story. Some even shared theirs, but they stayed quiet when we told them about bath-time, about how they washed us without giving us any painkillers, about the communal wards with ordinary beds, and about the infections they hid on purpose, letting so many of us die, devoured by multidrug-resistant germs. We get up, one at a time, from the table and go to the buffet to fill our plates. We're not hungry, but we must eat something. We spend the rest of the time allotted for breakfast consoling Iris, careful not to bring our own ghosts into the discussion, walking around them gingerly, like prisoners who have just escaped and are afraid to wake up the cruel guards.

The tears eventually dry and we just sit there, around Iris, holding each other's mutilated hands. With missing fingers or deformed ones, we touch our souls. They're not whole either. The cantina personnel notice our sadness. To cheer us up, K. brings us a tray filled with fresh fruit, cut in tiny pieces, especially for us. She comforts us as best as she can, by showing us that she cares and that she's seen the hurt that plagues us. Such a gesture of kindness means the world when you're on the edge of a gaping crevice, incapable of looking away. The starving eyes of nightmares stare back at you. And so do those of longing.

Sandra is the first one to leave. She has therapy scheduled at 8:00 A.M. The bruise left behind by the UVM device Frau H. uses to detach the sick skin grafts from the muscle underneath, so as to allow her body to move freely, is still showing on her neck. After the mechanical massage sessions, her body is speckled with purple and red. The superficial blood vessels in the scar tissue, still young and fragile, break when the device grabs the stuck skin, trying to release what lies under it. There is no other cure for such severe sequelae, and even though she's always offered strong painkillers here, she doesn't take them. She's used to far worse pain. Compared to bath-time, the procedures we're undergoing here are nothing, no matter how intense they are. I often meet her in the hallway, while I'm waiting my turn. She walks out of the ward, pale and shaking but with a smile on her face. She tells me she's going to her room to take a nap.

"Dozing off is my favorite painkiller, and since I can actually sleep here, I'm going to take advantage of it."

There was no rest for us at the Hospital for Burns. We used to spend our nights awake, feverish, and in pain, counting our beloved dead, devastated by the rot that was eating us inside out. The hidden decay they told us didn't exist. I don't tell the girls about the dreams I'm having. The small talk during breakfast is far better than what I'd have to say. We eat and chat until it's time for us to go to our scheduled therapies. The morning starts with a medicinal bath, followed by a scar massage for me. Iris and Anda are going to see their physiotherapists. What's the point of bringing up the sad chimeras that my mind conjures up from the darkness left behind inside me by the fire? I shroud the shadows in quietness and choose to talk about my days as a rock magazine editor instead, telling them funny stories, and listening to their own. Sometimes the change of topic is a success. Other times, a heavy silence falls between us, and nothing can lift it, not when we know that behind the eyes that look into our own, the fire has started to burn again.

I sit down on one of the cushioned chairs in front of the bathing ward. While I wait my turn, I examine the clean, freshly painted walls of the Manual Therapies Department. Everything looks neat, even though the clinic was built over two decades ago. Each year, an ample renovation takes place. The equipment is renewed, the rooms are sanitized, and the flooring is replaced. Opportunistic bacteria don't stand a chance here. Hygiene and prevention are sacred. Frau B. opens the door and invites me in. She's wearing single-use gloves because she just washed and disinfected the tub. It sparkles with cleanliness, as it awaits me, billowing with warm, nicely scented water. The nurse explains that I have to lie in the tub, allowing the hydrating substances she poured in to cover all my scars. They'll moisturize and soften the thick and rigid plaques, which will make the massage seem gentler. She sets the timer for fifteen minutes and leaves the room to give me privacy. I take my clothes off and, when I'm done, a sense of horror takes hold of me while I look at the immaculate whiteness of the tub.

I'm naked and alone in the room and I feel deeply vulnerable. Memories of strangers ripping the oozing bandages from my deep wounds in a different tub, worn and made from green rubber, gather in my mind, clouding my judgment. How I bled when the hard spray tore through my exposed muscles and tendons. How I cried because of that nameless pain, mad because of the agony, begging for painkillers that they refused to give me. The drain swallowed the red streams that poured from me, together with pieces of my ruined body: dead skin grafts that came right off, like sick lace dropping from an ancient dress, like flesh falling from a cadaver. The blue surgical threads surrounded them like wry halos, holding nothing in place. The stinging pierced through me, hollowing me. I felt like I was burning, just like I did in the container. Every day, again and again, at bath-time, I relived the experience of catching fire, devoured by the relentless water. Absurdly, cruelly, the blistering pain kept coming back, stuck on a loop, forever, and I thought I never actually made it out of the club. That I was stuck inside, smoldering, decaying. If it hadn't felt so real, so torturous, I'd have thought I died and went to hell.

Billy Idol's *Sweet Sixteen* starts playing on the radio. The song wakes me up from the nightmare that, for a moment, pulled me out of the German clinic and threw me inside the Hospital for Burns, at bath-time, and, as a finishing touch, trundled me through the hot ash in the club's container. I'm shaking because of the panic I feel. I have to lean on the edge of the tub to avoid falling. With difficulty, I climb in, nauseous, afraid. The water is warm and soft, and it ripples around me, surrounding me, like in an embrace. It isn't harsh and cold. It doesn't smell like burned flesh. It doesn't sting. I close my eyes and do the breathing exercises that the psychologist showed me. She calls these experiences PTSD – post-traumatic stress disorder, but for me they're just trips back in time. The four letters describe my journeys to a dark world that still exists somewhere inside me, as if the fire hadn't been extinguished, as if it was still there, burning, waiting for me. Maybe it won't get me today, but who knows if I've really escaped?

I take a deep breath and start humming the song, latching onto the lyrics like I would onto a rope that pulls me away from the horror and helps me tie myself to reality, one where the water doesn't hurt, and the flames are too far away to reach me. The alarm on the timer goes off, letting me know that my fifteen minutes are up. I put my clothes on hastily, say goodbye to the nurse as she walks in, and leave with my head low. I don't want her to notice the lingering terror in my eyes.

S. waits for me in the massage ward and greets me with unfeigned joy. I say hi and go right in, lying on my tummy, as always. She puts on her gloves and asks me how I'm feeling today. Would I like an analgesic before we start? I thank her, but it won't be necessary. I don't know if something broke inside me at the Hospital for Burns, but no pain seems great when I compare it to the torture I endured in the green tub. For a moment, I feel like telling her about the dream I had last night, about the tears Iris cried this morning, about the panic that took hold of me just before, during the medicinal bath. I change my mind. The therapist would listen carefully, and then she'd try to comfort me. She'd encourage me to stop looking back, to move forward. I'd approve, of course, and thank her because that's the right thing to do. I'd hide my fear that the future, at least the one I imagined for myself, doesn't exist anymore. There's a gaping void lying it its place, and it's so dark and shapeless that it can easily be confused with nothingness.

I choose to blather on about how beautiful the park is. I've explored it the past couple of days and it's enchanting. She starts the UVM device while I talk. She picks the medium head for the procedure, installs it, and selects the intensity with which the machine will detach the adhesions formed underneath the burn scars. She asks me if she can start. I approve, and I feel the weight of the robot on my back. She moves it over my body, while the head grabs the thick, clinging scars, lifting, and twisting them, to soften them. They're stuck to the muscles, tendons, and bones, and they have to be dislodged so that I can recover at least some of my mobility. The machine breaks the insides of the tissue, tearing apart the sick structures that have grown over my shoulder blades, spine, shoulders, and fingers, stretching like the tentacles of an evil octopus made from my own flesh. S. senses when I become tense because of the pain, so she lowers the intensity of the massage. Every once in a while, she stops and asks me if I'm all right, making sure I can go through with the procedure. "Shut up and take it!" isn't a thing here.

I think about Sandra's pale face and the purple bruises on her body. I think I'll take a nap myself afterwards. Forty minutes later, I'm done. I'm exhausted, but it was worth it, and S. congratulates me for my bravery. Like a caring friend, she helps me put my clothes on. She reminds me of my sister in a way. They have the same smile. I feel homesick now. I thank her and go back to my room to rest until it's time for my next therapy.

My body begs me for a reprieve, so I doze off. I wake up dizzy. It's time for the coordination gymnastics class and I have to put on my sports clothes. After the UVM massage, the scars keep "working" all day, as they say here, and the discomfort created by the inflammation is significant. I fight with the desire to lie back down in bed and manage to conquer it. In the sports hall on the ground floor of the clinic, the therapist, the other patients, and the girls are already waiting for me.

Today, we'll play with medicinal balls and get to know one another better. There's around ten of us in the room. Some people were injured in grilling accidents, others at work. One of them, a young man called L., was hurt in December. Even though his entire body is covered in grafts, his new skin is smooth, and his fingers, whole and straight, move and bend freely. The girls noticed too, and we take turns gawking at him, amazed, trying not to be rude. We're troubled by the same thoughts. If we hadn't caught the infections, if the conditions in the Romanian hospitals had been adequate, we too would have looked and felt better.

We're asked to form groups of two and the therapist, Herr K., explains the rules of the game. My teammate is a nice German lady, slightly older than the rest of the patients. When she throws me the ball, I try to move my arms forward to catch it, but the stiffness is so intense, I can't do it. The ball drops at my feet untouched, and I look at it, helpless. It's the first time I've tried to do anything remotely sporty since the fire, and the exercise reveals how disabled I actually am. The scars on my back climb from my lumbar region, up my shoulder blades, then descend to my shoulders and arms, forming a unified shield, only broken apart by a streak of healthy skin in the middle, where the strap of my bag protected me from the flames. They form a compact mass, like a rigid armor. The flesh doesn't stretch at all, and because of that, my arms can't move forward as they should. Even though it hurts, I pick the ball up and throw it back to my teammate, biting my lips. The scars burn under my clothes, and they swell with each movement I make, but I don't give up. 45 minutes later, wet with sweat, even though I'm overwhelmed by the stinging and the itching, I'm happy. I did it! Herr K. asks us if we're all right, as the therapists here always do, caring genuinely about our problems. We chat for a while, and then it's time for lunch.

The girls join me, and we leave together for the cantina. On our way there, we talk about the difficulties we faced during the gymnastics class. Sandra is holding her left hand with her right, resting it against her tummy. The thick and rigid compression glove has turned the tips of her fingers blue, and they're pulsating under the pressure. Pieces of gauze stick out from under the fabric, covering the voids where her nails used to be. I remember her pale face and teary eyes, while she told us, back in November at the Hospital for Burns, that they might amputate her hand. Her doctor – one of the exceptionals – fought until the end to save her limb, and he succeeded. Now, she has to move it constantly, work it, so that the tight, stuck grafts don't destroy her tendons, already invaded by adhesions.

"Does it hurt?"

"Oh, yes, but I'm used to it. It'll go away after I eat."

She jokes about it, just like we all do when we don't want our suffering to become contagious. When we arrive at our table, we notice that the vacant chair is now occupied by L., the boy in the gymnastics class. We introduce ourselves and he confesses that he's happy to share *Tisch Zehn*[4] with us. We talk about our injuries and how we got them, and he gives us a chilling account of his accident, which occurred on Christmas Eve. At one point, he tried to extinguish himself in the tub, but his burning flesh melted the shower head. He recounts the weeks he spent in a medically induced coma and tells us about the synthetic skin that the surgeons covered his burns with to help him heal faster. He tells us about his sterile ward, that only the doctors and nurses were allowed into, wearing special, single-use gear. While he speaks, his curious eyes wander over the odd-looking lacing of our scars, strange and swollen, unlike his. He asks us why they're so thick and inflamed and if there's something different about our injuries. It's our turn, so we tell him about the chaos in the Romanian hospitals, about the lack of hygiene, the common wards, the HAIs, and bath-time without anesthesia. The last part appalls him, and he explains, in a warm voice, that analgesia is sacred in Germany. The doctors do all they can to soothe the patients.

"They think that the shock of the pain can kill a burn victim. That's why they're so careful. I was in pain myself, but later, after they woke me up from the coma. I don't think I would have survived if I had to endure the first few days awake."

We, however, did endure everything awake the first few days, and then the rest that came. I know I'm wrong to do this, but I can't help myself from describing, in atrocious detail, how we were tortured in the green tub, screaming while the streams of red, bloody water, ran down the drain, until pieces of our rotting flesh clogged it, falling from us like they would off a cadaver. The harsh spray over our open wounds, penetrating through the muscles and the tendons, reaching the

---

[4] Table number 10, in German.

bone. I talk slowly, pressing the words in, as if I'm etching them upon stone. I talk about that nameless pain that's forever engraved on each one of our cells. I'm sorry I'm doing this to him, to us, to myself, but I think he must know. Everyone must know what was done to us. Maybe that way, they won't do it to someone else. I shut up after a few minutes, ashamed of myself, staring at my hands. I've gone to Hell again, and this time I took hostages. My scars are an ugly color, a shade of bruised violet that makes the crooked, fibrous skin look fake, like that of a wax figure from a museum of horrors. There's a wide dip in the middle of my right hand, where they made the decompression incision, slicing the flesh open so that it wouldn't burst. They couldn't sew it shut, so they just put a graft over it, which kept dying and being replaced, in an endless cycle of improvisations. I examine every centimeter of skin intently, absorbed. Because I can't raise my eyes and look at my friends. That's what we all do when something burns inside our soul. We've become the children who stare at their hands when they want to escape reality. But we can't. Our scars are here to remind us that what happened was real.

There's a heaviness in the air that can't be lifted. Our spoons make a monotonous noise in the soup bowl, mixing the hot liquid to and fro, like we're trying to create small maelstroms that can sink and drown our thoughts. Sandra clears her throat and starts talking, freeing us from the burden.

"How about we meet up tonight, after our therapy sessions, and go to the park? There's a bench with a nice table near the forest where we can sit. We can get a bottle of Coke from the cafeteria and enjoy it together. It's the 13ᵗʰ of May and I'd like to honor Mihai somehow."

We accept her invitation. Sandra's voice quivers when she mentions Mishoo, as his friends used to call him. He and his girlfriend, Cătălina, died together, the night we burned alive. He was Sandra's professor at the Architecture University, but more than anything, he was a dear friend. In a different world, a fair one, today would have been his birthday and he'd have turned 37. But in this one, all we have is the memories. Lunch ends and we must return to our therapies. Our minds are scattered, and our souls are in ashes.

B., my kinesiotherapist, has beautiful red hair and steel-blue eyes. She's made a mission out of fixing my crooked index finger. By now, it's completely bent in the palm of my hand because of the damaged tendons and the negligence of the

Romanian doctors. I've nicknamed it "the atomic sausage" and the German trans-lation, *das atomische Wurst*, amuses B. who, just like S., talks to me during our sessions, to keep my mind off the pain. I sweat and become nauseous because of it. I rest my head on the table and, when I feel like it's too much, I ask her to stop. She pats my shoulder and comforts me.

"Finger schmerzen gehen zum Herzen."

It means that finger aches are so bad, they go directly to the heart. We do breathing exercises together and start over, working until the forty minutes are up. She engineered a silicone splint for my finger, and she helps me put it on, fixing the finger in a more anatomically correct position. She asks me to keep it on for as long as I can. I promise I will, hug her, and we say goodbye, because it's time for my gym class. Herr O. and Frau F. are already waiting for me. They design a workout regime that will help me gain back the muscle mass I lost the past few months. Even though I'm too weak to commit to it fully, I find the weight exer-cises refreshing. For an hour, I don't have to think about anything else and I can enjoy the pleasant atmosphere in the gym. There are many severely ill people here, seeking healing, but the warmth and professionalism with which they're handled gives me hope instead of depressing me. Later, during the one-on-one physiother-apy session, Herr M. manipulates my limbs, bending and stretching them, stimu-lating the body so that it can learn to move wholesomely again. He's one of the nicest therapists and working with him is always great.

I really don't feel like seeing the psychologist today... I know I need to, but I'd like to skip this session. Actually, I think I'd gladly skip all the sessions. When I'm there, in the room, the pain shapeshifts and becomes things that I'm afraid of. Monsters are born out of my words and then, long after I've said them, they come back to haunt me. Sometimes, I wish I could just stay quiet about what troubles me. Maybe if I stopped voicing my ghosts out, they'd go away. They'd stop ap-pearing at the edge of my consciousness, with their ash-stained faces and peeling, burned skin. But if I shut up about it all, if I don't speak anymore, the nightmares become more frequent, and they get worse. I'm grateful to my therapist for not digging inside me for horrors. She lets me unearth them on my own, at a pace that works for me, according to which scares me the most. Another hour has run its course and I'm finally done for the day.

I go back to my room, take a shower, apply the medicinal creams, and put my compression garments on. My stiff and hard scars have been modeled, like clay sculptures, all day by the diligent hands of the therapists. Swollen and aching, they pulsate under the tight fabric, until all I can feel is a deep, rending throbbing. The pain becomes more intense by the minute, but I must resist the temptation to lie down. I promised the girls I'd meet them in the park in the evening and I use my commitment as motivation to conquer the hurt. My back and my left shoulder torment me the most. The feeling of laceration coming from inside of the congested tissue is shrill, restless, as if something was alive underneath the thick cuirass of my scars, some sort of merciless beast that wants to claw its way out of me. I wring and grab the smoldering flesh continuously, massaging it, tearing at it, in an attempt to bring myself some relief, but to no avail.

The itching that accompanies the pain is well known by burn victims and their therapists. Many patients take antihistamine drugs because they attenuate the pruritus and help them wind down. Sometimes, I can't bear it anymore and I remove my compression garments and throw them on the floor. Some nights, it's as if I'm locked in a cage made from synthetic fiber, and a feeling of suffocation comes over me. I must endure this for another 18 months, 23 hours a day. There's nothing I can do about it. I must heed the doctors' advice.

In the end, it's a miracle that I'm alive and a blessing that I'm here, at the M. Klinik, where there are no green rubber tubs or people who lie to hide a murderous truth. Every Monday, bath-time started again at the Hospital for Burns, after pausing during the weekend. By Sunday evening, Flavia and I were inconsolable. The loved ones who cared for us in the hospital told us that we always became sad, morose. The terror we felt at the thought of the inhumane procedure we were condemned to endure just a few hours later sealed our lips. When our parents went home, they took some of the horror with them. We gave it to them, like an infectious disease passing from one person to the other. Near dawn, fear turned into panic. When the nurse walked into the ward at 6:00 A.M. sharp, Flavia pretended to sleep, shaking and shivering under the thin, worn-out duvet.

And I... I cried. I cried to stay alive. I cried every day we had bath-time, before the procedure, out of fear, during the procedure, because of the unbearable pain. The tears fell down on my wounds, helping me stay whole inside while the water swallowed parts of my ruined flesh and scorched soul, devoured both by the multidrug-resistant germs lurking in every corner, on every surface of the hospital. The tears and Alina's voice, humming forgotten lullabies amidst sighs and screams. She didn't want to hurt me. She wanted to wash me so that I would heal. She didn't understand that, with each bath, the person I was before the fire faded and was replaced by someone else. A ghost, trapped in a decaying body, with a heavy heart that struggled to understand why people lie instead of saving. I still think about bath time every Monday.

The image of the bloody water haunts me. With 400 milligrams of Ketoprofen in my veins, and nothing else, I experienced the agony and the humiliation fully lucid, awake to an extent I had never been before, with every centimeter of my exposed nerves aware of the lacerating water and harsh words. I saw my body rotting, dying, with eyes wide-open, deprived of any form of sedation that could have alleviated at least some of the hurt. I felt an entire bestiary of pains each day, so diverse in their horror, it was hard to believe they were real. But they were because I felt them all, sober. Appallingly sober. At the end of each day, I closed my eyes and prayed to God. I begged him to help me survive another night, so that my mother and my sister wouldn't have to bury me like that, in dirty, oozing dressings, in the infected attire of the Hospital for Burns. With a disfigured face stuck forever in an expression of terror. With stiff hands clawing at the sullied sheets. In the "underpants" the orderly made for me from gauze to cover my shame, to hide the dirty wounds on my thighs, worsened by the diapers they let us fester in. We filled them with the rest of the countless antibiotic IVs they gave us, "prophylactically," because we were "sterile." They'd have to close the casket, I used to tell myself. This would be their last image of me. Their little girl, a decaying corpse before she was even dead. Please, God. Help me live.

I hear a knock on the door, and I come to. These jumps in time have been happening more often lately. My life is a sequence of interruptions and every fracture in the present means a return to the container or to the Hospital for Burns. I fight to stay here, at the clinic, where I was given a second chance at life. Sandra walks in gingerly and she sits on the chair next to my bed. She's come to take me to the park.

"Are you OK?"

"Yes, don't worry."

The empty table, surrounded by benches, is waiting for us at the edge of the forest. We spread our goodies all over it, starting with the Coke, fruit juices, sweets, and chips we bought from the cafeteria. The cashier opened the bottles for us because we couldn't have done it ourselves, with our mutilated, weak hands. It takes a while for the shyness to subside, allowing the conversation to flow naturally. We're not used to L. being around yet. He breaks the ice by talking about his rap band. He's very passionate about music and he admits he used to be a metalhead. We tell him about Goodbye to Gravity and play a few songs on our mobile phones. He loves them!

"These guys rock!"

He smiles, and we're delighted, but then it dawns on us. They used to rock, actually. Not anymore. When he finds out what happened, he sighs, saddened.

"Did they really die like that? On stage?"

"Yes. And then they perished, one by one, in the hospitals."

"Let's honor Mihai!" Sandra says. "Had he survived, today would have been his birthday. I find it so strange that, no matter what I do, no matter where I go, I'll never see him again. I still have his number. Sometimes I feel like calling him. Maybe he'd answer and tell me that he's OK, that he can't wait to catch up, that all of this was just a nightmare. It's absurd, I know, but I can't control myself."

With tears in her eyes, she fills a plastic glass with Coke and pours some on the ground.

"This is for you, Mishoo. And for all the rest. Happy birthday, dearest!"

We imitate her and take a sip of our soda. We're falling apart. L. looks at us and sighs. He can't fully understand our suffering, but he tries.

The rest of the evening is peaceful. We finish our snacks, and we empty the soda bottles. We clean the table and throw away the leftovers. Before we go back to our rooms, we watch the sunset. The sky is painted in a magical shade of pink. It's surreal how clear it is. The pale specter of the moon embellishes the vault where it's still blue. She's too weak to conquer it all yet, not while the sun is still fighting the coming of night, in a battle he's set to lose forever. The greenness of the forest and the elaborately winded branches, projected against the cloudless firmament, make the landscape seem unreal, as if copied from one of Caspar David Friedrich's paintings. I've traveled to one of the worlds he's brought to life, and the strokes of his brush leave traces upon my heart.

"Maybe they're watching us from above, happy that we're doing better," Sandra whispers, noticing how lost I am in contemplating the horizon.

Beyond the edge of the summit, where the sky turns into Heaven, our world ends, and theirs begins.

"Yes. I think so too."

We go back to our wards, with traces of the sunset in our heavy hearts. The schedule for tomorrow waits for me in the mailbox allotted to my room. It's filled with therapy sessions and classes, some of which are new. I also have an appointment with a surgeon, Doctor S., from the hospital in H. My hands begin to shake, but I calm myself down, reassuring myself that everything is all right, I'm safe here, and there's no reason to be afraid of him. Nothing can be worse than Doctor Moldovan, Silvia, or Pavel.

Professor S. is a middle-aged man, of an imposing stature. He's wearing a colorful bow that makes his otherwise somber outfit look more cheerful. His English is perfect, and his manners are impeccable. He consults me attentively, careful not to inflict pain. He's concerned about the state of my left shoulder and right index finger.

"Complex reconstructive surgery is needed to adequately address the seriousness of your case, but don't worry. We're highly trained. The shoulder and back have suffered massive damage, with major sequelae. Personally, I think that only full-thickness transplantation, either with skin substitutes or your own tissue, would eliminate the increased risk of malignity that comes with such scarring. As for the finger, I'm thinking either a joint prosthesis or an arthrodesis, which involves fixing it in an anatomical position. We'll treat the rest of your scars using a new procedure called surgical needling that is similar to laser therapy."

He is patient with me and answers all my questions. I agree to the suggested surgeries, and he tells me his team will schedule them for September. First, they'll straighten my index finger, remove some of the scars on my scalp, and perform the surgical needling over the rest of my body. Then, they'll gradually address the rest of my issues.

"Doctor, why do I look so bad compared to the German patients?"

"Because of the infections that resulted in multiple regrafting procedures done in the acute care phase. The bacteria don't allow the wounds to heal, they consume the transplanted skin, and the body reacts by creating new cells chaotically, desperate to cover the open sores, which are very dangerous. Sadly, the tissue resulting from such a pathological process isn't healthy. Normally, you're not allowed to graft healthy skin on an infected wound bed."

He doesn't say anything derogatory about the doctors or the medical act. He doesn't want to be unprofessional. Even so, he makes it clear why I'm in this situation, and once again, it's not my fault at all. After we finish, it's Sandra's turn to see him, then Anda's, and last in line is Iris. When we're all done, we meet up and talk about the future and what awaits us in the operating room. We promise that we'll be by each other's side and that we'll overcome everything with the help of our friendship.

The weeks pass quickly at the burn rehab clinic in Germany. Because of the intensive treatment regimen, we make a lot of progress. When I arrived here, I wasn't capable of being independent. Now, I manage fairly well with house chores, and I was very pleased when I washed my clothes all by myself, for the first time in months. I can also dress without help and tying my shoelaces is no longer the most difficult thing in the world. I use my left hand for almost everything I used to do with my right, and, as a result, the former has become stronger, to compensate for the deficit. Soon, we'll have to go back to Romania. I can't wait to see my loved ones, but it's going to be hard to say goodbye to the therapists. We've become close these past few months, and I'm very grateful to them for their dedication. I comfort myself with the thought that I'll have to return to M. Klinik in the fall, with the girls, for my surgeries and for another round of therapy. I'm nervous. I don't know how many reconstructive operations I'll need in the end.

After my last massage session with S., we both cry. She's the one I'm most attached to. With her talented hands, she's sculpted my flesh like an artist of healing.

"Alex, don't you dare hate your body! Your scars are signs of your immense inner power."

She tells me this because she knows how hard it is for a burn victim to accept that, whenever they'll look in the mirror, they'll relive the tragedy that maimed them. Because of her, I learned to love these smoldering designs, the prints left behind on my skin by the deadly touch of Hell. I made peace with the fact that they're a part of me, that this is my body now. The scars are not enemies that have to be destroyed at any cost. They're testaments of my resilience. Even if she was a stranger to me at first, S. showed me that beauty can still exist in a body marked with bizarre patterns, drawn upon it by the hands of fire and darkness. And by doing this, she became a friend like no other, she created a bond that can never be broken.

"See you when you come back in autumn, all right?"

She hugs me and wishes me *alles Liebe*, which means "all the love" in German. I say goodbye to the other therapists as well. Today's therapy sessions are filled with melancholy. The people here have become my guides on the long road back to normality. They're aware of the major role they play in the lives of their patients, and they give their best to help them, even beyond what the job requires of them. Every single one of them has left a piece of their knowledge inside me, in the movements I can now make, in the skills I've acquired since I came here, and, more than anything, in the trust I now have in other human beings. My physical recovery isn't the only crucial experience I've had at the M. Klinik. Learning to live again, to make friends, and to have faith in people are just as important to my healing as the therapy sessions. Here, I gained back some of my inner strength, and I feel like I'm better equipped to deal with the hardships and cruelty of what awaits me beyond this haven.

The last person I say goodbye to is Doctor Z. Before he discharges me, we have one final appointment. He examines my scars, takes notes of my progress, and hands me my medical papers. He gives me a stick with all the photos he took of me during my stay at the clinic. I smile and thank him. He doesn't have anything to hide.

"It was a pleasure to have you and the others as my patients. I'll be waiting for you to come back in the fall."

We shake hands and, after he wishes me well, he insists that I should try to continue at least some of the procedures at home, in Romania. I sigh and tell him that I'll look into it. In Germany, there are specialized clinics that offer outpatient physical rehabilitation services for burn victims. In our country, this is out of the question.

Adi is already waiting for me in front of the clinic. After I hand over the keys to my room, the receptionists hug me, telling me how happy they are that I'm doing better. I walk out into the courtyard and sadness overwhelms me. It's like I'm leaving home. After the fire, M. Klinik was the first place where I really felt that life can go on. I hope I won't lose the progress I've made because of a lack of treatment.

In Romania, nothing has changed. We're still on our own. Because I'm so stressed about finding a clinic where I can receive at least some physical therapy, the first couple of weeks pass quickly. I can't go back to Elias Hospital, that's for sure. Professor Ionescu summoned me to his office a few days ago for a check-up. He examined me from head to toe and concluded, rather disappointed, that things are looking good. However, he thinks I'd have benefitted even more if I hadn't given up on what he calls "electrotherapy."

"These folks from Western Europe are not as good as they think. We, on the other hand, have a lot of great devices here."

I stared at him, bewildered because I remembered the broken laser that would only start if the nurse slapped it repeatedly. The entire floor could hear the machine's jolting and hitching when it was brought to a patient or taken back to its storage place. There's no comparison between the equipment at the German clinic and what they have here, but I don't say anything. I don't want to offend the professor. I'm starting to think that maybe, so as not to go mad because of everything they're lacking, some people delude themselves into thinking they "have everything they need". In Professor Ionescu's case, I don't believe he's ill-intentioned or a liar, like Doctors Moldovan, Preda, and Pavel. Rather, he's the victim of his own elaborate, arrogant, and pathological illusion, which allows him to keep working in an impoverished, corrupted environment without losing his mind completely.

"You told me there was no room for me here anymore. Where was I supposed to continue the electrotherapy sessions?"

"As far as I'm concerned, we did everything humanly possible for you. We don't have any means to support you any longer. Anyway, it seems to me like you found a solution, right?"

After I left his ward, I put an end to the Elias chapter forever. It was clear to me that there was no going back. That part of my rehabilitation story was over. With the help of Flavia, I got an appointment at the Military Hospital. Mrs. C., the only therapist in Romania who still treats burn victims from the Colectiv Club fire, agreed to help me, even if she's exhausted. In a small and modest room, surrounded by worn-out physical therapy devices, Mrs. C. treats us and all the other patients in the hospital. We wait our turn patiently. Her hands are light, and I can tell that she loves her job. She massages my scars carefully, with genuine talent. She is discrete, gentle, and she does her best to allot as much time as possible to every single one of us, but she can't work for more than thirty minutes on each. She wouldn't be able to care for the others, who have not been burned but need her too. We understand the situation and don't demand more attention, even though we'd benefit from it. Resigned, we're happy with the healing an *exceptional* can provide, in a crooked system that doesn't show us – or her – any mercy. I ask her what happened to the other therapists who received training in Belgium. She doesn't know either. The months leading up to my second departure to Germany are spent like this, traveling from one corner of Bucharest to the other, in the scorching summer heat, in search of some relief. It's over 100 degrees Fahrenheit and I must take crowded buses, without any air conditioning, dressed in the thick and tight compression garments, to ride forty or fifty minutes to the hospital. My scars are boiling underneath the rigid fabric, and my face turns red while I get sicker and sicker, about to pass out. But I don't. I push through, clenching my teeth. I have to do this. I have to go, otherwise, I might lose some of the progress I made.

On my last day, Mrs. C. hugs me and wishes me good luck and much health. I look around at the tens of patients waiting for her care. Her tired eyes are surrounded by dark circles. She's just another victim of Romania, my beloved country, so overwhelmed by injustice. Even though she encourages me to return to her when I come back from Germany, I know she can't give me what I need. It's not because she's not capable. Rather, she's not given the necessary means. She's on her own, and a burn victim needs a multidisciplinary team. Like every *exceptional* out there, every day she fights alone against something bigger than her, and I hope that the system won't beat her one day. After we say goodbye, I'm convinced that this is the last time I'll see her as my therapist. There's no room left for me here either.

Sandra, Iris, Anda, and I travel back to Germany in September. Our first stop is at the hospital in H., where they have a big plastic and reconstructive surgery department. Professor S. scheduled five initial surgeries, which will take place at a distance of a few weeks. Sandra and I planned our stay together, so we're going to share the same ward. After we move in, we wait for Doctor K., our surgeon, to call us. He's a somber man who doesn't enjoy small talk, but he's also very kind. He sees us both in his consultation room and assesses the state of our scars. Paying special attention to my index finger, he makes sure to examine me thoroughly, so as not to miss something. After he's done, he leans against his study and looks at me, pensively. I ask him if I'll ever be able to bend the finger, and he shakes his head, disappointed.

"I don't want to scare you, but I can't lie to you either. Your finger is in very bad shape. I'll try to fix it in an anatomical position by using a technique called arthrodesis, but you must prepare yourself psychologically for the possibility of an amputation. Normally, you should have had surgery on it a long time ago, perhaps while you were still in acute care. It's quite late, but I'll try to save it."

His words take me by surprise. I sit down and force myself not to cry. "Normally, you should have had surgery a long time ago." Yes, just like Sandra had on her fingers. But who could have done that for me? My surgeons? They didn't know or care enough to get involved.

Doctor K. asks me if I'm all right with letting the medical students see me. H. is a university hospital and one of its purposes is to educate the new generation of physicians. I'm an interesting case and the surgeon thinks that examining me could benefit the residents. I accept being evaluated by them because I want as many people as possible to assess me so that everybody can see what happens when doctors lie that they "have everything they need." Using my scars as an example, the surgeon explains why the hypertrophic process occurs and gives insights into the negative consequences of acquiring multidrug-resistant bacteria. Here, the patients rarely end up having such ill-looking scars, mainly because their burns are not devoured by germs.

I return to the ward exhausted. I tell Sandra that this might be my last day with the "atomic sausage." I now understand her desperation at the thought of losing her limbs. I think about Anda and her missing index and middle fingers. God, the suffering we have to endure because of the negligence of the Romanian hospitals... Sandra sits next to me on the bed and puts her arm around me to comfort me. We stand there, staring out the window at the other wing of the hospital. The building is modern and stately. It's nothing like the ones back at home.

I turn around and look at the clean, modern beds equipped with remote controls to adjust their position. My mind runs in parallel to the memories of boxes filled with saline drip flasks that Felicia used to shove under the backs of our mattresses, to raise or lower our broken bodies. At the end of one of the bed's arms, there's a small tablet that can be connected to the wireless network in the hospital. We can watch TV on it or listen to the radio. As for the food, we can choose it ourselves from the big menu card. I'm used to the crackers with cheese or the sausages, served directly in a plastic bag, that they used to feed us at the Hospital for Burns. I'm amazed to see such a variety of dishes. H. isn't even a private hospital. It's a public one, without any preferential conditions. What I'm witnessing here isn't something special, it's simply normal, although, for me, it's exceptional. I have flashbacks of the cruelty and rudeness I endured at home, with things that happened during bath-time, like when the anesthesiologist accidentally walked in on my naked, emaciated body, eaten alive by infections, lying with wide-open wounds in a dirty rubber tub, and laughed at me, saying: "My God, aren't you a sack of bones!" It dawns on me that the sufferings I endured there were forms of abuse, torture disguised as procedures, hidden from prying eyes behind the tall walls of a place of healing. In reality, they hosted Hell itself.

For months on end, the inhumane treatments I was subjected to were advertised as normal. I was the crazy one for questioning them. "This is what burn care looks like everywhere in the world!" But no, it wasn't like that at all. In truth, what was being done to us was a sinister aberration, a corruption of all good practices. The real extent of the lie I fell prey to was revealed to me only when I left that place and came here. Once I understood that I was victimized on purpose, something broke inside me, and I don't think it will ever mend. The chance at decent care was denied to me in a deliberate, premeditated manner, by the people I trusted the most – those in medical uniform. I believed in them, not knowing that they were actually just the buffoons of the system, the lackeys of a monster that didn't care if we'd suffer and die as long as it kept the appearance of efficiency and capability. Those were concentration-camp hospitals, and we didn't realize that we weren't patients: we were prisoners.

One day, at the Hospital for Burns, a few surgeons from Germany came to see us. They wanted to help, but after they spoke to Silvia and to Dr. Moldovan, they changed their minds. They told us that the burn care protocol is similar to what they offer in their hospital. Yet here no one was washed without anesthesia. No one caught hospital-acquired infections. No one had central venous catheters inserted while they were awake. No one was left to soil themselves while they cried out for help. I'm convinced that they lied to those doctors, just like they lied to us. I'm certain that they had no idea what they were actually doing to us.

The anesthesiologist arrives after lunch and helps us fill out the consent forms. As I read, I stop at the part where they describe the risk of dying as a result of the procedures. I knew there was a chance our hearts would stop each time we went under, but I never saw the consequences explained so clearly, in black and white, on a sheet of paper. A shiver runs down my spine. I escaped the container. I survived the hospital in Romania, but I'm still in danger. I want to recover, so I have to do this. There's no other way than to accept that my life will be, from now on, a sequence of consenting to the possibility of death. I nod my head and pick up the pen. As I scribble my signature on the document, I realize that the countdown of victims of the Colectiv Club fire has not ended. At any point, either one of us can become the next in line.

At 7:00 A.M. the nurse walks in the ward and helps me take a shower. She teaches me how to put on the sterile clothing I'll wear to the O.R. She gives me a light sedative so that I don't feel nervous before the surgery. She changes the sheets and tells me to climb back in bed because they'll take me to surgery on it. An orderly helps her release the breaks on the wheels and I'm whisked away. From my bed, I climb directly onto the operating table. A young female doctor strokes my cheek and talks to me while the anesthesiologist looks for a vein to cannulate. Someone puts an oxygen mask on my face and asks me what I love more: the sea or the mountains. I don't hesitate. The sea! I adore it! He tells me to think about my favorite vacation spot while he counts to ten. Fear overwhelms me, but I know that I'm safe here. Before it turns dark, for the first time, I see waves instead of fire. They're billowing at the shore, and I'm watching them, fascinated. Then everything vanishes.

I open my eyes because of the pain. My right hand is lying in a splint and the thick dressings covering whatever surgical wound lies underneath are stained with blood. Something similar to a helmet made from gauze protects my scalp. They've excised parts of the scars on my head, and the pressure helps keep the sutures in place. A nurse asks if I need analgesics, and I answer that I do, with a faint, exhausted voice. She gives me something right away and I fall asleep. I wake up late at night, to the gentle sound made by the raindrops, patting against the windows. Streaks of artificial light crawl in the ward through the blinds, making odd patterns on the floor. Every once in a while, I hear the helicopter taking off or landing. It's bringing new patients in a critical state to the hospital. I can't move because my whole body hurts as a result of the surgical needling. I sit up with difficulty and press the red button on the remote, panicking. A nurse arrives with a doctor. Still confused after the anesthesia, I ask them if the surgeon amputated my index finger.

"No, no! Not at all! It wasn't an easy procedure, but you still have your finger. Don't be scared, but we also installed a central venous catheter. Your veins are filled with scar tissue as a result of the repeated cannulation you suffered during the acute care phase of your burn injury. We didn't think it was wise to use a regular cannula, so we took advantage of the fact that you were under anesthesia to put the catheter in."

Despite the discomfort I feel, I smile. "I've inserted catheters in pregnant women without anesthetizing them." This is proof that there are different, more humane ways to install the device. I breathe a sigh of relief when I find out that my atomic sausage has survived the surgeon's "attack."

The nurse tells me that it's time to go to the toilet because walking a little will help me recover faster. When I stand up, I feel sick, and I vomit on the floor. Ashamed of myself, I apologize. For a moment, I'm paralyzed with the fear that I'll be admonished for my bad behavior. But the nurse doesn't shout at me. It hasn't even crossed her mind.

"This happens quite often after the anesthesia. I'm the one who should have thought about bringing a tray."

Here, being ill isn't my fault. No one accuses me of rudeness because I did something I had no control over. When she's done cleaning me up, she takes me back to bed and tucks me in. I look at the bandages covering all my body and I feel horror. What do I look like underneath them? I lie down gingerly, so as not to put pressure on the wounds on my scalp. I look out the window again, staring into the night. The rain has turned a rusty color because of the odd shade of the light bulbs in the streetlamps. It's as if the sky is pouring copper over the world. God, how it hurts. But it still doesn't come near the agony in the green tub, at the Hospital for Burns. I compare everything to bath-time. It's become my darkest landmark.

After I while, I hear Sandra's sigh. She's woken up from the anesthesia and she's crying softly in her corner of the ward. I ask her what happened. She's in pain too, but it's not that. She's wailing because she needs some release. She understood that our struggles aren't over and she's having a hard time making peace with the idea. I comfort her as best as I can, but the words get tangled up on my lips and, at some point, I fall back asleep. The helicopter is humming in the distance, carrying precious lives aboard.

The first time I see my index finger, I burst into tears. The surgeon tries to console me. It won't always look like this. The important thing is that he managed to save it and, from now on, things are going to improve. He had to remove the middle joint altogether because it was too damaged. He had to excise it because, otherwise, he'd have had to amputate the entire finger. This way, he avoided a more invasive procedure. I'll have to wear a light splint, made from plastic, for eight weeks. To my surprise, it's actually quite comfortable. It's nothing like the huge, heavy cast they made for me at the Hospital for Burns, or like the metallic blade I used to accidentally cut myself with. Neither is it similar to the black crushing knob Silvia forced over the unhealed cut on my finger. When the nurse removes the dressings from the rest of my scars, I calm down. The scars have been pierced with a roll filled with needles in order to create small wounds in the tissue that will allow it to regenerate. However, I don't have any open cuts, which makes me happy. Everything is clean, albeit swollen and sore. The most discomfort is caused by the sutures on my scalp and the broken and reconstructed bones in the index finger. The analgesics help me endure the pain without falling apart physically and psychologically.

After we're discharged, we return to M. Klinik. The nurses take care of our wounds, sanitize them, change the dressings, and remove the stitches once the surgical sites have healed. We're not infected, so we're not feverish either. The chills, the nausea, the offensive words, and the cruelty are distant memories from our time in the Romanian hospitals. Because the hygiene protocols are sacred here, our surgeries are a success. If something hurts, we can always say so, and help will come right away. Every six weeks, we go in for more surgery. Our sequelae are severe, and the German surgeons are fighting against two enemies: the damages done by the fire, and those resulted from the improvisations and amateurism we fell victim to back home. The irrevocable verdict comes from H. after our fifth round of reconstructive operations.

"Unfortunately, you will need lifelong treatment. The problems you're facing are numerous and complex. We can't repair everything right away. We've done what we can for the moment, but it's not enough by far. If you want to recover and to maintain the progress you've made, you'll have to undergo procedures regularly, for as long as you live."

What I thought was going to be a temporary situation, like brackets in the stories of our lives, turns out to be our new normal. We'll have to get used to being patients forever. The alternative is to give up seeking medical treatment and end up witnessing, helpless, the deterioration of our scars, the loss of everything we've gained, the acquiring of new disabilities, and, ultimately, the development of skin cancer. We can't afford the luxury of being passive when our lives are at stake.

I've already forgotten what I used to look and feel like before the fire. I sometimes remember fragments of days, random moments, like I'm reminiscing about a movie I saw a long time ago, in a time of innocence. A naïve young woman is looking for the meaning of life in this big, careless world. The hazy scenes unfold like they're coming from an old projector, depicting her writing music articles for a rock and roll magazine. There's a spark in her eyes as she does this, a light only passion can ignite. Then I see her doubting herself, doubting her talent, doubting her purpose. And then there's the fire, followed by darkness. I still haven't managed to bridge the chasm between the two of us. I often stare in the mirror and fail to recognize myself. It's not because I look different, with short hair grown chaotically around the scars on my scalp, and a body that bears the permanent markings of the horrors I've experienced. It's because of the way my eyes gaze back at me haunted, like my soul is not fully there, like it's lost somewhere inside me, where the fire is still burning, stuck staring at the scars I carry within, that no one knows about but me. I wonder if there's a cure for them or if they're just as unhealable as those on my skin.

We find out about R. from a tabloid article on the internet. We decide to meet outside to talk, to find comfort, to honor him. We gather round a bench in the clinic's park. We can't utter a word. We sit in silence, without shedding any tears. It's not because it doesn't hurt. Something inside us has broken, and this fracture makes it impossible to react. There are no bones left in our hearts that this world hasn't shattered. We're paralyzed. We can't say it to one another, but we know that either one of us could have taken his place. In the late hours of the night, when darkness knows no boundaries, thoughts that we shouldn't entertain come to us to haunt us. They whisper fake promises about atrocious gestures that could end the suffering. The abyss R. dove into is no mystery to us. Often, we linger on its edge and stare into its depths until we feel the pull of the vertigo. It's only then that we take a step back. But we never go far away enough to stop seeing its hungry lips, to stop hearing them call to us. "No," we answer. "No."

"He posted something on Facebook a few days ago. I never imagined he'd..."

R. killed himself. It was too much for him. We understand him deeply. We wish him an easy journey through the stars, toward a world without nightmares and unredeemable longings. I get up first. The girls join me, one by one. We can't find words that would mean something. We return to our rooms and fall apart, appalled by R.'s choice and our own fragility. 65. What a horrifying number. The night of October 30th keeps smoldering inside us, poisoning our souls, even years apart. We're still on fire, even if we escaped the club. It's like a part of us is still trapped there, in the scorching container, drawing with ashes a six that it keeps adding numbers to. No. The countdown of the victims never stopped. I lock the door of my ward, draw the curtains, and sit down on the floor. Then I kneel and I start praying.

We undergo one reconstructive surgery after the other. The surgeons decide to make the most of each anesthesia by performing a variety of procedures at once. Because our sequelae are so severe, we'd need to go under hundreds of times, which is not sustainable. At some point, our bodies would break down, and to avoid that, the doctors work in teams to operate on as many areas as they can during one appointment. For the rest of our lives, we're going to depend upon reconstructive operations, surgical needling, and scar massage to improve and maintain our quality of life. All because they sewed healthy skin over infected flesh in the hospitals back at home. The bacteria sabotaged our chance at a normal life forever. The lies of the medical system never really ended. They'll linger forever in our sick bodies.

The week before my return to Romania, Doctor Z. consults and photographs me. I look a lot better than I did when I first came to the clinic. The improvements brought about by the surgeries and the rehabilitation procedures are obvious, even though I'm feeling fragile after so many operations.

"You will have to take a break from the surgical interventions. The blood tests we ran show that your body is weakened."

I know he's right, but I'm afraid that if I stop now, I won't be able to continue. "The Ministry of Health will only support us for a limited time. I have to go on, I must finish."

"I fully understand how hard it is to obtain the necessary funds for your treatment, but your needs won't simply disappear one day. You will never 'finish.' The sequelae are too severe, the burns were very deep. You will have to be taken care of and undergo rehabilitation procedures like massage, kinesiotherapy, and surgeries for as long as you live. Burn survivors often see new issues arise every year. Unfortunately, the story doesn't end once you no longer have open wounds. In many ways, that's when it actually begins. In Germany, burn scars are considered a chronic illness. That's truly what they are. They're not acute trauma that eventually resolves and goes away. Like any chronic illness, they're a lifelong affliction that requires specialized medical care, both surgical and rehabilitative."

My shoulders slump and I look down. The doctor's kind and honest words help me understand the magnitude of my predicament. Burn injuries know no real healing. I can't rush things. No matter how desperately I try to recover before the Ministry withdraws its support, I won't be able to. Horrified, I think about being left to fend for myself again, subject to the whims and the arrogant shallowness of the tyrant-professors of the Romanian medical system. They'll abandon us again just like they did then. They'll wait for our ulcerations and contractures to "go away on their own." "Even if you rub shit all over, you'll still heal." They'll never care about us. We'll always be the annoying problem-patients who ruined their reputation. That's why they won't see us as human beings. We're just liabilities in their dead eyes.

I put my hands in my pockets to hide that I'm shaking. I count the months I've got left to fix the ravages of "we have everything we need." Then I count the surgeries. No matter how I calculate, or what tricks I use, mathematics doesn't lie. It's impossible to get everything done in such a short time. Doctor Z. and I design a plan for future procedures. They're insufficient but, for the moment, my body can't handle more. After the appointment is over, I thank him, and he shakes my hand, moved by my sorrow.

"I'm really sorry. I wish there was more that I could do."

I smile. Doctor Z. welcomed us here with open arms, despite the infections we had acquired in the Romanian hospitals, the ridiculous demands of the Ministry concerning the paperwork they requested from the clinic, and, on top of it all, the payment delays. He never humiliated us. He never put pressure on anyone. After our country threw us away like garbage, he took us in wholeheartedly and gave us healing. When we thought we'd live a life a misery, he stepped up and saved us. He went above and beyond to help us. Out of compassion. Because he's a good human being. And still, he tells me that he wishes he could have done more!

It's not his burden to bear. The responsibility belongs to those who hurt us so badly that we ended up needing the services provided by specialists from abroad. Those who abandoned us once we left the Hospital of Neverhealing. Those who claimed that they "had everything they needed" and that they did "everything that was humanly possible." Those who didn't transfer us on time, who sullied our wounds with bacteria and denied it. Those who set our dreams on fire on a night of October that should not have ended in flames. The responsibility belongs to the eternally corrupt and dysfunctional systems they created in order to steal and plunder at ease.

One by one, the episodes of my abandonment resurface. I reminisce about the atrocious treatments I received during the acute care phase: the excruciating bathtime and the concealment of the infections that haunted those lairs of death. The moment I was discharged with open wounds, which were impossible to care for at home, also comes back to me. Then, I remember the untimely end of my rehabilitation procedures at Elias Hospital, together with the cheap show put on by Professor Pavel, who set up an appointment with me just to humiliate me for ten minutes, while I struggled to stand up, and he insisted I go back to the Hospital for Burns, to the "people who broke me." "It's a political thing and I'd make a bad impression." Finally, I relive the gaslighting I was subjected to by Doctor Moldovan and Preda who knew my infections had returned after they let me go home. They not only ridiculed me for my worries, but they discouraged me from seeking treatment: "Even if you rub shit all over, you'll still heal at this point."

This is what I'll go back to once the law that ensures our procedures expires.[5] I'll have to return to the hangmen who played God with me. If they abandoned me so many times before, they'll do it again now. To think that I didn't want to leave the country, that I kept giving chances to those beasts who mutilated me and then washed their hands of my fate. I didn't seek salvation elsewhere because I chose to. I did it because they rejected me. They don't want us, and they never will because they damaged us so badly, they have no idea what to do to fix us. Our only chance is to keep receiving medical care abroad. But where can we find support?

The tragedy is never going to end. Not as long as our bodies are unraveling from underneath, covered in these sinister shells that have replaced our skin as if to hide the decay. A burn injury is not the only thing that's chronic. So is the illness that afflicts Romania. A disease it doesn't want to acknowledge or cure, condemning us to the humiliation of begging the same people who mutilated us and killed our friends to now help us.

---

[5] Meanwhile, after many efforts, the law became permanent. I want this paragraph to serve as a testimony to the suffering we experienced when its status was uncertain.

"I've only seen sequelae like yours once when I treated a few patients who had war injuries. Immediately after they were burned, they were sent to campaign hospitals where they received improvised care. They were bathed in the sea. They healed poorly and their scars were very bad."

In the end, it's safe to say that we're also the victims of a war. One that has lasted for the past thirty years and is being fought by corruption against our lives. One that has moved from the field to the hospitals, which have become its derelict theaters, its human farms of death.

I don't know what I'm going to do. I can't think straight now. I walk out of the doctor's ward, thinking about the treatment plan he designed. There are tens of surgeries left to perform, spread across years. A surgical marathon is necessary in order to prevent the worsening of my prognosis. Then there are the annual rehabilitation procedures. "Physical therapy is a lifelong commitment." How will my needs be met when the countdown to the revocation of our support has already begun?

The evening before my discharge, I sit in the chair on the balcony, wrapped in a blanket, watching the serene end-of-summer sky. It's cool outside and quiet. The only sounds that make ripples in the ocean of silence are the gentle murmurs of the fountain in the garden and the chirps of the crickets hiding among the flowers. The thick scars on my left shoulder throb under the compression garment, and I massage them gingerly, careful not to stir up more pain. My once-crooked index finger brings a modest contribution to the process. It's no longer bent in the palm of my hand like it used to be. It's fixed in a straight position, immobile, and shorter because of the missing joint. I look at it affectionately and give it a silly little kiss, in endearment, amused by the ridiculousness of the gesture. Stumpy and odd as it is, it's a part of me, and it's been through a lot. Just like the rest of my body.

I don't want to leave, but there's nothing I can do about it. I read the discharge papers again and check the next admission dates. In two months, I'll have to come back and continue the rehabilitation procedures, until who knows when, while I'm still able to. I'm afraid of what the future might bring. I'm afraid of being abandoned again. When my scars grow worse, I'll end up back at the Hospital for Burns. They'll humiliate and mutilate me. I'm going to die. Shivers run down my spine as the left corner of the ceiling catches fire. It's bath-time again. Someone is skinning me alive in a dirty tub. The pieces of my dying flesh are splayed around, like in an exhibition of horrors, decaying, oozing. I won't get out of here alive this time. I cry, clutching the discharge papers, wrinkling them. I realize that I'm ruining the documents and try to get ahold of myself, to return to the present moment. For a second, I fell back into hell. I comfort myself that, at least for a while longer, I'm safe and I don't have to go back to those abodes of torment.

I put my hands together in prayer, close my eyes, and talk to God. Then when I'm done, I say a few words to my dad as well. As always, I ask him how he's doing. He can't answer me, of course, but I like to think that, sometimes, he hears me and he's happy that I'm reaching out. I don't bother him very often because I don't want to trouble him. Maybe the dead have their own lives up there, and when we, the living, keep bringing them up, we hurt them because we don't allow them to enjoy the great beyond, which is, for sure, gentler with them than the existence they left behind. I also speak to them, to the 65 who passed away, hoping that I don't burden them with my longing and that they don't know about my nightmares, the ones where we all burn again. "What will happen to me, Father?" I sigh, overcome with sadness.

The dark vault, pierced with bright lights, is mute. The sky looks exactly like it did one of the nights before he died. We used to spend hours on the balcony, hunting for falling stars. We didn't catch them often, but when we captured a wanton one, we celebrated our victory with giggles and laughs that broke through the silent, small-town evenings. Long after he went to seek them beyond the darkness, I searched for them alone, but to no avail. I saw one once, one year when I was vacationing at the seaside. Then they stopped showing themselves. Or maybe I just didn't look up anymore. I notice the brief, vertiginous flash of light and rub my eyes. It was real; I didn't imagine it. It broke off from above and it was gone. It only lasted for a second, but I saw it clearly. The emotion makes my heart beat fast, and even if I know something as little as a falling star doesn't have to mean anything, tonight I chose to believe that it's a sign. Somewhere, beyond all this, someone is watching over me. I remember my father smiling in an old photo. Then, I see my guardian angel, the one I made up to survive the hard nights in the Hospital for Burns, as I lay at the threshold of death. I know they're just figments, havens conjured up by the desperate mind of someone standing at a crossroads in life. But I allow myself to feel the hope they bring. In the end, what we imagine always becomes real, in ways that are often hard to comprehend.

Later, I put my earphones in without struggling. I manage to press the play button on the first try. Once, I used to hum lullabies to myself, prey to the fever and the fear that tomorrow wouldn't come. I don't see any other falling stars that could lead me out of the darkness, so I pick music as my vehicle of salvation. "Dark light, come shine in her lost heart, tonight."[6] And it does. Despite all the suffering, a part of me holds on to the hope that life can be beautiful. I'm no longer whole, but over the once gaping abysses within, steep in their descent toward the memories of hell, networks of laced scars have started to grow, intertwining like wildflowers. The stories their intricate designs tell are no longer only of pain and destruction, but also of redemption, and the latter have multiplied, with every surgery that succeeded and every kindhearted human being who healed instead of harming. I will seek the meaning of all the horror at the core of these patterns of salvation. I'll find it for myself and for those who can no longer search for it.

---

[6] Lyrics taken from the song *Dark Light* by the Finnish band HIM, written by lead singer, songwriter, and composer Ville Valo.

V
LIFE INTERRUPTED

It's 3:24 A.M. and I'm watching the city from the window of my apartment, gasping for air. My heart is racing as if I've been running, trying to escape from some sort of danger. The bright streetlights from Nerva Traian Boulevard have stolen the night's darkness, and their brilliance soothes me, killing the gloom within. I take deep breaths to calm the fear that something bad is going to happen, and after the terror passes, it's replaced with the deep sorrow that's been plaguing me ever since the fire. The panic is gone, but the debris it leaves behind after it barges in on my soul is hard to clean up. It burns when I try to rid myself of it, like incandescent fragments of nightmares, dug up from the entrails of a night that cannot be forgotten.

Suddenly, I remember moments from my life before the tragedy. Concerts, office days, a road trip to the seaside, and tears spilled for an unrequited love. My long hair dyed black on a whim, a dress I tried on at the Unirea store, in a hurry, a train I missed the night before Christmas. I feel like I'm staring at multicolored shards in the broken kaleidoscope of the past, trying to piece them back together, amazed by their chaotic beauty, which has become foreign to me. Was that girl really me? I close my eyes and lean my hot forehead against the window. My erratic breath draws circles of vapor on the glass, blurring out the image of the city that has fallen asleep with the lights on.

I take a sip of water and lie back in bed. It's only then that the abyss in my chest tears open, like a void spreading its famished arms, blood-hungry. Rilke said, in one of his poems, that solitude is like rain, and falls from the heavens. For me, it's the fire that climbs up from hell. The vertiginous sensation of falling makes me dizzy. Something powerful, a force beyond words, drags me toward the entrails of a merciless maelstrom. I see the poster with their faces, hung over the entrance in the alleyway that leads to the container. I feel the horror and the evil of it all, followed by the heartbreaking certainty that these people no longer exist, that no matter who I call, where I go, or how much I pray, I'll never meet them again. Then, like in the second act of a macabre play, the ceiling catches fire and the tragedy repeats itself, over and over.

Later, overcome with exhaustion, I manage to cry. The weeping frees me and, when dawn breaks, I finally fall asleep. I wake up a few hours later, to the shrill noises made by the first morning tram. It's 6:00 A.M. and, once, it used to be bath- time. By now, the terror had already taken hold of me. My body reacts to the memories with fear. To reassure the unconscious part of myself that still lies there, in the crooked hospital bed, awaiting the torture, that I'm no longer in the ward, I look around the room, paying attention to every object. That's the TV set over there. The desk with my laptop is right next to it, and so is the wardrobe, standing more to the left, filled with old clothes I can no longer wear. I'm at home, and I don't need to undergo the procedures from the Hospital of Burns anymore. Slowly, my heartbeat quiets down and the fear disappears. Sometimes, my body thinks I'm still in danger. Something inside wants to fight and save me, at any cost.

"You'll likely have some form of PTSD for as long as you live," the psychologist told me when I asked why I break away from the present and fall back into the past. It's not easy to come to terms with such a life sentence, but I'm working on overcoming it. I hope against hope that I'll learn to feel safe again. However, I don't know if Romania is the best place to start. We all have posttraumatic stress disorder here. You don't have to burn in the Colectiv Club to be afraid to walk down the street or end up in a hospital. We're severely traumatized by the dys-functionality we're subjected to by the incompetent governments that came and went, one after the other. We've been living in a sick, abusive environment for over thirty years and the whole of society is afflicted by PTSD. Normality is a luxury for Romanians, so we've accustomed ourselves to the unacceptable to pre-serve our sanity or a semblance of it.

It's been a few months since I've returned home, and I'm trying to find a way for myself. Working full-time is impossible because of the surgeries and the reha-bilitation procedures. I can't go back to the magazine either. Nelu would welcome me with open arms, but every time I walk into the office, I remember what I felt on the evening of October 30th, leaving for the concert. The memory of that past life, with its joys and sorrows, hurts too much. I'm no longer the same woman who believed in the profession she chose. By tolerating the precarious state of the alternative music scene, we enabled the habits that made the tragedy possible. Happy to have the chance to write about our favorite bands, we ignored the often-inappropriate conditions in the venues. We didn't understand that this blindness can have consequences. We thought we were protected by laws. By permits. Someone, a state authority, had allowed those clubs to function. People equipped to make such decisions. We didn't realize how bad things actually were.

Volunteering makes me happy. I get involved in charitable campaigns set up by NGOs that take care of children with advanced medical needs. I want to turn my pain into a guiding light for other people, to help them escape the darkness. However, it's not easy to offer such support. Every time I talk to someone who has been hurt by the Romanian medical system, I realize that nothing changed after the Colectiv Club fire. Loved ones of other burn victims, just like my mother and my sister, write to me, asking me to help them. Someone they care about cries in the green tub every day, and they don't know how to stop it. I refuse to lie to them. I tell them the truth that, to this day, the doctors keep hiding when they profess the same inanities: "We have everything we need," "the lab works are sterile," "their body wasn't strong enough." Hell is still there, wide open and inconspicuous, lying quietly amidst the Communist-era blocks of flats on Grivița Boulevard, in an old-fashioned building that passes for a hospital. To this day, they won't admit they're riddled with multidrug-resistant bacteria. They're still lying about infecting us, and all the other patients that they take in. Their refusal to acknowledge the HAIs causes avoidable deaths. The arch of the medical act swings between amateurism and torture.

Soon, I'll go back to Germany to continue my rehabilitation and undergo more reconstructive surgery. I sort through the papers that I have to hand over to the ministry officials so that I can receive financial support for my treatment. I make sure I didn't forget something. In a few days, I'll leave my small apartment for good. I gave it up because I can't afford to pay my rent anymore. Until I'm able to work full-time again, I rely solely on disability aid, and it's hardly enough to make ends meet in terms of independent living. I'll move back in with my mother, in my hometown. It's the only way I'll manage to save some money.

I leave home a little later than planned, holding the bulky dossier filled with documents under my arm. It's very cold outside. The thick winter clothing feels heavy on my fragile scars, making the aches and the itching worse. I can't find any relief. I sit in the tram, focusing on the music in my earphones, trying not to burst into tears because of the discomfort. The cold season is difficult because of the heavy clothing. Summer isn't much better because I have to avoid sunlight, something almost impossible to do in Bucharest, with its sweltering asphalt and lurching concrete towers. As much as I loved the sun before the fire, its rays upon my damaged body bring back memories of flames and burning. I dream of spring while the tram hitches and shakes along the tracks, heading toward the ministry's headquarters.

I knock and walk into Mrs. G's office with a shy smile on my face. Her coworkers raise their heads briefly, then lower them again, bored. Only Mrs. G and a younger colleague of hers greet me. Morose, the rest of the clerks go back to working on their computers, clicking away absentmindedly. Mrs. G tells me to take a seat and asks me how I'm doing. She's one of the *exceptionals*. Life among the austere souls that thrive in the emotionally arid environment of the ministry isn't easy for her, with her gentle, light, and kind heart. Every day, she fights to stay whole here, so she's determined to help me, making things more pleasant for me with her gentle manners and soothing words. I hand her the dossier and she gives me words of encouragement. She wishes me good luck for my next procedures, and I give her a clumsy hug in the decrepit room, studded with monotonous gazes from dead-eyed strangers.

I spend the rest of the afternoon at M.'s headquarters, the NGO I volunteer for. I help make Christmas cards for the children. It's the only place where I find peace and feel at home. When I'm finished, it's already gloomy outside. I say goodbye to everyone and leave, roaming the streets aimlessly, hoping that walking is going to help me put my thoughts in order. There are four days left until the holidays, and a snowless, desolate Bucharest makes me sad beyond measure. It's been a while since these once happy times have brought me any joy. Before, I used to examine my phone book carefully, making sure I didn't leave anyone out when I sent the Christmas greetings. If I tried to do this now, I'd realize that all that's left of many loved ones is just a sequence of numbers that I'd dial in vain. I couldn't bring myself to erase them. I don't think I'll ever be able to.

I stop in the bus station and take out my phone. I start searching for a song that can chase away the cold inside. Before I get to choose one, Monica calls me.

She greets me with warmth and tells me something about a dinner at Mr. Istrate's house.

"Narcis is going to be there too."

Every time she says Mr. Hogea's name, she sighs. Her voice becomes hazy because she tries to conceal the pain, which is only alleviated, to a certain extent, by their friendship born out of heartache. She once tried to save his son by helping to send him abroad for treatment, but she failed to rescue him, because his doctors lied about the infections.

Bus number 133 stopped in the station, picked up a few people, and left. It was my ride too, but I didn't take it. I talk to Monica about the holidays and how hard they are for those who have lost loved ones. Mr. Istrate and Mr. Hogea's sons died because of the Colectiv Club fire. Even though they managed to escape the container, they perished in the hospitals. Ever since, every year, they've hosted a dinner for their close friends, to bring some joy to their home, from which a soul is missing. They're orphaned parents, and it comforts them to have kind people around. I accept the invitation. After the call ends, I realize that my fingers hurt. All this time, I've been clutching the phone tightly, with desperation. I tell myself my hands are shaking because of the effort and the cold, but I know it's not true.

When I finally leave for Mr. and Mrs. Istrate's address, it's pitch dark. I'm very nervous. I wonder if the red wine I got them as a gift for the dinner table isn't too festive. I look out the taxi window at the crowded and bustling city. Even if it's dry and dreary, Bucharest still holds a peculiar charm in the cold winter nights. It comes alive with the Christmas decorations and the restlessness of the gift-seekers, walking in and out of stores in a frenzy. Once, I was in love with it. Today, I'm not so sure about my feelings. Beautiful memories give way to fragments of nightmares, and streets that used to take me home now seem foreign and threatening. The steps of my injured friends, tainted by ashes and blood, stumbled upon them in search of a salvation that never came.

I can't find the apartment building, so I call Monica to ask her for guidance. There's a tender kind of joy in her voice. I finally arrive and I take the elevator. She's waiting for me in the doorway, dressed in an all-black outfit. Her small and frail figure is surrounded by a luxurious halo of blonde hair. She's a fairy in boots, as gentle as she is fierce. She hides her sensitivity well because she has a fragile

December 2019. Surgical reconstruction of the scars on the left side of my body.

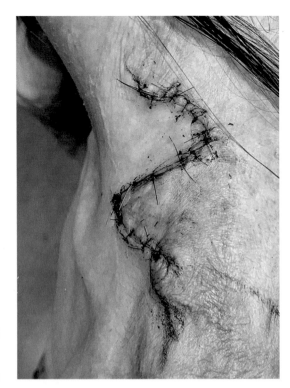

October 2018. Surgical needling procedure done to prevent the onset of complications like contractures and skin cancer.

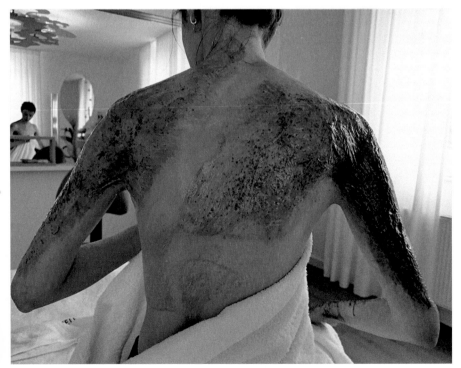

September 2017. Surgical needling procedure done to prevent the onset of complications like contractures and skin cancer.

After well over forty surgeries, I'll undergo a new surgical needling procedure in October, and next year three more. I will need medical treatment all my life. The diary gathers new chapters.

heart, and she doesn't want anyone to know about it. She hugs me tight and invites me in, where Mr. and Mrs. Istrate are waiting for me, together with the Hogea family. They're all smiling. They greet me as if I were one of their daughters, who they haven't seen in a while. It smells delicious, like warm, Christmas food. Mr. Istrate prepared everything for us, together with his wife. After the fire, Mrs. Istrate hasn't been able to cook like she did before, so he took on some extra chores, and now it's his pleasure to delight his friends with tasty dishes. He was in charge of the first course, and she came to his aid with the appetizers. They're such a great team!

We sit down at the table and make small talk. We joke and laugh at the puppy's somersaults. It's in the mood to play and it keeps climbing on our laps, in search of affection. Every now and then, Monica gets up and leaves the room to talk on the phone. Even today, she's busy helping people. She gives advice to some; she saves others. But she'd never admit it. She hates being told that she's a good human being, so she solves everybody's problems with discretion and comes back to us smelling like cigar smoke. You can tell she's been crying, but she says she's just tired. That's Monica in a nutshell.

"How are you, Alexandra? Is everything all right? Can we help you in any way?" Mr. Hogea asks.

I answer that I'm okay, but I have to constantly undergo reconstructive surgery and keep up with the rehabilitation procedures, otherwise I don't feel well. He wants to know more about the treatment protocol, so I start to explain. The orphaned parents look at me with compassion. They feel sorry about what I'm going through. Their eyes well up with tears and they sigh. All of a sudden, I feel like stopping because I'm ashamed of myself. Ashamed of the smallness of my pain compared with the void in their lives. Ashamed to talk about something that was denied to them: the chance to see their children struggling, but alive.

Someone changed the channel to VH1. Metallica's *The Unforgiven II* starts playing. Mr. and Mrs. Hogea's eyes shift from me to the screen, as if hypnotized. A cold shiver, akin to an electric jolt, runs through the room and, like they're remote-controlled, the parents get up from the table and sit down on the couch, in front of the TV set.

"It was one of Alex's favorite songs," Mr. Hogea whispers.

His voice is shaking, and his gaze is fixated on the video, as if he's trying to see beyond the frames, to the very core of the song, looking for something, or someone. Then, the thread of life is cut, and Christmas is interrupted by the suffering we share. It shears through us, tearing us apart. We fall out of the present moment, into the past, in a crooked world where nothing else exists except for the memories of the horrors. We haven't left the room where the Christmas tree lights cast happy, colorful patterns on the floor, but we're someplace else, with ashes under our eyelids, blind to the beauty, only aware of the terror. It's pitch dark again, like when the club lost power after we had burned alive. Our parents didn't see what happened, but they felt it all, and a part of that darkness was passed on to them and still lingers in their hearts.

By now, I've become an expert in the mechanics of these collapses into tragedy. Sometimes, they're set into motion by something concrete, tangible, like a song, or a picture, other times they just occur, like natural phenomena. They come out of nowhere and take us back to hell. I find myself lying in the dirt in the container. As for the parents, they're in a hospital hallway, hearing the news that Alex and Bogdan have died, over and over, like a broken echo. Big, quiet tears stream down the faces of the mothers. The fathers' eyes are downcast, staring at an inner void nothing can fill. James Hetfield sings and sings, but nothing can break the vast silence that has settled upon the room, like a vault being dragged over a tomb. It's the stillness left behind by their disappearance, and only the boys could chase it away, with their happy laughter, with their jokes, with their voices humming to the song that reminded us that we're not whole. But they're not coming, and I can't get out of the container either.

"I love this piece, Dad!" Alex once said, and his words reverberate around us, rising from every corner of the room, like an echo from another life.

He's here, among us, but he's irrevocably gone. The video ends and Eric Clapton's *Tears in Heaven* is playing now. We slowly climb back up from our common descent, gesturing to one another, as if surprised we're alive. Sighs turn into words that turn into sentences, and we're speaking again, talking about them. About how the parents found out that their sons were injured in a fire. About the war they waged to save the boys. About how late Alex was transferred abroad from the hospitals that couldn't offer us the necessary care but lied about "having everything they need." We discuss the criminal mindset of the authorities that didn't move a finger to give them a chance at life, and we praise the people who fought the system to try and remove them from the wards where they were devoured alive by multi-drug-resistant bacteria. Monica glares around aimlessly, broken inside. She can't stop recounting the horror of it all. Her story is interrupted only by her sighs when she mentions Alex. He'd be alive now had he left Romania on time. Just like Bog-dan. And the rest of them.

While I'm listening to her, my eyes shift to the scars on my fingers. I gawk at them intently, captivated by the elaborate patterns my flesh has drawn to close the once gaping wounds. It's a tic we all share. The survivors, as they call us. We've become the people who stare at their hands when they can't face the world. The anger chokes me up. I know that Monica is right. I know that this Christmas would have been different had the Romanian authorities done their job, instead of blocking the transfers and lying about the infections. I peer at my wounds, utterly absorbed by them, as if there, at their core, lie the words that could bring some comfort to the orphaned parents. Or perhaps a knot I could use to bind the sheared threads of our lives together. I can't find anything, and I fall apart.

"Forgive me," I tell myself. "Forgive me because I am here and they're not. Not a day goes by without feeling guilt, anger, sorrow, regret, and spite. I miss them, and I miss myself, the person I was before the fire. I miss Claudiu's warm black eyes, and the gesture he made when he propped up his camera and took his photos using just one hand. I miss Teo's curls, bouncing in the rhythm of her walk when she came to pick up her badge from the gates of the Roman Arenas. Sometimes I read the last messages we exchanged on Facebook, and I don't understand. I don't understand what happened. I'd give anything for your Christmases to be whole, uninterrupted. Forgive me. Forgive us."

We hear the cheerful voices of Mr. Hogea and Mr. Istrate's daughters, chirping away in the other room. We had forgotten about them. They're playing and laugh-ing at something, and their innocence breaks our fall, waking us up from the night-mare we got lost in. They run out and join us at the table, looking around, worried. The parents greet them with an immense and desperate love, chasing away their fears, making it look like nothing happened, like we hadn't just climbed back from Hell. They must be protected at any cost. For them, the Christmas tree, with its bright and colorful lights, must remain a beacon of wholeness, not a gateway into the dark. I raise my eyes from my scars and smile at them. No. They will never know about our collapse into tragedy. They'll stay here, above the horror, shielded from crashes, interruptions, and the fire. Life restarts, incomplete, putting the abyss in delicate brackets, always ready to shatter and engulf everything once again.

Time to go home. We say goodbye and they all hug me lovingly, careful not to put pressure on my scars by holding me too tight. They sit in the doorway, wringing their hands, fighting back tears. They thank me for coming and tell me I'm welcome to visit anytime. I leave with a heavy heart. I didn't get to ask for forgiveness. It wouldn't have made a difference anyway.

It's late and very cold. My shoulder begins to ache under the heavy winter jacket. I'm on an anonymous street in a city famished for dreams, but I can't see the apartment buildings around me. Behind my eyes, ravenous flames are devouring the ceiling. "It's going to fall! It's going to crash on us," someone screams. There's something else in the air beside the smell of frost. I can feel the chemical stench of burning debris and there's a stinging in my throat. The thread of life was cut once again. I shake myself, trying to return to the present.

A taxi is parked in front of me. Annoyed, the driver gestures, urging me to climb in faster. He doesn't know where I came back from. He's unaware that I'll leave ashes on his back seat. Cinders and clumsy knots I weave with nine crooked fingers and a stumpy one, that's too straight. He starts his red Renault and turns on the radio. Metallica is on. It was one of Alex's favorite bands.

"Nerva Traian Street, right?"

"No, change of plans. Take me to Tăbăcarilor 7, please."

"The place where...?"

"Yes, that's right. You can leave me right in front."

I get out, and the driver departs in a hurry. The squealing sound made by the tires on the dry asphalt break the ungodly silence of the night. I feel like it's darker here, in the square where we agonized, screaming for help, than anywhere else in the world. Our fear penetrated the walls of the buildings around us and nested there forever. Now, they reverberate with the echoes of our desperation, playing it back like a haunted record.

Someone washed off our blood from the streets then, but its shadow lingers, and no matter what they do, they can't cleanse it. Our suffering is etched here, permanent, and immutable, invisible yet perceptible, an eternal confession of the torment we endured. Because they witnessed its work, a great evil has taken hold of these surroundings. An evil for which there is no redemption. I sense it crawling its way to the core of my being and cold shivers of terror run down my spine.

Their faces smile at me from the photographs the parents left behind on the improvised altar erected near the entrance to the alleyway that leads to the club. A few candles are flickering between the frames of their portraits, ready to give in. Ana's right there, in the middle. Her picture is new. Claudiu and Teo are close by, a little bit to the side. I wave at them like they can see me. Alex's warm smile shines bright behind the quivering flame of a rushlight. Dressed in a neat suit, Bogdan is gazing confidently at the world, with enough dreams in his eyes to last him a lifetime. All turned to ashes when he died. I notice Delia last. I wouldn't have recognized her if Flavia hadn't shown me a picture of her one night, in the Hospital for Burns. She's wearing glasses and her long red hair falls in thick braids down her back. "God, how it hurts!" I remember her wails from the night of October 30th, when she begged and pleaded, lying in the bed which became her tomb. She kept calling the nurses, and they wouldn't come. "It can't be real," she cried. She wept and prayed by my side, and she died next to me while I was unconscious and incapable of helping her.

"I have to ask you for forgiveness too," I whisper and burst into tears. I don't know how long I sit there, lost in grief. When I come to, my legs have become numb, and, underneath the thick gloves, my hands are throbbing. I take out my right hand and stare at it. The index finger has turned purple, and it's swollen and sore because of the cold. I shake my arm, but the prickling sensation won't go away. I decide I'm going to stay a little longer so that I can pray. After I'm finished, I say goodbye to them, one at a time, heartbroken. On the night of October 30th, 2015, I walked here from home, strolling through the neighborhood, young and whole. Now, in another life, I'm going to make my way back, down the same streets, a different person, older, and incomplete.

I gaze at the illuminated windows etched in the tall, Communist-era apartment buildings on Goga Street. Once again, I imagine the lives behind their lights. I don't see the family of four anymore, but a smaller one, with three members. Someone is missing from the count, and no matter whether it's Dad, Mom or a sibling, the void they left behind is just as immense. The Christmas tree holds vigil over a disappearance that cannot be concealed. If anything, its flashy attire only makes the absence more obvious.

I make it to Nerva Traian Boulevard and head toward the crosswalk. It's deserted, just like it was back then. There's no angel there, waiting for me, willing to answer my questions: "What was the purpose of all this?" I'd ask him. "Why?" I look at the big metal gates of my apartment building. There's an ache in my chest at the thought of leaving everything behind. It's such a shame that I have to say goodbye to Bucharest. I walk past my place, going straight ahead, on the road that leads to *Maximum Rock Magazine's* headquarters. I take my usual route. Like before, I visit the non-stop store and buy myself a can of Coke. The cashier recognizes me and shakes his head.

"I'm so sorry for what happened to you," he whispers, nervous. "But at least you're alive!"

"Thank you," I answer. I don't know what else I could say.

I stop near the small entrance to the blind alley that encloses the editorial office. I open the can and spill from it three times, to honor those who have passed, the memory of my life back then and the memory of the life I could have had. I take a sip and grimace. What a poor choice for a drink in the freezing winter night... December wraps its cold arms around me, and I shiver, alone and lost in the darkness within. I've become like the woman I wanted to help that night, when it was raining, and she was seeking something she couldn't find. A street or a kind word. The lady with the melancholy eyes, wandering through this cruel world in worn-out boots. I spill from the can once more, to remember her lost soul. I hope she found her peace in the end. I hope I will too.

Big, stray flakes start to fall from the sky. Could this be a sign? It's too cold to stay outside anymore so I rush home frozen, thinking about the chills that shook me in the Hospital for Burns. I get in the white tub, so different from the green horror where I used to shed my flesh and take a shower that doesn't hurt. It warms me up and fills me with boundless gratitude. After that, I get dressed and sit on the wide windowsill, watching the snow cover Bucharest, as if strained through a magical sieve. It lays over my heart too. Over the asphalt in front of the club, still incandescent because of the pain it absorbed. Over their photos. Over the dying candle flames. Over my steps. Growing and concealing everything.

I lie in bed and stare at the ceiling. The brassy streetlights reflect off the left corner, creating strange patterns. Is something on fire? No, it's not burning. It just shimmers, it just shimmers... I pull the covers up to my chest with incomplete fingers, nestling in the comfortable warmth. Tomorrow isn't bath-time. It'll never be bath-time again. Will I wake up? Yes, I'll wake up. I can go to bed safely, without the threat of death looming over me, birthing nightmares. I'm not in danger. It's okay. Breathe in, breathe out. Every now and then, a car speeds by, scattering the snow in its rush toward an unknown destination.

Before I fall asleep, I allow myself to feel hopeful, to believe that maybe it wasn't all in vain. Perhaps, at least tonight, I won't burn again. From beyond the threshold, lying between our worlds, their searching eyes won't peer into mine, sad and questioning, wondering "why", expecting an answer. I wouldn't know what to say.

One day, I'll smile without flames burning in my heart or ashes smoldering in my soul. Someday, I'll give a meaning to all this horror. I'll draw straight maps to a better world using the crooked patterns the fire laid in my scorched flesh.

But not today. I close my eyes and count slowly, as far as I can before everything turns dark... 60, 61, 62, 63, 64, 65, 66.

VI
NINE YEARS LATER

I stare at the bleak October sky from the window of the German clinic's operating room. Like shields made from lead, thick clouds are lying on top of the autumn sun, as if they're trying to protect the planet from its dying rays.

While I wait for the lidocaine cream to numb me, I toy with the thought that the cold season is nature's attempt to heal Earth's skin, after it was burned by the summer. A shiver runs down my spine and through my scars, making me pull the sterile garment tighter around my body. Somehow, the image I conjured is hurtful, so I take my eyes off the window and look around. The O.R. is painted white, and it sparkles with cleanliness.

The new equipment is waiting for the surgeon to arrive, while he readies his tools in the room next door. It's the third surgical needling I'm having this year, and it was planned for October 29th. I have to undergo reconstructive and rehabilitative procedures all my life if I want to be all right. We all have to do this, so that our scars don't get worse with time. Tomorrow, it's going to be nine years since the fire.

"Alex, are you ready?"

Doctor Aust walks in the ward and his warm smile lights up the room. He's an angel dressed in scrubs. He takes out the surgical roll, studded with thin, long needles from its sterile packaging. It's the instrument he'll use to perform the procedure. During the surgery, he'll go over my rigid, adherent scars with it, making puncture wounds. Sometimes, he has to press harder to allow the needles to penetrate the thick tissue that has grown chaotically over the burns. The roll ploughs through the sick lacing of my skin, creating small holes that will be filled with new, healthy flesh, which will gradually loosen the rigid shell that suffocates me, like melted armor that has clung to my bones.

I nod and lie down on the operating bed. Doctor Aust puts his hand on my shoulder to comfort me and tells me that he's going to start. I feel the pressure of the roll on my left side, then millions of stings permeate the rough and deformed scar, as the instrument roams over me, creating surgical wounds that bleed profusely. The surgeon asks me questions about my family. How are my nephews doing? What about my mother? He talks to me to keep my mind off the pain. The procedure can be done under general anesthesia, but in my case, numbing with highly concentrated lidocaine cream is a safer option. The large number of reconstructive surgeries I underwent so far took a toll on my nervous system and the risk of side effects has grown. The physical suffering is significant, but safety is more important.

The surgeon checks with me constantly, making sure that the scars are still numb and that the pain is bearable. If it became too intense, he'd refuse to go on and he'd find a solution. There is no such thing as "you have to take it", "it doesn't hurt that bad," or "you're making yourself sick with all the crying" in his repertoire. Here, when the patient says it's too much, the doctor stops. At first, I was astonished that I could have such control over my own suffering. I come from a world where you're not allowed to complain.

As it penetrates my scars and moves back and forth over and through them, the roll makes a specific sound. It's as if tens of clocks have suddenly gone mad simultaneously and started ticking chaotically, counting backwards to 2015, etching all the seconds on my flesh. I listen to the ticktack made by the roll and think to myself that the pain doesn't even compare to the torture endured during bathtime, in the green tub of the Hospital for Burns. Doctor Aust stops often to ask me if I'm all right. He seems surprised by every "yes" I say but he doesn't falter. He wants to help me get better.

He knows our story. I told him about how they used to shower our burned flesh, without giving us anything for the pain. He was surprised when he found out because he didn't think something like that was still possible in this modern century, when burn care has evolved so much. I never admitted it to him, but I'm certain something broke inside me irreversibly when I lay in that tub, hunched under the weight of the pain, naked to the core of my being, while they skinned me alive in the hygiene ward of the hospital in Romania. I think a part of me – whatever was left of the girl who had managed to walk out of the container after the fire had fed upon her – died there. She lies buried within me, latching on to that pain – the pain of all pains, which makes all other suffering pale, holding it tight in her scorched arms. She doesn't want to let it go because if it escaped, it would burn everything in sight, bringing back the madness and the terror.

When he moves on to the back, the surgeon holds my hand. He works skillfully and fast, trying to shorten the duration of the procedure as much as possible. Near my spine, where the nerve endings in my skin are struggling to heal, the scar is more sensitive, and when the roll passes over it, the pain is strangely vivid, like a deep itch that nothing can soothe. The needles travel all over my body, drilling through the sick tissue so that the fresh blood coming out of the prick wounds can wash away from the inside the defective collagen fibers that have grown beyond measure, sticking to my bones, tendons, and muscles. It's a consequence of the hospital-acquired infections that didn't allow the burns to heal. My body tried desperately to erect some sort of fortress made from flesh, to protect me, but like soldiers of evil, the multidrug-resistant bacteria devoured everything that stood in its way. Every day, the new tissue was eaten alive, and the body had to start over, growing weaker and weaker, building shoddier and uglier structures, until it ran out of resources and gave up. The doctors in Romania used to sew healthy skin over infected wounds. Every time the surgeries failed, they had to clean up their mess, so they dug deeper, removing their botched grafts and everything underneath, in hopes they'd find clean tissue. But they couldn't. No matter what they did and how much they resected, we stayed dirty because they worked with contaminated instruments, in contaminated operating rooms, with contaminated souls. The hypertrophic process of the scarring is one of the most severe complications of infected burn wounds. It's also chronic, and it requires lifelong care.

Nine years after the Colectiv tragedy, the German surgeon isn't only fixing what the fire ruined, but also what was destroyed by corruption. For as long as we live, we, the survivors of the accident, will have to undergo various surgeries, procedures, and treatments. That's a lifetime spent in scaffolds, under repair, patching up parts of our bodies and our souls, to stop the darkness from seeping into us through the cracks in our beings. We can't allow it to reach our core. It would steal even the little that is left of what we once were.

The right arm is next, then the forearm and the hand. When the roll reaches the scar on my wrist, Doctor Aust stops again and asks me to take a few deep breaths. This part hurts really bad. Careful not to scare me, the surgeon starts slow. Then he speeds up. I turn my head to the other side and press my face against the pillows, searching for a soft touch to soothe myself. Even if such a gesture seems absurd, it helps me calm down. Sometimes, the surgeon and I sing until he's done. Other times we joke and swear. Usually, he tries to make me laugh by telling me funny stories that chase away the ugliest of pain's specters: the fear. I'm never afraid here, not like I was before when I thought I was going to die in the green tub or in my dirty bed, wrapped in bloodied sheets, sullied by fragments of my rotting flesh, dressed in nothing but the oozing diapers they always forgot to change, ashamed of my helplessness.

"We're done, Alex!"

Happy that everything went well, the doctor congratulates me for my bravery and calm. He pats my wounds with sterile gauze, infused with disinfectant and, once he's cleaned all the blood, rubs the healing vitamin oil all over the swollen and achy surgical sites. The growth factors in it will help me heal faster. The nurse walks in and helps me put the hospital dress on, making sure I'm feeling well. She takes me to my ward, which is just as clean as the O.R., and tucks me in bed, telling me to rest, but not before she reassures me that, no matter what I need, she's there for me and I shouldn't hesitate to call her. "If you're in any pain," she says, "just let me know." I nod and thank her, fighting back tears and the memories of shrugging shoulders and harsh words.

After she leaves, I get up and look out the tall window. It's drizzling. I listen to my heart. Its once heavy thumps are becoming lighter and lighter, until all I can hear is the murmur of the raindrops falling over the world. While Doctor Aust's needles performed their work, trying to sew me into a healthier body, it's gotten dark outside. The pristine whiteness of the room strikes a deep contrast with the leaden October sky that, nine years ago, on the 30th, watched over me as I walked across Tăbăcarilor Street toward a different life. I close my eyes and open them suddenly. There, behind my shut lids, flames are engulfing a ceiling I already know by heart from my nightmares. The gentle patter of the rain turns into the groaning of the fire and then into the screams of those who will never watch another October from the window of a hospital ward, bleeding but alive.

Slowly, the numbing effect of the cream wanes off, and the pain becomes more intense, but bearable. I don't need painkillers right now, but I know that if I asked for some, they'd give me the best, just so that I don't suffer, not like then, when they rolled their eyes and injected a few milligrams of Ketoprofen in my cannula to make me shut up. The thought that I'm far away from the fire, far away from those who showed me no mercy when I begged for help, when my world was falling apart in ashes and rotting flesh, comforts me. I lie to myself that there's no chance I'll ever experience something as horrifying as the fire or the inhumane treatment I received in the Hospital for Burns. But I am aware that, as long as Romania doesn't learn something from the Colectiv Club fire, I might as well end up back in Hell again. We all might, actually, burn victims or ordinary people. In the end, we're all one in the eyes of the heartless system. This certainty has become a haunting fear, which is impossible to conquer. It hurts me more than any procedure, except, maybe bath-time.

I try to close my eyes again. Now, I only see the illuminated ghosts of the neon lights in the ward. I want to fall asleep before the harmless specters turn red and catch fire. I don't have much time. The peace doesn't last long. The tragedy plays out in my mind once more, propelled by grief. For nine years, I've screamed inside, while my body begs for quiet. Nine years, I've wept, counting the surgeries, realizing they'll never stop. "Nine years," I say out loud, knowing that a lifetime of days like this await me, after one night in which thirty years' worth of corruption worked their evil upon me, like they did upon my country, itself a mutilated body, burning while dreaming of salvation. Nine years.

As darkness falls upon the small hospital, it brings with it unwelcome guests. Ghosts, dressed in tainted shrouds, of an evening that should not have ended the way it did. They rise like smoke from the entrails of my mind, crawling out, agonizing, billowing at the edge of sanity. They're just shadows of the past, I whisper to myself. Then why do their sad eyes stare at me, alight with desperation, begging me to help them? Their ashen faces are human, but I can't look at them. I'm afraid I'd recognize someone.

October 30th wasn't just one night. Because dawn never really broke over the nightmare. It went on and on, on the scorched asphalt in front of the club, where so-called rescuers stepped over raised hands that begged for help, in the hospitals, where the lies other crooked saviors told allowed the filth to seep inside our flesh, killing us, in the court of law, where justice makers put their dirty hands over truth's mouth, silencing it forever. Nine years since the Colectiv Club fire, and I'm still burning.

Epilogue
The Other October

She woke up the next day with a splitting headache. It felt like her eyes were burning in their sockets, and when she finally managed to open them, she didn't understand what she saw. She blinked a couple of times hoping that her sight would clear, but the room looked the same. A lipstick-stained glass of wine was resting on the small white table, and she was lying on the worn-out foldable couch. The TV set was on and some sitcom characters from Comedy Central were cracking bad jokes in low volume. The fake laughter added in postproduction tore through the ringing in her ears, making her grimace.

"I must be dreaming," she whispered, and closed her eyes again, trying to wake up. But nothing happened. The headache went on, throbbing, unusually real. Panicking, she got up, but was too dizzy to walk. She wobbled to the bathroom and fell on her knees in front of the toilet. Sick to the core of her being, she vomited violently, gasping for air, prey to the worst case of vertigo she had ever experienced. She recognized the small ceramic tub that Iulia used to wash her in after the fire. The neon light above the sink flickered, just like it always did. In the corner, on improvised plastic shelves, lay in disarray her numerous cosmetic products. She remembered how she packed them up hurriedly, throwing them in a big garbage bag, before she moved. She had scraped the delicate skin graft on her index finger with one of the containers and she bled profusely, amazed that a flesh wound could cause such damage. Still lightheaded, she pulled herself away from the toilet bowl, and looked at her hands in search of the tiny cut. She didn't find it. Instead, a cold shiver ran down her spine. The sick lacing that once decorated her burned body was gone. Her limbs were whole, unscathed. The black nail polish hadn't budged from her long nails, and her joints were flexible, healthy, able to bend at her will.

"What in God's name...?"

She leaned against the sink and got up. Shaking, she stared at herself in the stained square mirror. When she saw her reflection, her heart skipped a beat, then began to pound in her chest, deafening her with its desperate thumps.

"I don't understand what's happening."

Her old face gawked back at her, confused and terror-stricken. The glittery gray eyeshadow she hadn't worn in years was smudged across her cheeks. Her thick hair, dyed black on a whim, was tangled at the back, but was long and full, falling down her back uninterrupted by scars. Her back! Where did the scars go? The smooth skin listened to her, performing, with loyalty, every movement she demanded. Ioana put her hands over her mouth, as if to stifle a scream, and was shocked to see her fingers reflected in the mirror. They were normal again. She examined them, fascinated and appalled, waiting for the spell to break at any moment. But it never did. It wasn't a dream, a hallucination, or an illusion. It was real.

She ran back to the room, now steadier on her feet. She had to talk to Victor, but she couldn't find her phone. She ransacked every corner, rummaging through her things, annoyed that it was nowhere in sight. Then she realized that she was looking for the wrong one. Her small white Samsung, with its cracked edges, was lying on her desk, charging patiently. That's where she always put it before the fire. It was stuck on silent mode, and it displayed a dozen missed calls, all from her mother. She popped up on the screen again, and this time she answered.

"Ioana, what are you doing? Haven't you gone to work?"

"Mom, what date is it?"

"What?!"

Her mom kept scolding her about her "oddball" behavior and threatened her that she'd lose her job if she kept it up. She had to get dressed and leave right now! Seeing that her mother didn't take her seriously, she put her on speaker and stared at the phone screen. Amidst yellow and blue balloons, lay written, in a happy font, "October 29th, 2015." It was 8:45 in the morning. She froze in place. "What the hell? Have I... gone back in time? What is this? Victor doesn't even know me yet. There's no way I can talk to him."

"Mom, we'll talk later, okay? I must go to... the office!"

The minute she ended the call, she burst into tears. Through the throbbing of her headache, which had gotten even worse, she remembered fragments from the fight she had with Victor, which, in a logical world, happened yesterday. They went to bed upset with each other and, before she fell asleep, she wished, from the bottom of her broken heart, that he could get back the life he had with Lydia. She prayed to God and begged him to perform a miracle, to turn things around one way or the other. A few hours later, she woke up in October 2015. What else could this be but the fulfillment of her absurd wish?

"God, if you can hear me, please help me understand. What's going on? What am I supposed to do?"

But He didn't answer. All she could hear was the buzzing of the crowded boulevard and the happy chatter of the characters in the sitcom. Next to the white table lay a bottle of red wine, which was half empty. She remembered that nine years ago, one of her friends came over and they had a drink together to celebrate the girl's birthday. She poured what was left in the dirty glass and drank it all, coughing and grimacing. It had gone sour. Even if God stayed silent, she knew what she had to do. Now, nine years earlier, she'll save them all.

II

A few minutes later, she called in sick, lying to Tudor that she's too ill to come to the office. Upset, he gave her the day off reluctantly, making sure to point out that, whenever she felt better, she should write a piece or two for the webzine. His request made her chuckle. He hadn't changed yet. She promised him she'd oblige, fake-coughed in the receiver, and ended the call. She had to find a way to change the course of the things that had led to the fire.

There was no way that she could tell Tudor the truth, because then he wouldn't take her seriously. If she was being honest, she didn't fully get what was happening either. Her goal was to be as wise and tactful as possible, even if she felt like she was walking across the edge of a precipice. What she was experiencing wasn't natural, and she was afraid that, at any moment, her body was going to unravel and disappear, like a ghost in a horror movie.

She pulled herself together and came up with a plan. After looking at the situation from all angles, she concluded that, instead of stopping the concert from happening all together, it would be easier to prevent the fire from occurring at the venue. Colectiv was the only club where bands could still perform during the cold season, which meant that even if she found a way to cancel the show, it would be rescheduled and still take place eventually, likely with the same outcome. The key was for the gig to go on, but without the tragedy.

First, she'll call the pyrotechnics company. She'll claim that she's contacting them on behalf of the club owners, to make sure that they bring the right type of fireworks, appropriate for indoor use, and enough working fire extinguishers. Then, she'll pull the same stunt with the people from the venue. She'll get a hold of them and tell them that she's an ISU[7] inspector. She'll insist that, according to reports that have been made based on verified sources, their fire extinguishers were determined to be expired and, therefore, they have to replace them and install at least two new ones near the stage. Then, she'll demand that the sound-proofing foam on the pillars be covered in fireproof casing. And as a last measure, she'll buy a small fire extinguisher herself and take it with her at the concert, in a big backpack. Just in case her scheming didn't go as planned.

It wasn't hard for her to find the phone numbers of the pyrotechnicians and the club. All she had to do was run a Google search. She knew every detail about the fire from the legal documents she had read and the interviews she had watched. "Hindsight is an advantage that all time-travelers have," she emphasized, with a bitter smile. She cleared her throat a couple of times to make sure that her voice wouldn't shake, grabbed the phone, and rang.

"Hello, I'm calling on behalf of the Colectiv Club. You were commissioned for one of our events."

"Hi, yes. Let me check. Yeah, that's right. On Tăbăcarilor 7 Street, right?"

"Indeed. I'd like to ask you to please bring appropriate fire extinguishers because we've installed some soundproofing foam on the walls and ceiling that isn't fire-resistant. Also, I understand that you've recently bought some new fireworks from Bulgaria. We've had unpleasant experiences with those... before. They're not good for indoor gigs. Please bring something else."

---

[7] ISU is short for "Inspectoratul Pentru Situaţii de Urgenţă," which means the Institute for Emergency Situations, the Romanian authority in charge of reinforcing fire protection measures.

"The club isn't fireproofed? And... how do you know about the fireworks from Bulgaria?"

The woman was irritated. She spoke fast, awestruck. She was angry.

"We know from... some acquaintances. Be really careful with the fireworks, please. Bring something with a cold flame, and there won't be any problems. The ones you have right now are no good. They're only fit for outdoor events. I also have to emphasize the situation with the fire extinguishers. We want them inside, not lying around in the car, like last time."

"What last time?"

"It wouldn't be the first time pyrotechnicians showed up empty-handed and unprepared for the job."

"What do you mean, miss? What are we? Amateurs? Yes, we have some new merchandise, but we're professionals, we only work with the... best stuff. Of course, we'll bring, um, cold, um... fireworks. It's what we had in mind and what was discussed to start with."

Ioana could hear whispering and agitation in the background. The woman had put her on speaker and whoever was listening in on the conversation wasn't pleased with the direction it took. It was likely that her call threw their plans off course. If she wasn't so nervous, she would laugh at their amazement. They seemed flabbergasted, and it delighted her.

"I'm only doing my job and insisting that you do yours. Now that you're aware of our situation, you know what to do and what not to do."

"Yeah, of course, what can I say? Thank you, I guess. We'll change... I mean, we'll see what we'll use tomorrow, but it'll definitely be cold fireworks."

Things had gone smoother than she had expected. Aside from the woman's annoyed voice, she wasn't met with significant opposition. It was time to take care of the club owners. She rehearsed what she planned to say several times, changing her tone, trying to find the most authoritative and aloof one possible. She had to sound superior, arrogant even, but without really overdoing it.

"Good day. I'm calling on behalf of ISU with regard to the concert that will take place tomorrow evening in the Colectiv Club."

"Hello. Allow me to take a look. Indeed, we're hosting a rock concert."

"Yes. You'll have to change the fire extinguishers. They've expired and they might not be working properly. You have until tomorrow evening, before the show, to comply. Also, at least two have to be placed near the stage at all times. You have to provide people on the premises, who can operate them adequately in case of emergency. Don't forget to cover the soundproofing foam on the walls with a fireproof casing. For the safety measures to be complete, legally speaking, you must open a few secondary exit doors. We were thinking about the one that leads to the neighboring club and the lateral doors."

Pause. Then a long sigh.

"Hmmm, well... We'll take a look and see if the fire extinguishers are really expired. As for opening so many doors, um, are you sure it's necessary? I mean..."

"It's not only necessary but also paramount if you don't want to receive a fine that will run you out of business. I'm not here to negotiate safety terms with you, sir. If you don't do as I tell you, I guarantee that you're going to have very big problems. Take my word for it. Do as I say, and we won't have to take measures against you tomorrow... when we'll come to inspect the club *personally*."

The man gulps.

"Oh, I see. You should have just said so. We'll take care of everything, thank you."

This part wasn't that hard either. Could it really be this easy? Could it really be possible to save so many lives just by making a few phone calls and telling the truth instead of lying? She remembered the sensation of flames on naked skin, and the smell of burning flesh. She shook herself to chase away the ghost of a tragedy that hadn't happened yet and, for the next few hours, devoted herself to her plan.

After she took her makeup off, she washed her face, combed her hair in a hurry and got dressed. She left her apartment and came back an hour later, with a medium-sized fire extinguisher she bought from a specialized store. It fit perfectly in her mountaineering backpack and, even if it was very heavy, it was relatively inconspicuous. Worst-case scenario, she'd lie that Tudor asked her to bring it with her to the concert, without any further explanations. She spent the rest of her day reading the instructions manual and watching tutorials on YouTube to learn how to use it properly.

Should she say anything to Victor? How could she, now a stranger, write to him and tell him not to bring Lydia to the concert? It would sound like an indecent proposal, not like a warning, especially since, in this version of October, they didn't know each other. She had a day and a half left to stop the tragedy from happening, but she didn't know what else to do. She felt the anxiety rising, burdening her with terrible fears.

For a while, she read about time traveling, but there was no reliable information online. It seemed highly unlikely, yet here she was. Most of the articles were pure speculation. Some were even fiction. Truth be told, she didn't expect anything different. Her journey wasn't exceptional in any way. There was no tunnel of light or black hole. All she did was go to bed in 2023 and wake up in 2015. She read and read, but it only made her feel more confused. Having had enough, she shut down the laptop and lay down in bed, thinking about tomorrow and about Victor. Did she sell her soul for him, without realizing? Had she gone mad? She pinched herself several times to make herself wake up. Maybe it really was just a dream, a nightmare. She pressed down on her eyelids with her hands until she felt pressure and the darkness became tinged with tiny specks of light. She opened them, hopeful that she was going to see her and Victor's home, but all she saw were the familiar surroundings of her old apartment.

She pranced about the house, touching the couch, the TV set, the white table. They were all tangible, real. She felt the coolness of the surfaces or the texture of the fabric with hands that were whole, with fingers that were long and graceful. Scarless. While she made herself a cup of tea, she was struck by the ease with which her limbs moved. Stunned by how well everything seemed to be working. She could pour water and hold the pot seamlessly. Doing more things at a time wasn't a struggle anymore. But when she used matches to light up the gas stove, the hot and colorful breath of the fire frightened her. The fear she felt as the blue flames rose up from the hob, licking the bottom of the stainless-steel vessel confirmed to her, without a shadow of a doubt, that the tragedy had been real and that whatever she was experiencing was a mystery she couldn't solve.

She forced herself to believe that she had dreamed the fire. And Victor too. But the grief of losing him and the hope that perhaps now he'll hold on to his beloved were too intense to be an illusion. And look... flames terrified her. She was never afraid of such a banal thing before. The water boiled in the pan, making a rich, bubbling sound that silenced the gentle murmur of her crying. She poured herself tea and sat on the wide windowsill, giving herself to that strange night, from a past that had become present once again.

III

Darkness conquered the noisy city below, drawing over its loud mouth a black curtain of silence, torn open from place to place by the shrill streetlights. She could see the crowded boulevard from her window, packed with cars driven by impatient drivers who couldn't wait to go home faster. Autumn had settled in the heart of Bucharest irrevocably. Leafless trees grieved their nakedness by the side of the road, shaken empty by the cold wind. In the apartment building across the street, strangers were trying to hide their lives from sight behind flimsy drapes. She could see mysterious silhouettes moving behind them, drawing shadows of dancing, fighting, and kissing on the smoky canvas of October. Nine years ago, she would have never noticed the mysterious beauty of fall in the big city. She lived her life in a constant rush, blind to everything.

She was starting to think that maybe she too had received a second chance, not just Victor, not just the others. But somewhere deep inside her troubled soul, awestruck by the extraordinary things that were happening, she doubted that the ending of her enigmatic adventure would be entirely happy. Everything is an exchange in life, and she was about to find out what she had bargained with and what price she had to pay.

Like beasts hunting for prey, harrowing memories of the fire haunted her incessantly. The ceiling of the club burned above them as incandescent pieces of wood and plastic rained over her, hurting her. She was heading toward the exit, crushed between desperate bodies, writhing with pain. There she is, near the entrance in the container, walking underneath huge flames that descended toward her, licking her skin. One centimeter more and they would have devoured her. She was lucky. Others got trapped in the hall and died there. Once she managed to squeeze into the container, the fire came over them from behind, famished for their flesh, fed by the gust of air that seeped in when someone managed to open a door that led outside. They fell in the ashes, in what was left of them after the fire had been satiated, as if they were marionettes whose strings were cut by God. Before that boy dragged her out, she thought she had died. She couldn't feel or see anything. It was only afterwards, when she saw the asphalt and the bodies lying on it, that she realized she was still alive. She was surrounded by other people who had been taken out. A few of them weren't breathing and there was no one there to resuscitate them.

Someone helped her climb into an ambulance, and that's where the pain started. The skin on her hands and arms was gone. Its remnants hung from her body like the torn wings of an angel. She lost consciousness and woke up in the hospital, covered in oozing bandages. The pain was all-encompassing, undefeatable. Day after day, her wounds looked worse. She wasn't healing because of the infections she acquired in the operating room. Every surgery she had was a failure. They used to wash her in a rubber tub without giving her any painkillers. They skinned her alive. She cried when the harsh spray of the shower penetrated her gaping flesh. She wept until she vomited. Many of the people there were evil. A lot fewer were good and humble. Her friends kept dying, deepening her grief, until it became a bottomless pit of sorrow.

"The club didn't have a fire protection authorization," "the venue wasn't adequately fire-proofed," "the fireworks were not fit for indoor use," "the fire extinguishers were expired," "there was only one available exit, the rest were locked shut." Terrible mistakes had been made and the lies that were told were appalling. They had killed people who could have been saved had the truth come to light. Through the pain and the humiliation, her days in the hospital passed one after the other, identical in their agony.

The fear of death was everywhere. If someone died, the fault was theirs, their body had been too weak, their disposition too sad for the healing to take place. They told their loved ones that they had done everything they could. That they had everything they needed. But they didn't. All they had were dirty wards and hearts sullied by lies. And multidrug-resistant bacteria. They discharged her before Christmas, not because she was healed, but because they didn't want to take care of her anymore. She crawled out of that hospital a different person. Her soul was just as injured as her body, and blood seeped out from under the shoddy bandages that were stuck to her still open wounds. Iulia used to wash her in the small ceramic tub in her apartment. She doused her in antibiotics so that the infections wouldn't return. It was months before she was able to take a shower without crying because of the pain. There were moments when she wanted to die. When she didn't think it was worth it to see another dawn break over the ruins of her life and the lives of those she loved. One winter night, when the sky seemed darker than it had ever been, when thoughts of ending it all almost vanquished her, she decided, against all odds, that she was going to survive this. And then, as if it was a sign, it started to snow, and she smiled for the first time in this new life that had begun for her beyond hell.

The burn rehabilitation came next. It was winter, and she had to walk through the cold to get to the hospital. She still had open wounds that had to be bandaged and often the dressings would slip, exposing her injuries to the clothing that rubbed against them, making them worse. The physiotherapy sessions were brutal, and she often cried because of the pain. That's where she met Victor. He was a survivor of the fire too. They found solace in the jokes they told and in the music they both listened to, but that's not why she fell in love with him. She felt whole with him, and she liked to say that they met in spite of the tragedy and not because of it. But Victor's flesh was not the only thing that burned that night. His heart was in ashes too. He had loved Lydia deeply and when the flames engulfed her, when he couldn't save her, a part of him stayed behind with the memory of her, locked in a union that couldn't be shattered. Every kiss they shared, every tender embrace he gave her, was tinged with darkness, with fragments from a shadow that loomed over him, chasing out the light of another love. There was no room inside him for Ioana, at least not completely.

Most days she accepted things for what they were, without asking for more. Other days, the burden was too heavy to bear. She wept bitter tears hidden from his sight, cursing the night he had lost everything. No matter how hard she fought, there was nothing she could do to give him back the happiness that was taken from him. That's when she really felt how awful the consequences of the fire were, how terrible the revelation of the horrors that came after it, and of those that were still to come. She understood then that it won't ever be over, not as long as Victor held on to Lydia, until she became one with the hell that had killed her. With her loving heart, she tried to find a place for herself, in between the fire and the woman he had adored. She thought if she managed to fit somewhere in there, she'd be able to save him. But nothing she ever did was enough. They kept burning together while she watched from the sidelines. The years passed and sometimes the fire turned into ashes, while her memory rested in a locked vault only Victor had the key to. But then, suddenly, grief stoked the nesting flames, and a bonfire ensued, burning voraciously. The thick smoke took the shape of her beautiful face and set over everything they had built, suffocating their love. Like in an absurd play, the October night when they had burned alive repeated itself when they expected it the least, showing its cinder teeth and howling: "It didn't end, and it never will." At first, she thought that her love was bright enough to unravel the shadows that slept in the darkness. But they fed on anything they could find, including love.

When they fought, she had had enough. She confronted him, reproachful, telling him that he didn't love her as much as he had loved Lydia. He didn't say a word. The shadows had eaten his answer. He stared at her silently, his sad eyes looking inwards at the place in his heart where he and Lydia still burned together. "I love you, but in a different way," he whispered after a while, stretching his arms forward to hug her. She pushed him away and told him, as she wept, everything she had never dared to utter.

"I wish I could turn back time and stop the fire. I wish God would make a miracle and bring her back. So that you can return to your old life and share it with her. If I could cast a spell, I would. I don't care that we'd never meet. Maybe we were never meant for each other. At least not like this."

The weight of her words crushed them and sealed their lips. Victor let his arms fall soft along his body and looked at the floor, averting his gaze. She ran to the bedroom and closed the door. Late at night, when he joined her, he hugged her, humble and defeated. She nestled herself in his chest but kept crying with her face buried in the pillow, hoping he couldn't hear her, praying for the most terrible miracle in the world.

She opened her eyes and wiped her tears. Her love had fulfilled its destiny in that cosmos. Here, it was useless. From everything that had once been, only a distant and crooked memory had survived, and it was part of a world that no longer existed. In this one, he and Lydia knew nothing about the fire. They were sleeping peacefully at that very moment, locked in an embrace that nothing could break. And that didn't burn. Ioana's bitter wish had come true. How very strange... She had stopped believing a long time ago that love possessed a special power. When she was a child, she thought that it was a form of magic that gives meaning to life and that its purpose was to save people from the evil within and without. Now, as an adult, after years of heartbreak, she felt jaded. She had let her hope in love's miraculous nature die. But it turns out that she was wrong. It was indeed strong enough to pull Victor out of hell. To shatter the axis of the universe and turn the stream of time backwards. She shook her head and smiled.

On the leaden autumn horizon, dawn broke over October 30th, climbing from the rooftops of the dim apartment buildings, bringing with it the promise of a different fate for those who, once, on that Friday night, had left home never to return. Today, however, they'll all make it back, without ashes under their eyelids, without smoldering, infected wounds.

"He never loved me anyway. I sacrificed an incomplete love for hundreds of whole souls," she whispered in the quietness of the fall morning, rubbing her wet cheeks.

Her teacup was empty, and the apartment had gone cold. She realized she had forgotten to turn the heating on. The first tram of the day was already hurling down the rails, making a loud, metallic sound. No matter what awaited her, she was ready.

IV

Like on any other day, she talked to her mother on the phone and left for work. She didn't tell anyone about her plan. What could she have said to them? That she traveled back in time to prevent a tragedy from happening? She wasn't even sure about that herself. She still entertained the idea that maybe she had simply gone mad. Every once in a while, she looked up at the sky and demanded answers from God. If it's possible to wake up in a different year, in the past, then talking to Him wasn't off the table either. She sought a sign, an epiphany, anything that could explain how she had ended up in such a situation. But nothing happened. The divine order stayed quiet throughout her inquires.

Bucharest was just as impassive as always, reeling under the heavy traffic, deafened by the incessant honking, overwhelmed by the hundreds of people rushing back and forth, too busy to care about the supernatural. Nothing was missing from the sky. Stars didn't fall all around. No foreign moon embellished the vault with its mysteriousness. Everything was where it had always been and the world looked normal, boring even. And yet she was back in 2015, living a life she was torn out of nine years ago. It was clear to her that regardless of what this was, there was no chance that a foolish mortal like herself would ever fully understand what she was dealing with. A foolish mortal that had bent the source of time and forced it to flow backward.

"Maybe you regret what you did, and you chose me to fix your mistake," she scolded God, hoping to get his attention. "Maybe when you feel sorry about something, you play with time, and nobody finds out. It becomes your little secret. Who knows how many times you did it? But what about all the others when you didn't do a thing..."

She thought that by making Him angry, she would make Him react. But He hung in there, as the hours of October 30th, 2015, passed uneventfully.

She was the first to arrive at the office, so she made coffee for everyone. While she went over what she was going to say to Tudor, to convince him to be cautious that night and support her plan with the fire extinguisher, the espresso machine made a steady, purring sound that she was familiar with. She had decided that she was going to be honest with him and tell him the truth, leaving out the details that were too disturbing... or crazy. She stored the large backpack in which she had stuffed the extinguisher next to her desk.

"I'm glad you're doing better. Yesterday you had a pretty nasty cough," her boss said, not without irony, as he walked in.

"Yeah, it's probably just a harmless cold."

Her fixed stare must have rattled Tudor because, before she got to open her mouth, he asked her if she was all right.

"Tudor, I must tell you something that's going to sound strange. I had a horrible nightmare yesterday. That's actually why I didn't come to the office. I dreamed that we all died at the concert. We burned alive."

Normally, her boss would have made fun of her fears. He would have scolded her and told her that all the hours she had spent writing articles had affected her imagination. He'd have insisted that she take a few days off, then come back in much better shape. But Tudor wasn't laughing. All of a sudden, he was all ears, paying close attention to her words. She went on.

"I dreamed that the fireworks were not fit for indoor use. They should have been cold like the band members requested, but the pyrotechnicians had brought something else. They installed everything wrong too. The club owners had lied about their fire protection authorization. They didn't fireproof the venue and had put up highly flammable sound-absorbing foam on the pillars and ceiling. A tiny spark was enough to set everything ablaze. The pyrotechnicians had forgotten the fire extinguishers in the car, and the ones in the club were expired. They didn't work. The whole place caught fire, and we burned alive while we were trying to save ourselves. We ran toward the exit, but there was only one way out, the others were locked. The main door got jammed and we couldn't move anymore. We were trapped inside an incandescent cage. I got stuck under the flames and they melted my skin. Then, when I finally got into the container, the fire came from behind and tore through us, like a famished beast, hungry for our skin and blood. I can still see the pile of bodies on the ground. Yours was among them."

Her voice broke, and she remained silent. Tudor gulped and crashed into the chair. He examined her from head to toe a few times, then sighed.

"It's just a nightmare, Ioana, for God's sake. You have a way of recounting things that send shivers down my spine."

But he wasn't convinced. His dismissal wasn't wholehearted.

"Tudor, I bought a fire extinguisher yesterday. I brought it with me. It's in the big backpack next to your foot. Maybe you'll think I'm crazy, but please – I beg you – let's take it with us tonight. We'll sit next to the pillar near the exit."

He opened his mouth to say something, but changed his mind. He put his elbows on his knees and grabbed his face with his hands. After a while, he nodded and conceded.

"It's absurd, but all right. Let's do it."

She breathed a sigh of relief and thanked him with a hug.

"Okay, now let's work, shall we? You need to finish those interviews."

When she walked into the office, she was too stressed thinking about the conversation she was going to have with Victor to realize that she was back at her old job, at the magazine. The worn-out computer that made a weird clicking sound every time she turned it on waited for her patiently, filled with articles she hadn't finished writing and photos of bands she had to upload. On the right side of her

desk lay a pile of unsigned gig contracts. She sat in her chair and was overcome
with emotion. Nostalgia and joy washed over her, together with fear. She knew
what was happening wasn't natural, and it frightened her. The familiarity of the
space was in stark contrast with the acute feeling that this place had become utterly
foreign to her. Nine years had passed since she walked out as a young and hopeful
27-year-old woman since the skin on her hands was whole and her fingers danced
on the keyboard unimpeded and healthy. While Tudor was making the day's usual
calls, she laid her head on the desk and cried silently, happy, yet devastated by a
sadness nothing could soothe. She eventually came to her senses and decided to do
what Tudor had told her: finish her interviews. She didn't know how long the
spell, or whatever it was, would last, and she wanted to take advantage of the miracle to enjoy being whole again.

That night, before he left, Tudor pointed to the fire extinguisher.

"Do you want me to take it and bring it to the concert in the car?"

"Yes, sure. Can you pick me up tonight, too? I wouldn't want to walk to the
venue like last time."

"What do you mean?"

"Oh, nothing. So?"

"Yeah, of course. Wait for me downstairs in two hours or so."

"Perfect!"

Tudor grabbed the backpack and ran down the stairs in a hurry. She knew the
fast cadence of his footsteps by heart, and she smiled because she hadn't heard it
in years. "Like last time." He didn't understand what she meant by that, and it was
better that way. Back in the other October, she had left home late and decided to
walk to the club, through the neighborhood. She lived very close to the venue. She
remembered every detail of what she thought and what she saw on her way to
Colectiv. This time, she wanted to do everything differently. She was afraid that if
she repeated any part of that night, she couldn't stop the tragedy from happening.
Before she went home to prepare, she made a few more phone calls to make sure
everything was arranged. She talked to the club owners again, who confirmed that
they had taken care of things in preparation for the ISU inspection that evening.
Then, she spoke to the pyrotechnicians who, although annoyed, reassured her that

they had abided by her advice and took the necessary precautions: they had loaded cold fireworks in the car and had added in extra fire extinguishers.

She left the office earlier and arrived home before dark. She didn't stop at the store or see any old women on the crosswalk. An immense fear had taken hold of her, and she was rattled by mixed feelings. Had she managed to save them? Had her scheming worked? Even if she had failed, she still had the fire extinguisher as a backup plan. Why did she leave it with Tudor? Could she trust him? What if he threw it away or forgot to bring it? She took her clothes off in the hallway and jumped in the shower, hoping that the hot water would calm her down. She hadn't allowed herself a moment of reprieve these past few days. It was only now that she realized, lying naked in the tub, looking at her young, healthy body, how beautiful she had always been, and how blind she was to it. She gazed at herself, awestruck, touching her smooth, elastic skin with reverence, as if in the presence of a miracle. In the nine years that had passed, she had gotten used to the rigid, plaque-like scars that covered her. To the deformities and disabilities. She hadn't realized how much she had missed herself, the one before, the one... from now.

"Maybe if he had met me when I was beautiful, he'd have loved me more." But she chased that thought away, like she would a bad omen. There was no room for her love at this time, and she had to come to terms with that, just like she had come to terms with the scars on her body and the discomfort they caused her. In life, you learn to live with what you cannot accept.

She set aside the clothes she wore the night she burned alive. The black t-shirt with fashionable shoulder-pads was intact and smelled like detergent. She stroked it gently, careful not to stain her hands with the cinders she thought were still nestled in the fabric. But the palm of her hand was pristine when she stared at it, ready for the worst of revelations. The gray, high-waisted jeans were clean and stiff, not torn and bloodied. There were no shoe sole traces on them, from when the others had stepped on her, desperate to escape, not realizing she was still alive. They were nothing but rags, but she was afraid of them as if they were ghosts. She was wearing them when Hell had found her, and they terrified her with the memories they brought back. She picked a different outfit from her wardrobe: a long-sleeved black dress, and plain, opaque stockings. Then, instead of the new shoes, made from synthetic leather that had melted in the container, she chose a pair of ankle boots. She changed her hairstyle too and even wore a different perfume. She went downstairs early. Tudor was still nowhere in sight, but she decided to wait for him outside. It hadn't gotten very cold yet, but something inside her heart lay trembling, frozen by anguish. Her eyes, painted in dark colors, wandered over the streets, staring at the agitated passers-by who hurried over the crosswalks. Although the streetlights shone with intensity, they cast deep shadows on their faces, making them look unusually sad.

All of a sudden, she noticed her. She was sitting on the sidewalk, still among restless bodies that ebbed and flowed, like featureless waves. She recognized her melancholy blue eyes. She was dressed in an elegant coat and wore tall boots that were shiny and new. Her white hair was tousled, and she looked like she just came from the hairdresser. She stared directly at her and smiled. It was the same old woman who had asked her about Emil Gârleanu Street two weeks before the fire, the day it was raining profusely. On the other October, she was standing there alone, ignoring the green lights, wearing those wet ragged clothes. She had asked her for directions and after she gave them to her, she walked away. But her poverty and sadness stayed with her, so she decided to come back, to bring her some money, and an umbrella. To say a few kind words to her. By the time she returned, she was gone. She looked for her across the street, explored the surroundings in search of her, but she had vanished. At that point, she asked herself if the woman hadn't been an angel in disguise who tested her to see if she had a good heart. Disappointed that she had failed her, she left.

Every day she looked for her each time she left home, including on the 30th of October. But the woman never came back. Then, she burned alive and forgot about the poor wandering soul. To see her again here, to find her like this... Could this be the sign that she asked for? The woman hadn't taken her eyes off her and was still smiling. Her warmth enveloped the entire boulevard, making it look shinier, happier. There was no bitterness in her eyes. She radiated goodness and wholeness. People passed by her, oblivious to her presence, without touching her. Ioana started toward her because she wanted to talk to her. She wanted to know who she was, what this meant, but a loud honk distracted her and made her look away, at the car that had stopped in front of her building. From the driver's seat, Tudor was waving at her, pointing at Carmen, his wife, who sat in the back, holding the backpack with the fire extinguisher. Scared that she missed her moment, she stared at the sidewalk, but there was no one there. The outpouring of people had stopped, and the woman was gone. Her heart was racing in her chest, but then it quieted down. Peace had replaced fear. Tudor kept honking, worried, so she got in the car.

"What were you gawking at? You look like you've seen a ghost."

"Nothing. I thought I recognized someone, that's all."

The woman's smile had nestled in her soul. She started to hum one of the songs that the band didn't get to perform the last time. Now, they will.

V

When they arrived at the venue, the band was still doing sound checks. It was early. Tudor was holding on to the fire extinguisher, throwing cryptic glances in Ioana's direction. He probably thought she was crazy, but he had always been superstitious. He was afraid of death, so he'd much rather take the risk of looking like a fool than being caught off guard. She had done the right thing by telling him the truth. Or at least a version of it that wasn't so hard to believe.

Focused on the strings, Rareș, the bass player, was tuning his instrument. When he rose his head, still frowning, he noticed her, smiled, and waved. She said hi back, from a safe enough distance so that he couldn't tell that her eyes had welled up with tears. The last time she had heard his name uttered, was in the hospital ward. She was eavesdropping on the radio that the nurses had left on in their office. The reporter was counting the people who had died that day. To see him now like this, alive and happy, seemed surreal. But it was really happening.

The pillars had been dressed in some sort of temporary casing that covered the sound-proofing foam which had started the ordeal back in the other October. Someone had improvised an "Exit" sign with permanent marker on a piece of cardboard and had hung it over the now wide-open door on the side of the venue. It led to the neighboring club and had been locked... previously. The pyrotechnicians were installing two devices that looked like black boxes. They were placed directly on the stage, not on the metal scaffolding overlooking the audience. There were two big fire extinguishers on each side of the room. She got close enough to them to be able to check the expiration date: October 28th, 2023, the day she had fought with Victor. Ironic. Ioana shook her head. She looked around the room to check if he had arrived, but he was nowhere in sight.

She, Carmen, and Tudor found a spot next to the pillar that was closest to the exit. Her boss placed the open backpack with the fire extinguisher between his feet, so that he could take it out quickly if it proved to be necessary.

"Thank you for indulging me..."

"I told Carmen everything. I thought she'd say that you went mad, but she didn't. In fact, she actually encouraged me to listen to you."

"I've been having these weird dreams too," Carmen interjected. "It's hard for me to explain the feelings they left me with, but honestly... I'm glad we brought this thing."

It was as if a specter of the suffering they had experienced then traveled through time with her and nestled in their souls. Why else would they support her with such a crazy thing? Who goes out with a fire extinguisher in their backpack? She remembered Carmen standing in the door of her ward, crying. She came to check on her, to make sure she was still alive. She had just seen Tudor, who was critical. They told her that they didn't know if he was going to survive the night. But he did, only at great cost. Now, they were standing next to her, both whole, unscathed, making small talk, unafraid of losing each other. Every now and then, they remained quiet and stared at Ioana with somber, worried eyes. Somewhere beyond the threshold of consciousness, a part of them remembered something, reiterating the unlived horror that nearly cost them their lives.

One by one, people started arriving at the concert. Ioana recognized familiar faces, old friends, and acquaintances. She hadn't seen them in nine years. She could only visit them when she brought flowers to their lonely graves, as an homage to the youth they had lost forever. When Petru walked in, she went to him. She hugged him without saying a word and he hugged her right back, because he was kind like that. He giggled and gave her a pat on the shoulder.

"Well, now. If this isn't love, I don't know what is!"

"I'm so happy you're... here."

"Oh, yeah! Me too! I was afraid I wasn't going to make it."

They exchanged a few words, and then he joined his crew. She knew all of them and her heart was so full it nearly burst. An avalanche of feelings took hold of her: sadness, happiness, fear, grief, joy, all at once. She used to dream this exact scene in the rehabilitation clinic, after a long day of procedures, when the scars ached because of the tightness of the compression garments. They used to return to the club, all of them. The living said hello to the dead, and they looked at one another, amazed and appalled. Then, after they met again, the ceiling started to burn. They stared at it, hypnotized, while they caught fire. This time, nobody screamed. They just lay there alight, crying tears that never got to run down their cheeks. The fire would eat them up before they had the chance to fall.

"It won't be like that this time." She repeated the words to herself as if she was reciting a prayer or a mantra.

She put her arms around herself to stifle the shaking. That's when she saw Victor. She hadn't noticed when he arrived. He was talking to a group of people. Lydia was next to him, and they were holding hands. Every now and then, they exchanged intimate glances and smiles. She could tell how much they loved each other. Even if she had expected it to hurt, she realized she had underestimated the effect it would have on her. The more she looked at them, the worse she felt. She wasn't jealous. She was grieving. Finally, she had understood what she had wished for the night they had fought, and seeing it come true unraveled her. Her love didn't mean anything here. It couldn't save him. But it could rescue Lydia, and all the others. He lifted his eyes and glanced her way, but she avoided him. She didn't want to look him in the eyes and risk changing her mind.

"I did the right thing... I did the right thing..."

The concert started a few moments later, to the applause of the audience, which had gotten bigger. The band members were in great shape. Even though some things were the same as they were back then, others were very different. The songs were in the same order, so, after the first one, the fireworks went off. Their white light shone over the fans, illuminating their smiling faces. Ioana couldn't feel any heat coming off them. They were cold, just like she had schemed. Not sparks, but rather impressions of them.

"They used the cool ones, see?" Tudor said, breathing a sigh of relief.

"Keep the fire extinguisher close, just in case."

He scoffed and pulled the zipper of the backpack all the way down. Ioana counted the songs in her head and, when she recognized the beginning of the eighth one, she started praying. She wanted to chase away the ghosts that haunted her and the fear that enslaved her. Soon, her life would break in half, splitting into "before" and "after." Tens of people would die. She heard their screams and saw the tears evaporating from their cheeks. You can't cry in Hell. The flames won't let you. The boy to her right recited *The Lord's Prayer*, muttering meaningless things in between verses: "it's not happening," "it can't be real." Then, she could only hear him howl in pain: "I'm dying! I'm dying!" His voice became one with hers until she didn't know which one of them was shouting. Their bodies cradled together, pushing against each other, shoving, desperate for salvation that no one could provide. Then, after the flames engulfed them, they fell down in the muck, in the ashes they made with their skin, writhing, burning harder and harder. The air had become blistering and had started to scorch their insides, killing them.

The fire's groan had silenced everything. She could no longer hear anything else. Their screams were swallowed whole by the deafening roar of death. She thought the light would blind her, but instead it was pitch dark. The hungry fire licked her eyelids and, for an instant, she saw a bright flash that quickly sunk into the nothingness of obscurity. A black, smoldering curtain fell over them and silence took hold of their bodies, like grief settles into a house where the dead lay in vigil. It only lasted for a while. The time for crying had come. She thought she had gone blind, but she managed to discern the contours of devastated silhouettes, bobbing around, like shipwrecked marionettes, lost at sea. As if someone had punished angels by tearing off their wings, their flesh hung from their arms, fluttering in the gust of air that reached them from beneath the bodies piled up in the door, like a morbid monument erected in the name of death. What had they done wrong to deserve something like this? They were so innocent in their youth and their love of music. They collapsed and got back up, they crawled and were trampled by others, too injured, too desperate to escape to realize what they were doing. Then, someone grabbed her by the arms and pulled her out. But a part of her stayed inside forever, with bleeding wounds stuck to the dirty, sweltering floor, choking on the smoke and the ashes. And now she's back there again.

The song was almost done, and, after the last guitar note, a new jet of fireworks sprang out.

"Our Father, who art in Heaven, hallowed be thy Name..."

Just as white as the first ones, they fluttered in the air for a few seconds, splashing the room and the people with light. Then they faded away without a trace.

The fans unleashed a round of applause and they started to chant the band's name. Back then, they screamed meaningless fragments of words, distraught by the horror and the pain.

The roaring voices and thundering claps deafened her. In her troubled mind, they mixed together with the sorrowful weeping and the desperate pattering of their footsteps as they ran for the exit. But then, they came apart. The cheering conquered the cries and cast them away. The seconds bid farewell to minute 32[8], multiplying, taking her with them to a different future that she had built from her hopeless love, which had fulfilled a different purpose.

When she opened her eyes, Carmen was holding her hand. The ninth song was playing as the concert moved forward naturally. Petru smiled at her from the corner of the stage and took a picture of her, amused by the weird reverie she seemed to have fallen into. He was surrounded by his photographer friends, and they were busy trying to capture the most important moments of the show. Their photo albums won't be scoured in the days to come by journalists, looking for the exact moment when the ceiling caught fire. The stills will be ordinary mementoes of a Friday night just like any other.

"Are you okay? You're shaking."

"I'm fine. I'm just a little dizzy, that's all."

She felt like all vigor had been drained from her soul, that life itself had left her body. As the concert neared the end, she became weaker and weaker, until she thought she was going to collapse. Their beautiful faces, so alive in their joy, the passion of their youth, now untouched by horror, proved to her that she had made the right choice. She had paid a big price, indeed. Perhaps one that was not yet settled. But she saved them! God, she saved them! She looked at each one of them, mesmerized, in disbelief that it was so easy. So little stood between them and this version of "after?" A few honest confessions and more thoughtfulness? Yes. Her heart ached with sadness.

After the encore, the fans stayed behind in the club to talk about the show. Tudor went backstage and came back happy and a little smug.

---

[8] The fire erupted at 22:32, according to the surveillance cameras.

"Cold fireworks! That's why we didn't feel any heat near the stage. The pyro-technicians brought these devices that don't use live sparks. You had no reason to be afraid, Ioana. Did you see how many fire extinguishers they had back there? And all the exit doors? Truth be told, such precautions are a rare occurrence here, but still. We were never in any real danger."

The band members were putting their instruments away. They were sweaty and tired, but deeply happy. They were cracking jokes about the drum player who was moving slowly, as usual. How beautiful and alive they were! But was it really over? She squeezed the backpack with the fire extinguisher between her ankles until her bones felt sore. Then, all of a sudden, she let go. Enough. It was done. She was exhausted.

"Can I take it to the car?" Tudor asked her, pointing at the backpack.

"Yes... sure. I'll walk out with you to get some fresh air."

Tudor went to look for his car, which he had parked somewhere in the square, and she stayed behind. She sat outside the club, looking around, still awestruck. The cold autumn wind swirled the dust in the alleyway around, piling small mounds, then tearing them down again, like a child playing with sand. She let loose and started to cry. She didn't know if she was weeping because she was happy or sad. Terrified or euphoric. She saw her with the corner of her eye. When she approached her, she took a step back in fear. But then she recognized her. It was the old woman from the crosswalk! She was smiling.

"There, there. It's over. You did it!"

"But how..."

"How do I know about the fire?"

"Yes..."

"Once, it happened here. Many souls rose up to the heavens from the ground, from where you're standing right now. But that won't be the case now. Your pray-ers have been answered, child."

"Who are you?"

"Oh, I don't think it matters. Then, in the other October, you knew. And you know now too."

When she hugged her, she broke out in tears and gave herself away in the embrace, laying the entire weight of her mutilated soul to rest in the woman's arms. As she wept, the angel lulled her, rocking her like a baby.

"Will I die now?"

But she didn't get an answer. The embrace became so strong it felt like it was lifting her above the ground. She had the distinct sensation that her feet didn't touch the floor anymore, that she was floating above everything. The woman stroked her head and sang to her, just like Alina used to, when she sat in the green tub. But she didn't remember where or when. Or who Alina was. She was flying now and the fragments of nightmare, the scorching fire, the screams became one with the sound of big wings soaring through the heavens. She was convinced she was somewhere above the clouds now. All she could hear was that strange music, noteless, voiceless, like a monotonous flutter carrying her heart to peace. Her father gave her a kiss on the cheek and told her he was proud of her. Her grandfather was there too, and he was smiling. They had finally left their quarrels aside. They were happy. Then they started to fade away, waving at her as she descended lower and lower, like a feather drifting to the ground, in a gentle fall.

"Ioana, are you sleepy?"

Tudor was standing in front of her, examining her from head to toe. He seemed concerned.

"What?"

"You were standing here alone, with your eyes closed and rocking from side to side. Where were you before? When I came back, you were gone. I thought you went home."

"I don't know... Maybe you just didn't notice me," she answered, with honesty.

"Come, now. Don't be silly. Let's go get Carmen. Everybody's leaving. The place is almost empty."

She turned around to join Tudor, who darted toward the entrance at his usual, impossible pace. Because she didn't want to lag behind, she rushed after him and almost knocked over a guy who was coming out of the club, holding hands with his girlfriend.

"Oh, sorry!"

"No, no, I apologize. I wasn't paying attention. My boss is waiting for me."

"Hey, no problem. Fun night, right? Do I know you?"

Ioana took a step back and stared at him, confused, as if trying to remember something she had forgotten a long time ago. The tall, brown-haired man looked familiar. But no. He was wrong. They'd never met.

"Hmmm... maybe from the gigs?"

"Yes, you're right. Anyway, have a nice evening!"

"Yeah, you guys too!"

She watched them leave. Their steps merged as they strolled off, becoming one. They were obviously very in love, and that made her happy. She felt some sort of strange nostalgia she blamed on the exhaustion. There was something about the way he moved that made her think that this wasn't the first time he walked away from her. He or someone like him. But it was late, and she was beat. It was time to go home.

She, Tudor, and Carmen were the last to leave. It was cold outside, and the leaden sky had become stormy. They jumped in the car, and she huddled in the back seat next to the fire extinguisher. When she saw it, she laughed at the nightmare that had scared her. She couldn't remember the details, but she was so frightened, she asked Tudor to bring it with him, in case something caught fire in the venue. She was ashamed of herself now, but he never held it against her. Embarrassed, they all giggled and rolled their eyes. When they arrived at her address, they asked her what she wanted to do with it.

"I'll take it upstairs as a souvenir!"

"All right. Well, see you tomorrow at the office."

She stood in front of her apartment building for a while. The streetlights made the boulevard shine brighter than ever. It was past midnight and silence had taken hold of the empty street, grateful for a few hours of rest from the daily chaos. That night of October 31st was somehow special. It seemed different, even though nothing had changed. Everything felt more whole somehow. Yes, that was the word she was looking for. Bucharest was complete. Nothing was missing from it, the soul count was correct, and everyone was resting, sheltered by its heavy concrete arches. The promise of goodness, of a new life, and of joy floated in the chilly autumn air.

An older couple was crossing the street gracefully. They were so beautiful to-gether. The woman turned her head, smiled, and winked at her as if they were privy to some shared secret. As if she had known her for centuries. She probably mistook her for someone else or simply wanted to be nice. She smiled back, con-fused. Then, they vanished in the shadows cast by the large trees from Emil Gâr-leanu Street, heading toward God-knows-where. As soon as she walked into her apartment, she crashed in bed. She giggled for no reason. It was as if a crushing slab had been lifted off her soul. Nothing special happened at the concert, but she felt as if it did, as if something akin to redemption had taken place there. As if she was finally rid of a great evil that had troubled her for years. She shook her head, amused by her strange thoughts. She yawned and stretched, her body heavy with exhaustion. She was tired, but happy. Deeply happy. She dozed off as soon as she put her head on the pillow. When the dawn of October 31st washed over the city with its shy rays, she was still smiling in her sleep, bathed in light, far away from the fire. Her whole life lay ahead of her, ripe with beauty.

The price had been paid, God had fixed His mistake, and time returned to its normal course, leaving no trace of its transgression. Nobody suspected a thing.

ABOUT THE AUTHOR

Alexandra Furnea is a Romanian author, book editor, journalist, and social activist. She has a bachelor's degree in philology and a master's degree in American studies. She is a survivor of the deadly Colectiv Club fire that took place in Bucharest on the night of October 30th, 2015. Her memoir, *Diary of 66: The Night I Burned Alive,* is an intimate account of the suffering she endured as a result of the tragedy, which was caused by the corruption that still plagues many Romanian institutions. The book was a bestseller in Romania and earned the praise of renowned authors like Gabriel Liiceanu, Radu Paraschivescu, and Marius Chivu.

HISTRIA

BOOKS

HISTRIA
PERSPECTIVES

HISTRIA PERSPECTIVES
BOOKS TO CHALLENGE AND ENLIGHTEN

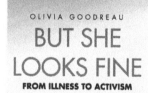

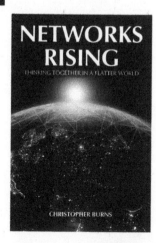